BROKEN PROMISES

**CONTEMPORARY CHRISTIAN
COUNSELING**

BROKEN PROMISES

HENRY A. VIRKLER, Ph.D.

**CONTEMPORARY CHRISTIAN
COUNSELING**

General Editor
GARY R. COLLINS, PH.D.

Unless otherwise indicated, Scripture quotations are from The New International Version of the Bible, © 1986 by the New York International Bible Society. Used by permission of Zondervan Bible Publishers.

Permission to quote from the following sources is gratefully acknowledged:
  Hermeneutics: Principles and Processes of Biblical Interpretation by Henry A. Virkler, copyright 1981. Published by Baker Book House.

  Speaking Your Mind Without Stepping on Toes by Henry A. Virkler, copyright 1991. Published by Victor Books.

  Out of the Shadows: Understanding Sexual Addiction by Patrick Carnes, copyright 1983. Published by CompCare Publishers.

  The quote on page 217 from a "Dear Abby" column by Abigail Van Buren, © 1963, is reprinted with permission of Universal Press Syndicate. All rights reserved.

Library of Congress Cataloging-in-Publication Data:

Virkler, Henry A.
    Broken Promises : understanding, healing and preventing affairs in
  Christian marriage / Henry A. Virkler.
       p. cm. — (Contemporary Christian counseling series)
    Includes bibliographical reference and index.
    ISBN 0–8499–0838–8 : (hc)
    ISBN 0–8499–3374–9 : (tp)
    1. Marriage counseling—Religious aspects—Christianity. 2. Adultery. 3. Marriage counseling. I. Title. II. Series.
  BV835.V57 1992
  248.8'44—dc20
                                                                    91—39489
                                                                         CIP

2349 LB 987654321

Printed in the United States of America

To my parents
Clayton and Lillian Virkler
from whom I learned the
meaning of faithfulness
and commitment

Contents

Introduction

INFIDELITY IS ONE OF THE MOST painful, devastating experiences that a married person can encounter. It is the most universally accepted grounds for divorce, and is even a legally accepted justification for murder in some states and many societies.[1] It is difficult for someone who has not experienced a partner's affair to understand the wracking pain that comes when someone who pledged to "love, honor and cherish you, forsaking all others," betrays that sacred promise. In movies, in magazines, and in everyday social life we hear humorous talk about infidelity, but people invariably are shaken to the very core when it happens in their own marriages.[2]

The statistics indicate that in the coming years many of us will be involved in affairs ourselves, either as the betrayer or the betrayed one. Alfred Kinsey shocked the world in 1948 when he reported that 50 percent of American husbands had been unfaithful.[3] More recent surveys indicate that this number has increased. Twenty-five years later Dr. Bernard Greene, drawing on 750 case histories of married men, stated that 60 percent of his subjects had been unfaithful.[4] In 1981 Shere Hite reported in her study of over 7,000 males that 72 percent of men married more than 2 years had cheated.[5] More than 15 percent of men report having a series of affairs.[6]

In 1953 Kinsey found that only 25 percent of married women had been involved in affairs. By 1982 Atwater found that this number had risen to 50 percent.[7] In 1987 Shere Hite reported that her survey of several thousand women indicated that 75 percent of women married five years or longer were having or had had an affair.[8]

Even if these percentages were to remain at their present levels, it would mean that infidelity would occur in at least three out of four marriages of those who are young and middle-aged couples today.

But isn't the picture different in the Christian world? Perhaps not, for it should be remembered that these statistics are drawn from the general population, where approximately 30 percent identify themselves as evangelical believers. We do not have the same kind of research data available on evangelical Christians as we do on the general population, but we have a number of observations from those who have written and worked in this area. When I began counseling some fifteen years ago (my counseling has been primarily with Christians), about one in ten marriage counseling cases involved an affair. In recent years at least three out of ten such cases is precipitated by an affair. Other Christian counseling colleagues agree that they too have seen a significant increase in the number of Christians becoming involved. The pastor of a very fine evangelical church recently said: "We're having an epidemic of affairs in our congregation!"

Carol Botwin, the author of *Men Who Can't Be Faithful,* stated: "Although some earlier studies indicated that men who were religious were more likely to remain monogamous, other, more recent ones have shown that religious men are as apt to have affairs as those who never enter a house of worship. That goes for some religious leaders too."[9]

Charles Mylander, an evangelical pastor and author of *Running the Red Lights*, says: "What comes as a surprise to many is that Christians may fall into extramarital affairs even when they are not looking for them. Too often well-meaning believers make unwise moves and suddenly realize they are in love with someone other than their spouse. The 'If I had only known what was happening . . .' revelation dawns too late."[10] Perhaps our percentages as evangelical Christians are not as high as those of the general population, but nevertheless affairs are wreaking havoc in the lives of Christians we know and love.

There are at least two reasons why we are likely to see a continuing increase in the number of Christians involved in affairs. One is that Christian men and women will continue to work long hours with members of the opposite sex. Such working relationships consistently have been shown to be associated with an increase in infidelity.

The second reason is more speculative. After sitting through the pain of infidelity with more than a hundred couples, I have come to believe that Satan has found infidelity to be one of the easiest ways he can destroy a Christian family, a Christian ministry, or defame the name of Christ. In our day, I believe that Satan will launch an increasing attack against the church through the temptation of infidelity.

Intended Audience, Goals and Stylistic Issues

In writing this book my primary intended audience is Christian counselors, pastors, Christian counselors in training, and seminarians. My secondary audience includes Christian laypersons who are interested in the topic. The latter may wish to focus on chapters 1 through 5, 11, and 12, with less emphasis on chapters 6 through 10, which have to do with counseling those who have been or are involved in affairs. Those whose partners have become involved in affairs may also wish to read chapters 7 through 9.

My goals for readers are that this book would help you understand how affairs get started, how they develop—even among those with strong Christian beliefs, how to help a person break the emotional bonds that hold him or her to the affairee, and how to encourage forgiveness and rebuild trust in a marriage. My hope is that not one reader of this book will subsequently become involved in an affair and say, "I didn't know it was happening." For this reason I wish every Christian married couple would read chapters 1 through 5, and chapters 11 and 12.

All names and identifying data have been intentionally changed to protect the identity of those whose stories are discussed in this book. One last stylistic issue: In these pages square brackets are sometimes used within quotations; the words enclosed within brackets have been added to make a statement more understandable or to replace offensive wording.

This book can be divided into three main parts: Why and how affairs happen is discussed in chapters 1 through 5. What can be done when they do happen is the subject of chapters 6 through 10. Chapters 11 and 12 focus on how to prevent them from happening.

NOTES

1. Frank Pittman, *Private Lies: Infidelity and the Betrayal of Intimacy* (New York: Norton, 1989), 33.

2. Dr. Ruth Westheimer, quoted in an article by Susan Jacoby, "After His Affair," *McCalls*, February 1982.

3. Alfred Kinsey et al., *Sexual Behavior in the Human Male* (Philadelphia: W. B. Saunders Co., 1948).

4. Bernard Greene, Ronald Lee, and Noel Lustig, "Conscious and Unconscious Factors in Marital Infidelity," *Medical Aspects of Human Sexuality*, September 1974: 87–111.

5. Shere Hite, *The Hite Report on Male Sexuality* (Garden City, N.Y.: Alfred A. Knopf, 1981).

6. Laurel Richardson, *The New Other Woman: Contemporary Single Women in Affairs with Married Men* (New York: The Free Press, 1985), 1.

7. Lynn Atwater, *The Extramarital Connection: Sex, Intimacy and Identity* (New York: Irvington, 1982), 15–29.

8. Shere Hite, *Women and Love: A Cultural Revolution in Progress* (New York: Alfred A. Knopf, 1987).

Readers may note that the statistics given here are significantly different from those cited by Andrew Greeley in his article "Faithful Attraction," in *Good Housekeeping*, June 1990, 132–37. Greeley found that 90 percent of his telephone respondents in a randomly selected population said they had been faithful during their present marriages. There are several possible explanations for the differences between Greeley's findings and some of these other researchers: (1) Greeley's sample was 1/20 the size of Shere Hite's; (2) Greeley's respondents were responding to questions about faithfulness within their present marriages only; (3) a written survey (as Hite's) may elicit more honest responses than a telephone survey from an unknown caller (as Greeley's: some suspicious respondents may have wondered whether the "survey" was an attempt by their spouses to elicit incriminating data from them); and (4) other factors may have confounded the data (for example, if Greeley's respondents were answering the telephone interviewer's questions while some member of the family was present, they may have been less than candid about their infidelities.

9. Carol Botwin, *Men Who Can't Be Faithful* (New York: Warner Books, 1988), 14.

10. Charles Mylander, *Running the Red Lights: Putting the Brakes on Sexual Temptation* (Ventura, Calif.: Regal, 1986), 29.

PART ONE

Understanding How Christians Become Involved in Affairs

Chapter One

Contributions of the Unfaithful Partner: Personality Disorders and Sexual Addiction

STAN AND BRENDA WERE DEEPLY COMMITTED CHRISTIANS who had been married ten years.[1] Stan was the pastor of a three hundred-member conservative evangelical church, and Brenda was a conscientious pastor's wife, involved in a number of church activities, and the leader of two women's ministries. She invested her time in her husband, her children (Ricky, eight, and Jennifer, six), and her church activities. Neither she nor Stan ever considered the possibility of being unfaithful to each other.

One summer, due to a series of unusual circumstances, a Christian man named Bill spent four months in their home. At first somewhat shy, Brenda eventually began to appreciate Bill's friendship, especially during the many evenings when Stan was involved in church activities. Gradually she began to realize how little she and Stan ever talked or shared in depth with each other, and how good it felt when someone would do so. She began to be aware of the various areas where she and Stan had had frustrating disagreements, and had unconsciously chosen to deal with those frustrations by not discussing those areas anymore. Meanwhile, she began to experience the excitement of having a deep friendship with Bill.

Eventually she recognized that she no longer felt in love with Stan. She realized she was deeply frustrated by the lack of intimacy in their relationship, although she knew that this was at least partly her fault. At the same time she realized she felt "in love" with Bill, even though these feelings contradicted everything that she had believed and taught about marital faithfulness for many years.

At first the affair remained hidden, although Stan suspected that something was not right. Eventually it became known, and Stan reacted with predictable fury. As their congregation became aware of the relationship, they responded with shock and sadness. Stan's job, their marriage, Brenda's relationship to her children—all were on the line.

Over the next six months, Brenda and Stan, and Bill and his wife, each fought to retain what they thought was essential to their happiness. Eventually Bill and Brenda parted, and Stan and Brenda began the difficult task of rebuilding their marriage. The process was not smooth, and more than once they almost gave up in despair. Ultimately they succeeded, and began to develop an intimacy that they had never known before. They eventually developed a ministry to other Christian couples caught in the throes of infidelity.

MYTHS ABOUT AFFAIRS

Brenda and Stan realized they had been caught completely off guard by the affair. They came to see that some mistaken beliefs caused them to be unprepared when temptation came. They were vulnerable to an affair because they held several mistaken beliefs about infidelity. Twelve such beliefs, often held by Christians, are:

1. *The majority of affairs start because of lust.* Various research studies show men and women become involved in

affairs for primarily different reasons. Rarely do women initially enter an affair for sexual reasons. Almost always their primary motivation is a relationship in which they can meet their emotional needs for friendship and security. For some men the motivation is primarily sexual. For others it may be anger at one's spouse for not meeting his social or sexual expectations in the marriage. Many men initially seek a relationship, and that relationship eventually develops a sexual component.[2]

For Christians the most common way an affair begins is through a friendship, usually an innocent and well-meaning one. Though sex eventually becomes part of most affairs, the major motivation for the majority of Christians in affairs is the desire for relationship, the yearning for a deep friendship.

2. *A strong personal faith in Christ inoculates a person against an affair.* A strong personal faith in Christ probably *reduces* to some degree the likelihood of an affair, but the inoculation is far from 100 percent effective. Although we will discuss this further in this chapter and in chapters 2 through 5, I think there are at least four reasons why strong believers still fall. First, affairs happen in large part because we, although believers, still partake in the humanity common to all. We don't cease to experience normal human emotions, needs, and desires simply because we become believers. Second, most affairs develop very gradually, usually over a period of several months and sometimes even years. Because they develop so gradually, they don't trigger the spiritual alarms they might if they were developing more rapidly.

Third, many of the inner dynamics that move a person toward an affair happen at an unconscious level, and thus bypass our consciously held values and commitments until our feelings are so strong that they have more drawing power than the values we once held so strongly.[3] We will talk more about this in chapter 5. Fourth, we must never forget that we are in a *spiritual battle* (Ephesians 6). Satan is determined to destroy our happiness and testimony for Christ, and he will use any means at his disposal. When our emotional needs are not being met by our partners, Satan recognizes our vulnerability.[4]

3. *We don't really need to worry about an affair in our marriage because they rarely happen in good marriages.* I wish this were true. As we have seen in the Introduction, an affair is likely to happen within three out of four marriages of young and middle-aged couples in the general population. Making a conservative prediction, we probably can expect that one out of two Christian marriages will experience an affair. Having a good marriage reduces the chances of an affair. But those involved in affairs—particularly men—will often say they had good marriages and that dissatisfaction with their marriages was not the reason for extramarital involvement.

4. *If a person is an evangelical believer, a strong biblical confrontation will usually cause him or her to stop the affair.* Scores of evangelical pastors could testify that this usually does *not* work—generally it only results in losing a parishioner. By the time an affair has become apparent to others, it has usually reorganized a person's perceptions, values, and emotions to such a degree that a strong biblical confrontation will only build a wall between the person and his or her confronter. There is another way, however, to motivate a Christian to move back to biblical obedience (it is discussed in chapter 6).

5. *An affair indicates that the straying person's mate is not an adequate husband or wife.* Sometimes an affair points to a problem in the relationship that needs to be changed. In such a case, it is important to help the couple understand the problem so they can give attention to that part of their marriage. However, affairs also occur because of the personality the straying partner brings into the marriage, and because of unrealistic expectations that he or she holds. An affair does not always indicate that something is wrong with the straying person's mate.

6. *A man having an affair will almost always choose a lover who is physically more attractive than his wife.* This is a common belief, related to the idea that sex is the most important ingredient in an affair. Sometimes the affair partner is more attractive than

the man's wife, and at other times the affairee and spouse are equally attractive; but in a significant number of cases the affairee is considerably less attractive than the spouse. The most common bond between an affairee and a man is *emotional attraction* rather than physical attractiveness.

7. *Most affairs, even if carefully responded to by the faithful partner, result in dissolution of the marriage.* Frank Pittman, a well-known family therapist, analyzed his caseload of one hundred married couples where one or both were involved in an affair. He found that 53 percent eventually divorced and 47 percent stayed married.[5] In my own counseling practice I would estimate that between two-thirds and three-quarters remain married. The difference is probably because the majority of clients I work with are Christians, and have a stronger commitment to permanence in their marriages and biblical standards for their behavior.

8. *If you are so sure of your and your partner's commitment to faithfulness that you can say, "An affair could never happen in our marriage," you're probably on safe ground.* Writer Ellen Williams has said, "If you are thinking to yourself, 'An affair could never happen to me,' you are in trouble. To believe that we are immune leaves us wide open and unprotected."[6] This is because of the reasons mentioned in relation to Myth Number 2: (1) Most affairs start as innocent friendships, not as sinful relationships; (2) most affairs develop so gradually that a person's biblical defenses are not aroused; (3) much of the psychological change that permits an affair to occur happens unconsciously, and therefore the married person involved does not recognize what is happening until the affair is well developed; and (4) Satan looks for the area in our lives in which we are most vulnerable at any point in time.

9. *A Christian woman who is a close friend of another Christian woman will not betray her by having an affair with that woman's husband.* There is a certain unwritten code of honor among Christian women that they should not make passes at their friends' husbands. Somehow those kinds of affairs happen anyway. A significant number of affairs among Christian

couples develop when they become good friends and start spending significant time together. The affair may even continue in secret for a considerable length of time—months or in some cases years—with the two couples continuing to carry on a pleasant friendship with each other (it doesn't stay that way long once the affair is discovered). This does not mean that all Christian couples should immediately retreat from their couple friends, but that they should realize that these friendships do increase one's vulnerability. Therefore, some of the precautionary steps outlined in chapter 12 should be taken.

10. *An affair can improve an uninteresting and dying marriage.* It is true that an unhealthy marriage can be shaken out of its lethargy by an affair that forces both spouses to take a careful look at unmet needs in their marriage and make necessary changes. A year or two after an affair ends a couple will sometimes say, "Our marriage is better now than it was before the affair." However, an affair is an extremely painful and costly way to improve one's marriage. There is much less trauma if a couple can recognize, without an affair, that their marriage is not healthy and seek to make changes before that state of unhealthiness leads one or both into an affair.

11. *If a person has an affair, that proves he or she does not love his or her mate.* In some cases this is correct. A person may have become so filled with anger that few, if any, positive feelings are left. However, in more cases, particularly in the Christian realm, the straying partner loves both the mate and the affairee, but with different kinds of love. The romantic *love* for the affairee often obscures one's awareness of his or her *commitment love* for the marriage partner, a love which has developed through years of sharing struggles together, of creating and raising children, and of many other shared experiences.

12. *When a spouse's affair is discovered, it is best for the offended party to pretend not to know, and thereby avoid a crisis.* This approach is often taken out of fear of the consequences should a spouse be confronted. What if he or she leaves?

In times of crisis we often rationalize why we do things a certain way. A Christian woman may say that she is remaining silent out of submission and a willingness to give up her rights. Unfortunately, the longer a spouse remains in an affair, the more he or she becomes accustomed to living in disobedience to God, and one's conscience becomes deadened. Also, the longer one has an affair (or several), the more one feels entitled to it. Furthermore, the longer a person lives in a state of unfaithfulness and deception, the less respect he or she has for the spouse. Marriage counselors who have worked with people having affairs are unanimous in stating that confrontation is important, as soon as one partner is aware that the other is having an affair, and as soon as he or she has developed an appropriate way to confront. (How to confront a mate will be discussed in chapter 7.)

If you (or one of your counselees) have a spouse who is involved in an affair and you (or the counselee) are not convinced that confrontation is a necessary and helpful thing to do, please read James Dobson's excellent book, *Love Must Be Tough: New Hope for Families in Crisis*. I don't think any other author, secular or Christian, deals more excellently with this topic than does Dr. Dobson. If you need further convincing, *Back from Betrayal: Recovering from His Affairs*, by Jennifer Schneider, is also excellent.[7]

WHY DO AFFAIRS HAPPEN?

Most people do not set out consciously to have an affair. Why, then, do they happen so frequently?

Many different answers have been given. If we examine the literature on affairs, at least ten categories of reasons emerge. As with every discussion of human personality, these categories overlap; many affairs occur because of a combination of reasons rather than a single one. These ten categories are:

1. Personality disorder of the unfaithful partner [8]
2. Sexual addiction of the unfaithful partner
3. Developmental crises

4. Temptation-filled situations
5. Unconscious, unrealistic, or uncommunicated expectations of the unfaithful partner
6. Failure to meet realistic, communicated expectations of the unfaithful spouse
7. Failure to meet the ego needs of the unfaithful spouse
8. Unconscious, unrealistic, or uncommunicated expectations of the faithful partner which are expressed in unhealthy ways
9. Psychopathology, including codependency, of the faithful spouse
10. Other "systems-related" reasons

The first five factors above are primarily the responsibility of the *unfaithful* spouse, and will be discussed in the first two chapters. The next four are ones in which the faithful spouse *produces a situation where his or her mate is more vulnerable to an affair*. Notice that this is different from saying that the faithful spouse *causes* the affair. We are each responsible for our own actions, and unless the faithful spouse holds a gun to the unfaithful one's head and commands him or her to have an affair, the unfaithful one is responsible for his or her own behavior. However, faithful husbands or wives may behave in such a way that they fail to meet legitimate needs in their partners' lives, and this contributes to a situation in which their partners are more vulnerable to temptation.

The tenth category, systems-related affairs, includes situations where responsibility varies from one partner to the other or is shared by both. The last five categories are discussed in chapter 3 and 4.

Some might argue that since all affairs are sin, it would be more straightforward and accurate to give affairs a single explanation (sin), rather than trying to identify the many situations in which they tend to occur. But when sin comes knocking on our doorstep, it comes in disguise. The following chapters attempt to describe the variety of disguises sin can take, so that we can be better prepared to recognize it when it does come.

Vulnerability to affairs may be discussed in terms of both remote and immediate causes. *Immediate causes* refer to situations that have recently occurred which make a person more vulnerable to an affair. *Remote causes* include those experiences that affected us many years before the affair, frequently during childhood and adolescence, and that may have led to the development of unhealthy personality styles which predispose one to an affair. The next two sections of this chapter will deal with affairs due primarily to remote causes. Affairs due to immediate causes will be discussed in later sections and in chapter 2.

FEMALE PERSONALITY DISORDERS OFTEN ASSOCIATED WITH AFFAIRS

The two female personality styles most often associated with affairs are histrionic personality disorder and borderline personality disorder. People with *histrionic personality disorder* have a need always to be the center of other people's attention.

The borderline personality is more difficult to describe. These persons form very intense relationships with one or two people, and then vacillate between excessive dependency and excessive anger at those people. Because they are unhealthily dependent, they become very anxious or angry if they think the other person is abandoning them. Their relationships are usually stormy. Borderlines are impulsive, have rapid mood changes, and are often involved in frantic efforts to avoid real or imagined abandonment.

Those who have seen the movie *Fatal Attraction* were exposed to a partially accurate picture of a borderline personality. Some borderlines are sincere, committed Christians, while others may have little commitment to the Christian faith but use their association with Christians to meet their emotional needs. Either of these groups can pose grave threats for caring Christian male counselors or pastors; their skillful use of emotional and sexual seduction can lead men into an affair who had no intention of becoming so involved.

MALE PERSONALITY DISORDERS OFTEN ASSOCIATED WITH AFFAIRS

The three male personality styles most commonly associated with affairs are technically known as narcissistic personality disorder, histrionic personality disorder, and antisocial personality disorder.

Persons with narcissistic personality disorder focus so much on meeting their own needs for power, prestige, and money that they do not consider others' needs. Those with histrionic personality disorder have a need, as mentioned above, to be always the center of other people's attention. People with antisocial personality disorder appear to have no conscience, and chronically violate legal and ethical norms in pursuit of their own pleasure.

Less-Technical Conceptualizations. In less technical terminology, those males who frequently have affairs that are part of a long-standing personality disorder have been categorized by Botwin as

- HE-MEN: those who attempt to defend against feelings of personal inadequacy by acting hyper-masculine
- WOMEN-HATERS: those who express their slightly veiled hatred of women by using them as sex objects
- IMPULSIVES: those who always give in to temptation
- PRINCES: those whose mothers treated them like little messiahs, who now continue to expect to be treated in similar ways
- TRIANGLE-MAKERS: men who thrive on the enjoyment of having two women fight over them.[9]

This same group of men (the three technical personality disorders or the five less-technical categories of Botwin) have been referred to by other writers using different names. Pittman groups them all into one category, and refers to *philanderers*. He defines their behavior (philandering) as "that habitual sexual activity that . . . is motivated more by fear of and lust for the 'opposite sex' than by any forces within the marriage or the immediate sexual relationship."[10] Kreitler was probably referring to this same group when he spoke of the "Western affair," a type of philandering in which a man keeps score of his "conquests," similar to the way in which a Western lawman put a notch in his gunbelt for every badman he killed.[11]

To illustrate the Western affair, one unmarried woman who was involved with a man for several months was constantly frustrated by the amount of time he was free but did not spend with her. One day while at his apartment she went to make a telephone call and happened to see his appointment calendar lying partially open. Her curiosity aroused, she began paging through the appointment book and found that each day he had drawn in one, two, or more bullseyes. Realizing that this was some kind of code, she confronted him with the daybook. After an angry exchange she found out that it was a code: Each bullseye represented a woman he had had intercourse with on that particular day!

The narcissist has a tremendous lust for power, prestige, and money. He constantly uses others to meet his own personal needs, seemingly experiencing no guilt about using people in this fashion. The narcissist who acts out sexually may be interested in a woman only until he has seduced her, then he casts her aside. He has no true empathy for those he uses, is afraid of closeness, and so keeps everyone at a distance. A man who fits the description of narcissist in the way he used women sexually recently rose to national prominence and just as rapidly fell in disgrace. His associate resigned, describing his boss as someone who had a "dangerous sense of being divine and above the rules."

Time-Related Conceptualizations. Narcissistic, histrionic, and antisocial males who act out sexually have been divided into three categories based on the length and depth of the extramarital relationships they develop. The "one-night stander" enjoys a kind of pseudo-intimacy for an evening or two, but avoids emotional involvement by never seeing a person longer than that. He may have several different "one-night stands" with a month. The "one-night stander" usually isn't discovered. If he is he rationalizes it by saying "it was only sex; there's no relationship," an explanation which usually doesn't bring a great deal of comfort to his wife.

The "occasional strayer" views himself as basically monogamous. He says he's a one-woman man, *except* when his
mate is out of town (or when he's angry, or when some gor-
geous woman comes on to him, or when his self-esteem is low
and he needs some reassurance about his masculinity). Unlike
the one-night stander, he allows some of these relationships to
develop a little depth, but backs off as soon as he senses that
commitment is expected.

The "long-term lover" is paradoxically monogamous—with
two persons—the spouse and a second person. The spouse
meets certain needs, and the lover meets others. Both relationships are long-term, and he believes he needs both to survive.
Most frequently the relationship with the spouse provides stability and security, and the relationship with the lover provides
excitement and romance.

Men who are unfaithful frequently prefer one of these three
modes of operation, but may on occasion use another mode
for a brief time.[12] I am not aware of any similar studies that
have been done on the patterns of women who are unfaithful.

OTHER PERSONALITY DISORDERS THAT CAN LEAD TO AFFAIRS

Other people, who also have fears of intimacy, may not fit
one of these diagnostic categories. Some men and women with
a fear of intimacy express that fear by becoming perfectionistic
toward the spouse whenever that spouse wants more intimacy
than they feel comfortable with. By faultfinding, these people
create hurt and anger in the relationship, which rapidly produces the psychological distance they (unconsciously) feel they
need.[13] Because there is no true intimacy in the marriage, they
sometimes seek out the pseudo-intimacy of an affair.

Another way of producing distance in a relationship is to
have one or more affairs, and thereby not feel overly dependent on any one individual. One man's description illustrates
how this works.

> I was really hooked on Ruth, but I was [going to bed with]
> other girls all the time. I would tell her terrible stories. I
> would go out at night, telling her I would be back, but

sometimes I didn't return. It was a confused situation. Although I said I was in love with her, the [going to bed with other women] and not showing up sometimes was a way of not getting too involved, because, with her, I would have fallen head over heels, and I couldn't lose that kind of control. I was scared stiff of getting into the thing. At times I felt helpless, I was so sappy, smitten with her.[14]

This fear of intimacy, fear of loving and needing a wife so much, can happen in even "happy" marriages. Botwin observes: "Infidelity then becomes a faulty solution. It's a way of relieving anxiety through running; without understanding what is really happening, the single man may find himself overwhelmed by a sudden urge to switch partners or begin another simultaneous relationship. The married man may find another woman irresistible."[15] This same mechanism may be also used as a faulty way to relieve a man's increased sense of responsibility at the birth of a first child.

Although the behavior of the narcissist, the histrionic, and the borderline all looks like a classic case of sin on the surface, most of these people have both a deep desire for true intimacy and a deep fear of it. This approach-avoidance conflict causes them to settle for the pseudo-intimacy of sexual affairs instead. This has sometimes been referred to as "go away-come closer disease." The person may be starving for contact with the spouse but avoids contact like poison when it is offered.[16]

CONFRONTING THE SIN COMPONENT OF SEXUAL ACTING OUT

The people described above may have deep fears of intimacy, not because of their own sin, but because of events that happened to them during childhood or adolescence. Sometimes the incidents were occasioned by the sin of others, and sometimes they were caused by events common to all human beings because we live in an imperfect world. People who deeply fear intimacy may have been raised by parents who provided no model of healthy intimacy. They may have lost an emotionally significant person during childhood, or perhaps several such persons. Or they may have experienced several rejections from significant others when they were young. They may have a fear of being overwhelmed or suffocated if they were to allow a person to become truly close. Further, they may fear the dependency that usually accompanies marital intimacy. Their poor self-images may cause them now to try to keep everyone far enough away so that their flaws will not be recognized.

As believers we cannot condone the sinful sexual acting out of Christians with histrionic, narcissistic, or borderline behavior. Yet we also should be aware that their personality development may be traced to factors other than personal sinfulness alone. Their unhealthy (and sinful) behavior is often based on mistaken assumptions about how to meet their needs for love and acceptance, and those mistaken beliefs are often due to experiences during childhood over which they had little control. I believe we need to reach out caringly to such persons at the same time that we point out the mistaken beliefs underlying their behavior. We need to reach out caringly because most of these people are very sensitive to rejection. If we confront their sinful behavior *strongly*, they are likely to believe that we are rejecting both them and their behavior, and will likely not return for further counseling.

Perhaps the story of Ron can illustrate this in a more personal way. Ron was forty-five years old, the father of three children, and a committed believer, even though he had had five affairs during his twenty-year marriage. He was grieved about the affairs, had confessed them to his wife, and did not want to repeat his mistakes.

I asked him to make a written analysis of each of his affairs, trying to understand the drawing power in each one and how they related to the larger scope of his life. He soon saw a pattern. While growing up he had an enmeshed relationship with a very critical mother.[17] Repeatedly he tried to earn her approval, but never could. Ron's constant memory of his father was of him yelling; Ron never successfully gained his acceptance either.

He married with the unconscious hope of sharing his life with someone who would accept him as he was. And during the months just prior to marriage, he thought he had found such a person. After marrying the situation changed rapidly. Ron was not well organized nor was he a good decision maker, and soon he was experiencing the same kinds of criticism from his wife that he had known from his parents.

While doing his written analysis for me, Ron soon realized that each of his affairs was an attempt to find someone who accepted him for who he was, someone who would not criticize him continually. Those women were not bothered by Ron's disorganization or his lack of wise judgment to the degree his wife was, and he felt that they gave him the unconditional positive regard which he so much wanted.

Anyone who struggles with low self-esteem, as did Ron, is more susceptible to a lover who promises, either explicitly or in one's imagination, to accept him unconditionally and shelter him, temporarily, from further criticism. Through his analysis Ron was able to understand why he kept repeating his pattern of extramarital affairs and why he kept falling into them despite his desire not to do so. I believe that if I were to have confronted his behavior only as sin, which it admittedly was, he would never have gained the insights that hopefully will help him resist the temptation the next time he experiences it. Confrontation usually causes people to become defensive. A conversation with someone whom we know cares about us is more likely to help people such as Ron look more deeply at themselves, their unconscious assumptions and behavior, and agree that they need to change than will a confrontation.

SEXUAL ADDICTION OF THE UNFAITHFUL PARTNER

The concept of sexual addiction has only become well known within the last decade, primarily through the pioneering work of Patrick Carnes and his two books—*Out of the Shadows: Understanding Sexual Addiction* (1983) and *Contrary to Love: Helping the Sexual Addict* (1989).

An argument might be made that this category could be combined with the previous one. I have not done this because some people with histrionic, narcissistic, and borderline personalities rarely or only occasionally act out sexually, rather than on a daily or weekly basis as is common for sexual addicts. They do not seem addicted to sexual arousal in the way the sexual addict is. Some of the behavior that is common for a sexual addict is rarely used by those who have personality disorders. For this reason I am treating the two categories separately although there is some overlap.

LEVEL 1 ADDICTION

Dr. Carnes divides sexual addicts into three levels, with each level representing an increasingly more serious state. Five behavioral components characterize the sexual addict in Level 1.

1. Compulsive masturbation. Frequently the addict masturbates four or five times a day for years on end. Masturbation becomes a central part of his or her life. The sexual addict comes to use masturbation in a way parallel to the way a substance abuser uses drugs or alcohol. Masturbation is resorted to in order to cope with feelings of loneliness, anger, fear, anxiety, boredom, or depression. This compulsive behavior continues even when the body may be harmed by it. Compulsive masturbation often starts in childhood or adolescence when the person is exposed to physical, emotional, or sexual abuse. It becomes a way to escape the pain of reality and enjoy a few moments of pleasure.

2. Sexual affairs. Most sexual addicts show acceptance of a spouse or sexual partner(s) in direct relation to how such people meet their sexual expectations. However, addicts eventually become habituated to each sexual activity and want something more. They lead their partners into more and more degrading activities in order to satisfy their own obsession with sexual experience. Addicts may resort to multiple affairs, often simultaneously. Usually the affairs are not satisfying, and they want to move on to another relationship as soon as sexual

intercourse is achieved with a new partner. It was estimated that one addict had had nearly one thousand affairs.

3. Centerfolds, pornography and strip shows. Dr. Carnes has stated:

> The addict can transform even the most refined forms of human nudity into his own particular fusion of loneliness and arousal.

> The absence of a relationship and the desire for heightened excitement are the twin pillars of the sexual addiction. Nowhere is this more clear than when the addiction is visual. . . . Endless hours [are spent] browsing in a porno bookstore, sitting in the beach parking lot, driving around a college campus, tennis courts, and shopping malls, a nightly habit of stopping at the topless bar. Soon the time takes its toll. Work does not get done and excuses are made. Lies are told to the family about the long work hours.

> Money becomes a problem. For instance, money needed for family expenses is spent on pornography and sexually explicit magazines or an expensive videotape machine used for porno films. . . . The worst is that after a time, the obsession becomes more important than being in an important relationship. The watching becomes a more important "high" than healthy contact with family and friends. But, rationalizes the addict, there is no harm in watching.[18]

4. Prostitution. For the sexual addict, the compulsive use of prostitutes often occurs. Again, Carnes says:

> Addicts like prostitutes because [they offer] an immediate fix with few entanglements. Often [the sex] is anonymous. Yet, the consequences of prostitution are high. The lies are often elaborate. There is risk of disease. There is the possibility of it becoming public knowledge. Yet, the biggest factor for most addicts is the expense. A habit of three to four visits a week is expensive to sustain. . . . For family men

even more lies are required [in order] to explain where the money has gone. When addicts tell about themselves, their stories are frequently punctuated with deep sobs as they tell of the times when they would come home after spending a hundred dollars on a prostitute, only to realize that their children and wives were doing without something they needed. However, as in all addiction, painful realization does not stop compulsive behavior.[19]

5. Homosexuality. For homosexuals who also happen to be sexual addicts, Carnes states:

Compulsivity simply compounds problems of acceptance and shame . . . his sexual compulsiveness [is] an obstacle to developing significant relationships. . . . The addiction is even more complicated for men who consider themselves heterosexual, but are compulsive only in homosexual ways. . . .

Level 1 addicts seldom stay with one behavior category. More common would be an addict for whom prostitution, affairs, visits to porno shops, and occasional visits to hot johns form an overall picture of obsession. The accumulated effect is that the addiction can become the center of the addict's life—rooted in a complex malaise of deceit, isolation, and shame.[20]

LEVEL 2 AND 3 ADDICTIONS

Level 2 includes exhibitionism, voyeurism, making obscene telephone calls, and touching women in crowded situations such as buses and subways without their consent. Level 3 includes compulsive rape, incest, or child molestation. A sexual addict at Levels 2 or 3 usually is involved in several of the behaviors of Level 1 as well.

Common characteristics of addictions. As a sexual addiction progresses, more and more of the sexual addict's entire waking life is spent either planning to satisfy his or her addiction or actually satisfying it. Other relationships (if the addict had any healthy ones before the addiction began) become less and less healthy as the addict's energy and focus becomes completely absorbed by the addiction. This is similar to the progression in alcohol or drug addiction, where the addict's life eventually becomes entirely oriented around preparing for or actually using their drug of choice.

Another defining characteristic of an addiction is that addicts gradually lose the ability to exert voluntary control over their behavior in the area of their addiction. When under extreme threat, sexual addicts can suppress their behavior for short periods of time, but this ability to suppress is of limited duration. They have become addicted to sexual experience, and in a way similar to alcoholics or cocaine addicts, can find no rest until they receive a "fix." Chapter 6 will discuss some of the treatment options available for the sexually addicted.

KEY IDEAS FROM CHAPTER 1

Affairs can result from a personality disorder of the unfaithful partner, a sexual addiction of the unfaithful partner, a developmental crisis, temptation-filled situations, and unconscious, unrealistic, or uncommunicated expectations of the faithful partner.

The four personality disorders most often associated with affairs are narcissistic, histrionic, borderline, and antisocial personality disorders.

Sexual addicts become dependent on sexual experiences to help them cope with life in a way similar to a substance abuser's misuse of alcohol or drugs. They become enslaved to needing ever-increasing sexual experiences and lose control over their behavior.

NOTES

1. This illustration is a composite of several real-life examples.

2. In a recent study by Yablonsky, almost 50 percent of the men who were having affairs stated that the primary reason for their affairs was *the desire for a relationship* (cited in Daniel Dolesh and Sherelynn Lehman, *Love Me, Love Me Not: How to Survive Infidelity* [New York: McGraw-Hill, 1985], 35). Similarly, sociologist Laurel Richardson found that most men and women who are

involved in extramarital relationships are doing so out of a desire for relationship: "Another World," in *Psychology Today*, February 1986, 23–27.

3. I use the word *we* throughout the book to emphasize that all of us, even
if we have not had an affair, have the potential for having one.

4. Gary Collins, personal communication.

5. Frank Pittman, *Private Lies: Infidelity and the Betrayal of Intimacy* (New
York: Norton, 1989), 121–25.

6. Ellen Williams, "The Day the Fairy Tale Died," *Today's Christian
Woman* (Winter 1981–82), 49–51.

7. See Appendix A for complete bibliographic details on these books.

8. Note to lay readers: An unhealthy personality style that occurs with
some frequency in the general population is called a "personality disorder."

9. Carol Botwin, *Men Who Can't Be Faithful: How to Pick Up the Pieces When
He's Breaking Your Heart* (New York: Warner Books, 1988), 85–96.

10. Pittman, 133.

11. Peter Kreitler with Bill Bruns, *Affair Prevention* (New York: Macmillan,
1981), 28.

12. Alexandra Penney, *How to Keep Your Man Monogamous* (New York:
Bantam, 1989), 56–69.

13. Technically we might refer to this as a mixed personality disorder, with
schizoid and compulsive components. The schizoid component describes the
fear of closeness a person has, and the compulsive component indicates that
he or she uses perfectionistic behaviors to defend against those fears.

14. Quote found in Botwin, 127. Some might label this as
counterdependency. The individual is unhealthily overdependent, but tries
to act in ways that disguise this reality.

15. Botwin, 125.

16. From Ken Kesey's novel, *Sometimes a Great Notion*, cited in H. Norman
Wright, *Seasons of a Marriage* (Ventura, Calif.: Regal, 1982), 55.

17. An *enmeshed relationship* is one that has an unhealthily high degree of
closeness, where the child is not allowed to differentiate his own thoughts,
feelings, needs, and attitudes from those of his parent.

18. Patrick Carnes, *Out of the Shadows: Understanding Sexual Addiction*
(Minneapolis: CompCare Publishers, 1983), 32–33.

19. Carnes, 34.

20. Ibid., 36.

Chapter Two

Contributions of the Unfaithful Partner: Developmental Crises, Temptation, and Expectations

IN THIS FIRST SECTION WE WILL LOOK AT those developmental changes, traumas, and difficult or unpleasant situations that can sometimes lead to extramarital sexual liaisons. Some developmental periods, even though they do not involve a specific crisis, can also lead to increased risk, and we shall look at them as well.

This discussion is not a complete listing of crises and situations that produce anxiety. Almost any change can awaken insecurities. These insecurities can lead to healthy problem solving or to a variety of unhealthy ways of distracting oneself when a problem needs to be solved or a change needs to be accepted. One such unhealthy way to deal with anxiety is through neurotic sexual behavior. Listed below are the most common of such developmental crises or situations that can lead to either healthy or unhealthy problem solving.

MAKING THE TRANSITION FROM ROMANTIC LOVE TO MARRIED LOVE

Most of us have experienced the razzle-dazzle of "being in love." If we have been married for any length of time, we probably recognize that romantic love does not continue to be experienced in marriage in the same way as it did during the dating period. In the last section in this chapter we will discuss more fully how and why this change occurs. Many people are unprepared for the change that gradually occurs, usually during the first several months of marriage. As it is occurring, infatuation (a feeling produced by a highly idealized notion of who the other person is) is gradually giving way to a more realistic view.

This change is usually accompanied by some degree of disillusionment: The greater the difference between the idealized vision of our mate and the realistic vision that is developing, the greater the degree of disillusionment. Prior to marriage the less psychologically healthy person is likely to suppress or repress recognition of any unfavorable traits in the beloved. Such a person wants desperately to believe that marriage to the other partner will meet all his or her psychological needs and that they will live happily ever after. Thus, those who are less psychologically healthy are likely to experience the most disillusionment when postmarital reality breaks in.

When people initially recognize that they no longer feel the strong surges of romantic love they once did, they may conclude that they have "fallen out of love." And if they are strong fans of country and Western music, romantic novels, or daytime "soaps," they may decide that there is nothing left of the relationship. They may be tempted to rediscover that feeling of romance in the arms of someone else.

DECIDING HOW TO NEGOTIATE DIFFERENCES

One of the most important developmental tasks of a young married couple is clarifying the role of husband and wife and deciding how they will negotiate differences. Sometimes the decision-making process during this time will become quite heated. If either partner is an impulsive personality and has had a history of sexual promiscuity, these heated disagreements may lead to sexual acting out early in the marriage. More commonly, if these agreements are not resolved in healthy ways that respect the dignity of both people, this failure will lay the seeds of frustration that may grow into an affair five or ten or fifteen years later.

DECIDING ON THE RELATIONSHIP
BETWEEN SEX, LOVE, AND INTERCOURSE

The majority of women want sexual intercourse to be a manifestation of love, and only that. Most men want sexual intercourse to be an expression of love sometimes, but at other times they will want to be sexual when they are lonely, frustrated, tense, or bored. For them, sex provides a helpful antidote by serving as a distraction and producer of good feelings at these times.[1]

This difference in expectation, which usually is not articulated by couples this clearly, often causes resentments about sex that can lead to affairs. Women often feel that they are being used if their husbands want them to have sex as anything other than an expression of love: They may either refuse to participate outright or they may express their unhappiness in more indirect ways. The man may feel that his wife is denying him something that is rightfully his by refusing to have sex when he wants it. The usual result is that both give in somewhat to each other (women have sex with their husbands some of the time when it's being used as a tension reliever, and men get turned down some of the time when they want to use it as such), but neither person feels happy with this compromise.

WORKING OUT RELATIONSHIPS TO PARENTS

Another of the most important developmental tasks for young married couples is working out healthy relationships with their parents. The God-given formula for marriage is that a man shall leave his father and mother and cleave to his wife (the word *man* is undoubtedly being used generically here to refer to both persons in the marriage psychologically "leaving" their parents). If this is done, husband and wife should feel closest to each other, and the relationship to their parents should be secondary, though still respectful. Problems develop if either person feels that the other's relationship to his or her parents is more important to that spouse than the relationship they share as a couple. Parents can cause problems here if they are unwilling to allow the marriage relationship to become primary. While a failure in this process may not lead to infidelity immediately, it can begin to produce alienation that can cause problems later.

BIRTH CONTROL DISAGREEMENTS

Couples sometimes disagree as to the timing of their first child. Sometimes a male, who during the courtship had agreed to have children, changes his mind and repeatedly attempts to postpone the time they will start "trying." In such situations a woman may feel that her husband is breaking a very important promise. Depending on her age, a woman, afraid that her "biological clock" may be running out, may decide to take matters into her own hands by unilaterally discontinuing birth control measures without informing her husband. If she becomes pregnant and her husband learns that she suspended birth control procedures without his consent, he may have a "revenge affair" during the latter part of the pregnancy or after the child is born.

PREGNANCY, BIRTH OF FIRST CHILD, MOTHERING

A prime time for a first affair by a male is during the last few months of pregnancy, shortly after birth, or during the first two years of a young child's life. Prior to this in their courtship and marriage, he has become accustomed to being the center of his wife's attention. During this time the woman usually is extremely sensitive to her husband, watching his nonverbal behavior carefully, trying to anticipate his desires, and generally doing whatever she can to make him happy.

With the coming of the latter stages of pregnancy this all changes. She may not be as responsive to his needs and wants because of her own discomforts. She may not be able to meet his sexual needs comfortably. Her focus, because of hormonal changes and because of the mothering responses that she is experiencing, is shifting from her husband to their unborn child. She may have fears about the baby's health or about her delivery, and these fears may further decrease the attention she gives her husband.

Once the baby comes, the six-week period of recovery that follows for the wife may seem like an eternity for the husband. And after that a woman's energy and attention is primarily focused on meeting the needs of the infant. If she is nursing, this takes an additional portion of her energy. Her psychological need to be needed is met by her child, not by her husband. By the time they retire at night, she is usually so exhausted that she has no desire for sex. Even when they do have intercourse, they may be interrupted at any time by a crying baby.

A husband frequently becomes angry, believing that his wife cares more for the baby than she does for him, and yet he feels guilty or foolish about voicing this complaint. His psychological and sexual needs have not decreased at all during this period—only his wife's ability to fulfill them. For these reasons the latter stages of pregnancy and the first two years of a child's life are times when a husband is more likely to be unfaithful.

EXTRAORDINARY STRESS AT WORK FOR EITHER PARTNER

If a husband's workload increases at work, he may come home exhausted and have very little to give to his wife, yet he still wants to receive as much or more support from her as when he was more fully meeting her needs. His wife may feel sympathetic to his situation and try to give increased attention, but, being human, if the imbalance continues for an extended period of time she may grow resentful and reduce the amount of support she is providing. In such a situation both partners are at increased risk of an affair.

If a wife's workload increases at work, the resentment may be even worse. We still have enough of the psychological double standard present that even if both partners are working full-time and the husband is giving his primary energy to his work, his wife is expected to give her primary energies to the marriage. If her workload and pressures increase dramatically, she may simply not have enough time and energy to continue to put his needs and wants first. A similar situation may occur when a husband has an hourly job that permits him to come home at the end of eight hours, and his wife's job requires her to work longer hours. Those late afternoon and early evening hours when he wants her home attending to his needs can be brooding hours that put his fidelity at risk.

FAILURE OR REJECTION

Whenever we have a goal that we fail to achieve, we experience a variety of feelings. These may include depression, discouragement, embarrassment, or anger. (Because depression can be of varying kinds, susceptible to differing treatments, an extended discussion of it is added in Appendix D.) The healthiest response is to deal with the failure or rejection by talking it out with another person, with God, or with both. Sometimes, though, the negative feelings are not talked out, and may be acted out through one or more affairs. The affairs may be an attempt to distract ourselves from the negative feelings, or they may be a neurotic attempt to prove that we are acceptable and adequate despite the failure.

AWAY FROM HOME TOO MUCH

Some jobs require that the employee spend long hours at work, or be away from home several nights each week. Only those who have traveled for a living can appreciate the boredom and loneliness of eating alone in a restaurant and sleeping alone in a hotel, especially if this continues month after month. At home, loneliness, boredom, or resentment may also be growing. Thus these kinds of situations put both partners at increased risk for an affair. If there are one or more small children to care for, this usually (but not always) precludes the chance for an affair by the wife, and only the husband is more at risk.

SUCCESS

Surprisingly, success is also a risk factor. Success may carry with it increased work hours, increased responsibilities, and increased attractiveness to the opposite sex. These in turn may result in a person being less able to give quality time and attention at home. As this diminishes, the partner may also reciprocate, intentionally or unintentionally, by giving less to the marriage. Also, success has a way of "going to our head." We start to believe our own press reports, and this pride in our accomplishments may make us more vulnerable to temptation.

PEERS WHO ARE DIVORCING AND ENJOYING THE SINGLE LIFE

This is probably not as much of a factor for Christians as for non-Christians. For a nonbeliever who feels stuck in an unsatisfying marriage, who doesn't feel respected and accepted by his or her mate, for whom sex is infrequent and unsatisfying, the allure of being free of all the negative involvements with a mate and able to enjoy single life again may be very attractive. This is likely to be more of a temptation for a male, for whom independence and autonomy are primary needs, than for a female, for whom security is usually a primary need.

MIDLIFE

The midlife crisis is usually experienced by females between thirty-five and forty, and by males between forty and forty-five. There is disagreement among writers and researchers about what percentage of the population experience a period of drastic emotional turbulence. Some writers claim a rate as high as 90 percent, and others say it is as low as 15 percent. We all must come to terms with certain realities as we go through the midlife period. Some of us may experience and deal with these developmental realities one at a time, and so may pass through several midlife transitional periods; others may experience these realities in a more condensed period of time, and may have an identifiable midlife crisis.

Some midlife realities include:

- dealing with the facts of aging as it affects our physical strength and prowess
- dealing with the facts of aging as it affects our attractiveness to the opposite sex
- dealing with unaccomplished career goals we had set for ourselves
- dealing with the fact that we may never gain the fame, prestige, or wealth we once hoped for
- dealing with the reality that we have given most of our adult life to provide for our mate and children, and they may not appreciate the personal sacrifices we have made
- dealing with the fact that accomplishing some of the goals that we thought would bring us happiness and fulfillment has brought us neither
- dealing with our aging parents and realizing that one day they will leave us
- dealing with our own death

In the following paragraphs are some of the developmental changes and thought processes that may make a midlife person susceptible to an affair. (I am using the entire midlife period from thirty-five to fifty-five in this discussion.) These paragraphs are more highly weighted with regard to males because more research and writing has been done regarding the male midlife period.

Feeling entitled to appreciation. At midlife many men want to be appreciated for their hard work and the sacrifices they have made. Many don't feel appreciated and may say, "I've gone to college, worked fifty hours a week for my wife and kids and company. Now the kids are grown and don't think I'm too great. Nor does my wife. I'd like to meet someone who thinks I am somebody."[2]

That feeling of having sacrificed and not being appreciated can lead to a feeling of entitlement. After all his years of supporting the family, a man believes he is entitled to some good feeling himself. This can, consciously or subconsciously, serve as justification for entering into a relationship that gives him some of those good feelings.

Male/female changes in assertiveness. Another factor is that a man in midlife often tends to become more passive (more traditionally feminine). A woman in midlife tends to become more managerial (more traditionally masculine). She may also refuse to live in his shadow. Not knowing how to cope with this change, but feeling uncomfortable with it, he may select a younger woman who will be passive with respect to him and who will be content to live in his shadow.[3]

The desire to be accepted and not criticized. In the play *Fences* by August Wilson, a black, middle-aged American named Troy confesses his affair to his wife Rose, and tries to explain what it means to him:

> It's just she gives me a different idea . . . a different understanding about myself. I can step out of this house and get away from the pressures and problems . . . be a different man. . . . I ain't got to worry how I'm gonna pay the bills or get the roof fixed. I can just be a part of myself that I ain't never been. . . .
>
> I can sit up in her house and laugh. . . . I can laugh out loud . . . and it feels good. It reaches all the way down to the bottom of my shoes. Rose, I can't give that up. . . .
>
> When I saw that gal, she firmed up my backbone. . . . Rose, I'm trying the best I can to explain it to you. It's not easy for me to admit that I have been standing in the same place [he hasn't moved forward career-wise or financially] for eighteen years.[4]

This same need to be respected, to be unconditionally accepted, is echoed in the words of middle-aged Sam Toffler.

> I want someone new and fresh, who knows me and loves me as I am today. Not someone who knows I lied on my income tax, not someone who knows I cheated on my final exams. I've changed in the thirty years I've been married, I've grown in all kinds of ways. I'm filled with new ideas,

bursting with new thoughts. Yet my wife still sees me as I was thirty years ago.

I want someone who loves this Sam Toffler. All I've become. All I am today.

I don't want someone who reminds me to floss my teeth, who tells me my socks don't match, tells me to go easy on the butter. I don't want a mother.[5]

There are some who would say that what middle-aged men want is more than respect—that they want to be adored or worshiped. Such a person is Joanna, a woman in her early thirties involved with a man in his fifties.

"The greatest aphrodisiac is not an oyster," Joanna said with a smile. "It is a worshiper. A worshiper is irresistible. Men do all their brilliance during the day. They want to come home and not have to deal with anything, not have to think. They want someone who is more pliant. . . .

"You hear the old chestnut that men leave their wives for someone who understands them. That's [nonsense]. They leave their wives because their wives understand them *too well*." Then with a wink and a sly smile, she concluded, "And understanding does not make anyone an adorer."[6]

A young woman as an aphrodisiac. There are several other reasons a younger woman may function as an aphrodisiac for a man struggling to adjust to middle age. Many men experience sexual problems, the most common being impotence, sometime between forty and fifty-five. When this happens his wife may make some critical comment about his inability to perform. The next time they attempt intercourse he is genuinely anxious, and his anxiety causes him to be impotent again.

He becomes aware that he can become sexually aroused in the presence of an attractive younger woman. He then arranges an encounter with such a young woman to see if he is permanently deficient. The novelty of the situation, her youth, and her willingness to work with him may often allow him to bypass his anxiety and not be impotent. In the presence of his wife his anxiety returns, and so does his impotence. Only in the presence of a younger, attractive woman who is willing to work with him is he able to maintain his sense of masculinity.[7]

Another attraction of the younger woman to the older man is what has been called "the trophy factor." The trophy factor refers to the enjoyment a middle-aged man receives being with a young woman because he thinks that by having a young, attractive woman on his arm, his standing will be enhanced in other people's eyes.

Sex with a younger woman may also be more exciting than with his partner because he is rebelling against the unwritten taboo that a fifty-four-year-old man should not be having sex with a twenty-four-year-old woman. Her spontaneity, her willingness to indulge a little fantasy and a little playfulness in their lovemaking also enhances the experience for him.[8]

Many middle-aged men become involved with or even marry women half their age because such women make them feel younger. A physician in his forties who divorced his wife and married a twenty-one-year-old said, "It's starting over; it makes a man feel he is winning and attractive, powerful and dynamic."[9] We like people who make us feel good about ourselves.

A younger woman keeps a middle-aged man active, performing his best. And functioning at his best is positive for both of them. She encourages him to live out his best fantasy of himself. Some men marry young women because they believe younger women make *them* feel and act younger.

What an older man provides a young woman. One might ask what possible attraction such an arrangement could have for the young woman in these situations. One young woman answered that question this way: "Jeremy, my fifty-five-year-old lover, is my one safe place, where I can lean, relax, say I'm tired, say I'm scared, ask for help. He's so understanding, he loves to advise me and help me. He makes me feel special."[10]

It is likely that this young woman reflects the feelings of many others. An older man may provide a sense of caring, of protection, of specialness that meets certain important needs in herself. Undoubtedly there are other factors, some of which may be unconscious in some women, but very much in the conscious awareness of others. For example, someone has made the point that young women don't fall in love with *poor* middle-aged men, only with *well-to-do* middle-aged men.

Such relationships have their critics, to be sure. Author Joseph Heller quipped, "When I see a couple where one member is much older than the other, I know there's something wrong with both of them."[11]

Connie White discussed her own experience as a young woman married to a much older man:

"When I became his wife, I had to be perfect because I was his wife. I realize how you must deny your feelings to be happy with older men. It took me fifteen years, then I realized what was happening. I had to be an ornament, a dear little doll. Oh, I was wrong, so wrong. This was not a good daddy; he was a cruel parent. It was tyranny, not strength, but I didn't know that then."

She then goes on to say that she believes her experience is far from unique:

"Everyone I ever met who was a younger woman with an older man is somebody who in some way feels worthless. Later they recognize they had to deny their feelings to stay in the marriage, and then they realize there's nothing for them. It's all domineering, controlling; they're treated like dirt. The trips and the furs and jewels aren't worth it, but you don't know that until you've been in it for a long time."[12]

The phenomenon of middle-aged men with much younger women reflects our male failure to come to terms with the issue of aging, a neurotic acting out of the desire to stay young. Not only is it a vain attempt to try to maintain a sense of youthfulness when we are growing older; it's usually a sinful way of responding to the issue of aging, for it often means breaking faith with the wife of one's youth, and seducing a young woman into an unhealthy relationship that sometimes will prevent her from having a healthier one.

Throughout this section on developmental crisis we have seen that change often produces anxiety. We want to go back to the safety of an earlier relationship or situation, but cannot. We have a choice: to clearly think through the situation and develop a plan of action to deal with the anxiety in a way that is within God's moral will, or to act out the conflict through the use of alcohol, drugs, or sexual encounters that distract us from the difficulty or produce pleasant feelings, but in a morally unacceptable fashion.

TEMPTATION-FILLED SITUATIONS

SOCIETAL FACTORS THAT INCREASE TEMPTATION

At least six factors make our present environment an increasingly temptation-filled one: (1) Opportunities for adult males and females to be alone together have increased. (2) The opportunities for men and women to work or interact for extended periods of time have increased. (3) Our expectations for what we want out of marriage have increased. (4) The time and energy we believe we have available for our spouses has decreased. (5) Our sense of entitlement to emotional happiness and sexual fulfillment has increased. (6) In some ways the consequences of going outside marriage to meet our needs have decreased. It should be helpful to discuss these briefly.

Opportunities for men and women to be together for extended periods of time have increased. The visitor to the Washington Monument will be treated to an interesting bit of American folklore that illustrates just how much ideas have changed. When a mechanized elevator was first installed in the monument during the last century, it took several minutes for the elevator to ascend from ground level to the top. It was considered inappropriate for men and women to be together in a confined space for such a long time. Therefore, gallant men that they were, it was decided that men could use the elevator and women had to climb the stairs.

Today many people find it incredible that such segregation of the sexes was then thought to be necessary. In contrast, now regular opportunities exist for unmarried men and women to be alone together, not just for a few minutes, but for hours at a time. It has been shown empirically that when persons of the opposite sex are in constant contact, such regular exposure enhances interpersonal attraction.[13] As Penney states, "The relationship between a man and his secretary, the female 'buddy' in the next office, the colleague who works on a deadline project, the co-worker who accompanies him on a business trip—these are the 'high-risk conditions' that induce a familiarity that is all too easily transmuted into emotional and sexual intimacy."[14] As people develop good working relationships, positive feelings emerge and it may be only a small step from a good working relationship to an affair. In addition, it is not uncommon for men and women to be alone together in a variety of contexts without the social disapproval they would have encountered only a few decades ago.

Today we are expecting more from our marriages than did our parents. We want more intellectual and emotional intimacy than our grandparents and parents did. At the same time, in many marriages both partners work full-time outside the home, and so have less energy and time to give to their marriage. Thus in many families each person wants more from the partner, but has less to give in return.

Entitlement is a term that appears more and more in the psychological literature. At first this term was used primarily in reference to narcissistic personalities, people who believed they were entitled to be treated with extra courtesy and respect. But now a great many more people believe that they are entitled to romance and sexual ecstasy in their marriages. If they don't find it there, they feel "entitled" to seek it elsewhere.

Simultaneously, *the consequences of looking for intimacy outside of marriage have decreased.* With the advent of no-fault divorce, more effective birth control, and greater social acceptance of affairs—plus a cultural milieu that even encourages "open marriages"—fewer punishing consequences are left within American culture to deter a person from looking for romantic fulfillment outside of marriage.

SPECIFIC HIGH-RISK SITUATIONS

In his book *Affair Prevention*, Episcopal minister Peter Kreitler lists seven high-risk situations in which he believes an affair may easily start. These are The Friendship Affair, the Be a Good Neighbor Affair, the Cup of Coffee Affair, the Seize the Moment Affair, the Old Acquaintance Never-to-Be-Forgotten Affair, the People-Helper Affair, and the Office Affair.

The Friendship Affair. Probably the relationship most in danger of becoming an affair is a friendship between two people of the opposite sex. This may occur at work, at church, or within one's extended family (i.e., your spouse's relatives). Frequently the relationship begins to deepen when a Christian man sees a female who is experiencing difficulty and asks, out of Christian love, "Are you OK?" She may share with him some of the problems in her life. His original motivation is Christian concern, but he soon finds that it feels good to be able to give comfort to her. It also feels good to her to have the attentive concern of a man. Meeting their reciprocal needs through each other reinforces further sharing and attentive listening, which can eventually lead to an affair.

Various writers refer to the frequency with which a friendship can turn into an affair.[15] Carl Broderick says:

> I am convinced that more people get themselves into the pain of infidelity through empathy, concern and compassion than through any base motive. The world is full of lonely and vulnerable people, hungry for a sympathetic ear and a shoulder to cry on. . . . With a little help from rationalization, the sympathy leads smoothly into tenderness, the tenderness to the need for privacy, the privacy to physical consolation, and the consolation straight to bed.[16]

The Be a Good Neighbor Affair. Another high-risk situation is when neighbors become good friends with each other, and begin spending considerable time in each other's homes. This

becomes especially risky if two unmarried people of the opposite sex are alone for significant periods. Consider the story of
Rick, Diane, and Peg as told by Rick:

> We had this next-door neighbor, Peg, whom Diane and I
> became good friends with. Peg was divorced and had a ten-
> year-old girl who enjoyed playing with our daughter, who
> was nine. They often played together while we would talk
> or play cards. Then Diane got transferred from the day shift
> at her job to the evening shift. Peg and I continued to get
> together to talk while our daughters played together. One
> night Peg and I just ended up in bed together—it's hard to
> explain how it happened. Since then we go to bed when-
> ever the kids give us a chance.

The Cup of Coffee Affair. The Cup of Coffee Affair is a friendship that develops over as innocent a thing as the coffee break.
This may begin when a man and a woman are casually introduced by mutual friends. The relationship may start on a very
light note, and the two may see one another only sporadically
at first. As one or both senses an attraction, they are seen more
regularly together for coffee, often with other people. Then,
having a cup of coffee by themselves becomes their habit. From
there the story is quite predictable.

The Seize the Moment Affair. Two people who meet each
other and are away from their natural constraints, and who
develop a warm relationship easily, may be tempted to "seize
the moment." Ross and Betty were both high-school music
teachers, and met at a national music teacher's workshop far
from either one's home. They struck up a light and enjoyable
conversation during the afternoon break, and attended the
same workshop later in the afternoon. Since neither of them
knew anyone else at the convention, they decided to go to
supper together. After a pleasant supper Betty invited Ross
back to her room, and they spent the night together. The next
morning they both agreed never to tell their spouses what
had happened, and not to keep in contact after the convention
ended. They have not seen each other since.

The Old Acquaintance Never-to-Be-Forgotten Affair. Seeing an old friend from years past and having a pleasant interaction with them is likely to trigger pleasant transference feelings from the past. We may remember the good times we had together. Especially if two people had dated in high school, it may not be uncommon for former schoolmates from many years before to have a one-night affair after a high-school reunion if their spouses are not present.

The People-Helper Affair. People are often more open with a counselor than with anyone else. Because many counselors try to show unconditional acceptance, this kind of relationship can easily lead to powerful transference and countertransference feelings. Those situations in which a male counselor holds private sessions with a female client who has either a histrionic or borderline personality are especially risky. Counselors are prohibited by their professional code of ethics from becoming sexually involved with their clients, and most maintain these standards. When romantic feelings develop between a counselor and a client, and when those feelings distract them from working effectively on the issues that brought the client into counseling initially, it may be wise for the client to transfer to another counselor.

The Office Affair. Perhaps no one can explain this kind of situation more clearly than does Alexandra Penney:

> Of all the conditions that men describe as "high risk" for infidelity, there is one which is absolutely treacherous: It occurs when he says "I have to stay late at the office."
>
> If I were asked to locate the exact territory at which a large percentage of infidelities take root, it's when he starts working longer hours. This may seem obvious, but when you hear it over and over again as I did in talking with men, you begin to realize just how prevalent the office or work-related affair is—and to what disasters it can lead.
>
> "There are high-risk and low-risk situations," observes a forty-five-year-old monogamous stockbroker from New York. "In business situations you leave early because if

you leave late, the atmosphere becomes more charged, more close, more open to connection on an intimate level. I bring work home if it's a matter of staying late. The few times I left the office after six, I almost broke my lifelong pattern of monogamy. If you've made the conscious decision to be faithful, it's easier to withstand pressures, but there are always occasional snares and I think most men who work late in offices can much more easily succumb to them."[17]

In my experience as a counselor, I have not seen many Christians who became involved in casual affairs (e.g., the Seize the Moment Affair or the Old Acquaintance Never-to-Be-Forgotten Affair). For committed Christians, the more high-risk situations seem to be the relationships that develop gradually over a long period of time, often very innocently. As reciprocal needs are met between two people, those relationships very subtly become more than a friendship or working relationship. High-risk situations for Christians include the Friendship Affair, the People-Helper Affair, and the Office Affair.

THE SEXUALLY ASSERTIVE WOMAN

Single women. Perhaps the highest risk of all to monogamous marriages is the growing number of single women who are willing to be sexually involved with married men in return for benefits that they enjoy, and who are becoming increasingly assertive in seeking out men. Richardson, Chapman, and Denholtz identify several reasons why single women may choose to become involved with married men. Women can use such men to augment their finances and to treat them to restaurants and social events that they could not otherwise afford. Lesbian women can use an occasional affair with a male to cover their sexual orientation.

Having an affair with a married man gives the other woman a sense of control—she doesn't have to deal with all the expectations of marriage, and yet has some of the benefits of it. "Today's Other Women generally have a different agenda than did women who became mistresses in the past," notes Laurel Richardson. "Today's woman wants to finish her education, build a career, recover from a divorce, raise her children, explore her sexuality. Getting married is not necessarily her primary goal. Indeed, she may see marriage or a marriage-like commitment as a drain on the time and energy better spent achieving other personal goals. Yet she may still want an intimate relationship with a man. As an Other Woman, she believes, she can have both."[18]

Women who have been newly promoted to high-level management positions cite another psychological motivation for their affairs. This same author reported, "Some career women I talked to said that their liaisons helped relieve major conflicts in their personal and professional lives. Many women still feel insecure in their roles as professionals and top-level managers. Some fear that their femininity will be compromised; others fear that they are frauds, incapable of doing the work that their high-level positions entail. Although a woman can get some guidance and reassurance from female mentors and colleagues, most of those I interviewed still placed a higher value on a man's judgment and approval.

"In a relationship with a married man, I was told, a woman can risk expressing her fears and showing her inadequacies without the risk of exposure to others. She can be vulnerable and weak, a luxury she denies herself in her professional role. When the married man listens and offers support, he also strengthens the woman's emotional attachment, increasing the probability of a long-term affair. As one executive woman commented, 'I hadn't realized how much I needed a safe harbor. A place where I didn't have to know everything and make all the decisions. That's what swept me off my feet.'"[19]

The generally satisfied but bored homemaker. There is another kind of high-risk situation, one that goes against the belief that an affair is always a symptom of an unsatisfactory marriage. These are women who are not experiencing problems at home. Their marriages are not intolerable. Their husbands are not abusive. These women simply want more "benefits"—adventure, fun, and recreation—than monogamy can provide. They love their husbands and want their marriages to continue, but they also want the extra adventure of having an affair.[20] (I have not known any Christian women who fit this category.) In *Having It Both Ways*, one woman expressed it this way:

> "Marriage gets boring, and the excitement of a new man keeps me going. I know it can't last forever—affairs come to an end. And I want to keep my husband. But when boredom sets in, an extramarital affair soothes me over the bumps.
>
> But I don't want to leave my husband. I'd be crazy to trade him in. He's a nice man. We've got two little kids. It surprises me that I don't feel guilty.
>
> Everyone wants a little extra. That's how I get mine."[21]

Women who immediately ask for sexual contact. Another high-risk situation is one in which a woman, from her first contact with a man, indicates her interest in having sex with him. While the majority of affairs develop around a relationship or friendship first—and sex is secondary and remains secondary—a small number of women take the initiative by letting men know they are sexually attracted to them and are available.[22] To have a woman indicate that she wants to give herself to him is, for most men, a tremendous ego boost, particularly if his wife "only has sex to please him." Even if his wife is a willing sex partner, it is still a tremendous boost to his ego for a woman to say of her own initiative that she is sexually attracted to him and would like to go to bed with him. Few men have the strength to turn down such a proposal from an attractive woman, particularly if they are in a situation where they believe they could carry off the encounter without danger of discovery or repercussions.

A new era in male-female relations. Men have long been criticized because some among them have tried to initiate sexual relations with women to whom they had no permanent commitment. Often, women's unwillingness to be sexually involved without a commitment put limitations on adultery.

Such "safeguards" that once existed against adultery are no longer there with the strength they once were. Instead, an increasing number of women are willing to be sexually involved with men because it meets their personal, emotional, or sexual needs. We Christian men need to be prepared for a new era in male-female relations: to be prepared not only to not initiate improper relationships with women, but also to say no when women seek to begin such relationships with us.

OTHER RISK FACTORS

Doty lists a number of other factors that he believes can increase vulnerability or susceptibility to an affair. They include:

- Partners' parents had affairs
- Frequent sexual experience before marriage
- A background of cheating (by either partner)
- Schedules that allow for unaccounted time
- Partners who are alienated from each other
- A partner who is extremely jealous of a spouse
- A partner who wants out of the marriage
- When there is no creativity in the sexual relationship
- When one's partner is overweight
- When one's partner is facing chronic physical illness[23]

How can we summarize this section on high-risk situations? I think it indicates that increasing numbers of work and recreational situations exist where individuals can be seriously tempted to be unfaithful. Many Christians fall into extramarital sin because they are unprepared for the sudden seductiveness of someone who wants a sexual liaison. Because temptation is much more prevalent today than in previous generations, it is crucial to make improvement of our own marriage one of our highest priorities, especially where the marriage is unfulfilling for either partner. If our partner is reluctant to begin improving the relationship, then *we* must take preventive steps. Otherwise, something much more serious than dissatisfaction with the marriage may occur. The days are gone when we can safely say, "I know my partner's not happy with this, but he (or she) will get over it." Alexandra Penney, in her book *How to Keep Your Man Monogamous*, gives a warning that both husbands and wives should apply, even though Penney is writing to women:

> Tell women that when they've not paying attention to [their] man, or when they're not there for him, it's just too easy for another [woman] to fill the bill.[24]

Unconscious, Unrealistic, or Uncommunicated Expectations of the Unfaithful Partner

Many writers, researchers, and family therapists have made the point that we all bring a host of expectations to marriage. These expectations include what we are to do and not do, and what we expect our partner to do and not do. Many of these are unconscious—we're not aware of them until our partner either transgresses one of them or starts to expect something from us that we didn't think was part of the original marriage agreement. We may become aware of our expectations when our partner fails to meet them and someone outside the marriage starts to meet them instead; when this happens we may feel emotionally attracted to that other person.

The Problem with Unconscious Expectations

When we have unconscious expectations, we have not thought about whether they are realistic or unrealistic, and whether they are fair to both persons or are overly self-centered. We become frustrated whenever an expectation is not met, whether it be a realistic one or an unrealistic one, fair to both or overly self-centered.

An unconscious expectation of our partner, unmet, can generate frustration that may propel us toward an affair. Thus it is important, when we feel frustrated with our mate, to identify the unmet expectation that is causing that frustration. By making it conscious, we can judge whether it is realistic and fair to our partner and ourselves. We may decide that it is a realistic and fair one. We can then talk about the issue with our partner and attempt to find a resolution that satisfies both.

Sometimes we won't need to talk with our mate. After evaluating it we will decide it is an unrealistic or overly selfish expectation: By letting go of it we can let go of the frustration that was generated by it. J. Allan Petersen has said: "When anyone expects something out of marriage it was never intended to deliver [i.e., has an unrealistic expectation], he is doomed to feeling disappointed, disillusioned, and angry. This can become an excuse for an affair or an opportunity to grow up."[25]

FOUR COMMON EXPECTATIONS

H. Norman Wright has identified four expectations that are often unconscious, unrealistic, and uncommunicated. Because they are unrealistic, they usually cannot be met in a marriage. Paraphrasing Wright somewhat, we may expect that: (1) our relationship will always be the way it was in the early days of marriage, (2) our romantic "in-love" feelings can and should last forever, (3) if our spouse really loves us, he or she will know what we want without our needing to ask, and (4) if we really love each other, we should both think the same way, feel the same emotions, and want the same things.[26] We will examine each of these in a little more detail.

Expectation number 1: Our relationship will always be the way it was in the early days of our marriage. Frank Pittman has said, "Every marriage is a disappointment. Everyone who marries expects to be adored, pampered, and served or supported in style. They expect their status to rise, they expect the world to envy them. They expect to live happily ever after. When this doesn't happen, they are disappointed, and they do whatever they do when they are disappointed—they pout, or they cheat, or they fight, and they make life even less wonderful."[27] While Pittman is obviously using hyperbole to make his point, there is some important truth in what he says here. We need to let go of the unrealistic expectation that our spouses exist primarily to meet our needs and make us happy. Their primary goal should be to love and serve God, as should ours. The goal of meeting each other's needs, while important, is not to be our all-consuming focus.

Expectation number 2: Honeymoon fever can be maintained or recaptured. Although this has been discussed briefly under developmental changes a couple must adjust to, the importance of this phenomenon merits further discussion. According to Pittman, being "in love is . . . a form of temporary insanity. . . . Romance is wonderful and smells like a new car and fades about as fast and has nothing to do with real life."[28]

Elaine Walster, recipient of a National Science Foundation grant to study romantic love, found that "6 to 30 months is the average duration of the kind of heart-stopping, I'm-about-to-faint romantic frenzy we all think of as being in love."[29]

For many people, there is the unconscious expectation that that state of being "in love" will continue throughout the marriage, and that if it does not, something is seriously wrong with the relationship. According to Robert Johnson, the author of *WE: Understanding the Psychology of Romantic Love,*

> Romantic love doesn't just mean loving someone; it means being "in love." This is a very specific psychological phenomenon. When we are "in love," we believe we have found the ultimate meaning of life, revealed in another human being. We feel we are finally completed, that we have found the missing parts of ourselves. Life suddenly seems to have a wholeness, a superhuman intensity that lifts us high above the ordinary plane of existence. For us, these are the sure signs of "true love." The psychological package includes an unconscious demand that our lover or spouse always provides us with this feeling of ecstasy and intensity.[30]

Another writer has said:

> The truth about all highs is that they gradually fade. You gradually get to know the guy and he becomes predictable. Or you get to feeling overly secure. . . . The barriers fall. The

limits are exceeded. The tingle fades, and there you are wondering where your "happy" went, and if you really want the tingle, the tension, the "high," then you have to go looking for another Prince. And another one after him, and another one after him. There's nothing wrong with wanting highs. The only problem with it is that if you only get sexual romantic highs and that's all you want, you're probably going to spend a lonely and disastrous old age. Princes get few and far between when you're forty. . . . Remember: some women only think they're "happy" when they're "in love." Which means that some women are really fouled up with the Wretched Habit of Romance.[31]

The above is probably one of the most important points to be made in this book. The "high" of being "in love" (romantic love or infatuation love) will not last when a couple has come to know each other well and the constraints against their being together have been removed. In a healthy marriage, being "in love" matures into the state of giving and receiving love. This does not mean their love has died, but rather that it has matured into something we might call "commitment love"— what Scripture calls *agape* love.

We can regain the "high" of romantic love by developing a secret relationship with another person. If we do, many of the same conditions that produced our initial feelings of being "in love" (perhaps years ago, with our mates) will be present again. The excitement factor of coming to know someone who is new and mysterious, the excitement factor of doing what is forbidden, the making of plans, the excitement of not being discovered, the in-love craziness—all of it will come back.

When contrasted with the high of romantic love, the intensity of commitment love seems to pale in comparison. In such an instance, some people think that in order to be true to themselves, they must pursue the relationship in which they are "in love" and leave the relationship that seems "dead." The fault in this reasoning is that depth of love is not related to the intensity of emotions the person is experiencing in the two relationships. Someday in the future the emotions he or she feels in this second relationship will be the same as the emotions now felt toward one's first partner. This change from the emotional intensity of romantic love to the emotional stability of commitment love is a normal developmental part of every relationship.

Expectation number 3: If my spouse really loves me, he or she will know what I want without my needing to ask. The corollary to this expectation is: If I have to ask for what I want, that spoils it and it is no good, even if I get what I ask. In response to this I would paraphrase the words of marital therapist Helen Singer Kaplan: "Learning to become a good lover without feedback from your partner is like learning to target-shoot blindfolded." I cannot read my partner's mind, no matter how much I love her, nor can she mine. We need to replace the unrealistic self-talk that it spoils the romance of an action if I have to ask my partner for something, with the more realistic notion that it is her willingness to respond to my requests rather than her ability to read my mind that indicates her love for me.

Expectation number 4: If we really love each other, we should think the same, feel the same, and want the same things. This is a misinterpretation of the phrase "and the two will become one flesh" (Eph. 5:31). The biblical author was not saying that a married couple will always have the same perspective on every issue. Rather, he was teaching that part of the total commitment that a man and woman make is the willingness to give themselves sexually to each other.

Part of the beauty of men and women both being made in the image of God is that together each sex sees part of God's reality that the other is prone to miss. By sharing those additional perspectives with each other we grow in our understanding of God's creation. Expectation number 4, when carried out in a marriage, leads to enmeshment, an unhealthy kind of closeness that does not leave room for healthy individuality and personhood. A healthy marriage must leave room for partners to see things differently as well as to agree.

KEY IDEAS FROM CHAPTER 2

When some people meet a new developmental situation or crisis, they act out their emotional stress sexually through affairs. Developmental situations that can lead to sexual acting out include making the transition from romantic love to married love, pregnancy and birth of first child, extraordinary stress at work for either partner, experiences of failure or rejection or success, being away from home too much, and midlife crises.

Some of the factors that make our present world a more temptation-filled environment include the fact that opportunities for adult males and females to be alone together have increased, the opportunities for men and women to work or interact for extended periods of time have increased, our expectations for what we want out of marriage have increased, the time and energy we believe we have available for our spouses have decreased, our sense of entitlement to emotional happiness and sexual fulfillment has increased, and the consequences of going outside our marriage to meet those needs have decreased.

High-risk situations that often lead to affairs include the Friendship Affair, the Be a Good Neighbor Affair, the Cup of Coffee Affair, the Seize the Moment Affair, the Old Acquaintance Never-to-Be-Forgotten Affair, the People-Helper affair, and the Office Affair.

Another high-risk situation for Christian men are the increasing numbers of women who are willing to be sexually involved with married men in return for benefits that they enjoy, and who are becoming increasingly assertive in seeking out men.

Unrealistic and often unconscious expectations that may make a spouse dissatisfied with marriage and therefore more vulnerable to an affair include the ideas that a relationship will always be the way it was in the early days of marriage, romantic "in-love" feelings can and should last forever, the belief that if my spouse really loves me, he or she will know what I want without me needing to ask, and the belief that if we really love each other, we should think, feel, and want exactly the same things.

NOTES

1. Some women like to use sex in the way described here as usually used by males. One female wrote: "Extramarital [sex for emotional relief] isn't exclusively a male reaction. It relieves my tension. I couldn't get through law school without it." Quoted in Elaine Denholtz, *Having It Both Ways: A Report of Married Women with Lovers* (New York: Stein and Day, 1981), 132.

2. Barbara Gordon, *Jennifer Fever: Older Men, Younger Women* (New York: Harper and Row, 1988), 54.

3. Psychologist David Gutman, cited in Gordon, 19–20.

4. Cited in Gordon, 256–57.

5. Cited in Gordon, 39–40.

6. Cited in Gordon, 58–59.

7. Adapted from Gordon, 8.

8. Gordon, 85, 75.

9. Quoted in Gordon, 17.

10. Quoted in Gordon, 10.

11. Quoted in Gordon, 18.

12. Quoted in Gordon, 196–97.

13. S. Saegert, W. Swap, and R. B. Zajonc, "Exposure, Context and Interpersonal Attraction," *Journal of Personality and Social Psychology* 7 (1973), 25.

14. Alexandra Penney, *How to Keep Your Man Monogamous* (New York: Bantam, 1989), 75.

15. Willard Harley, *His Needs, Her Needs: Building an Affair-Proof Marriage* (Old Tappan, N.J.: Revell, 1986), 12–14. H. Norman Wright, *Seasons of a Marriage* (Ventura, Calif.: Regal, 1982), 111–12.

16. Carlfred Broderick, *Couples* (New York: Simon and Schuster, 1979), 163.

17. Penney, 74–75.

18. Laurel Richardson, "Another World," *Psychology Today*, February, 1986, 25.

19. Richardson, *Psychology Today*, 26.

20. Denholtz, 197, 214.

21. Denholtz, 127.

22. Penney, 82.

23. Dale Doty, "Treating Marriages Recovering from an Affair," a paper presented at the International Congress on Christian Counseling, Atlanta,

Georgia, 1988.

24. Penney, 74.

25. J. Allan Petersen, *The Myth of the Greener Grass* (Wheaton, Ill.: Tyndale House, 1983), 63.

26. Wright, 16–17.

27. Pittman, 85–86.

28. Pittman, 93.

29. Cited by Denholtz, 98.

30. Robert A. Johnson, *WE: Understanding the Psychology of Romantic Love* (New York: Harper and Row, 1983), xii.

31. *When Your Happily Ever After Isn't* (Denver: Raj Publications, 1981), 12.

Chapter Three

Contributions of the Faithful Partner: Failure to Meet Expectations and Ego Needs

IN THE FIRST TWO CHAPTERS WE LOOKED at five sets of factors, primarily related to the *unfaithful partner* in a marriage or to the situation he or she is in, which can lead to an affair. In this chapter and the next we will look at four more sets of factors that are somewhat different. Each of these relates more closely to the *faithful partner's* behavior. By responding or not responding in certain ways, the faithful partner may fail to meet some of the reasonable human needs of the other partner. As a result, the potential adulterer becomes more vulnerable to temptation and may accept someone else's overtures. A final category includes situations in which each partner shares in various ways in things that contribute to a marital affair. The five categories are:

- Failure to meet realistic, communicated expectations of the unfaithful spouse
- Failure to meet the ego needs of the unfaithful spouse

- Unconscious, unrealistic, or uncommunicated expectations of the faithful partner that are expressed in nonassertive ways
- Psychopathology, including codependency, of the faithful spouse
- Other systems-related reasons for affairs

If you, the reader, have recently been betrayed—it can certainly happen to counselors or to pastors, for whom this book is primarily intended—it may be difficult for you to hear the message of this chapter. Especially if the infidelity is a recent happening, the pain, humiliation, and sense of outrage you feel may prevent you from accepting any blame for the betrayal of the wedding vows. These are normal feelings. If they are so strong and the anger is so intense that you cannot concentrate on the message of this chapter, then the contents may have to be introduced slowly. It may be best to put the book down, pray for the next week about what God may want to say, and try to read this chapter later.

Each marriage is unique—even those where affairs have intruded. The material in this chapter may or may not apply to any given situation. In some affairs the contributions come almost entirely from the unfaithful spouse. However, in many affairs both partners contribute something to the situation from which the affair arises. There is a consensus among marriage counselors about one point: Those marriages that survive an affair are those where both people are able to recognize and accept what they have contributed to the infidelity. Those marriages where partners do not get past the blaming stage rarely survive, and if they do the marriage never becomes a healthy relationship. We will turn now to look in detail at each of the five categories.

FAILURE TO MEET REALISTIC, COMMUNICATED EXPECTATIONS OF THE UNFAITHFUL SPOUSE

Susan Squires has written, "The affair is a sign of a need for help, an attempt to compensate for deficiencies in the relationship due to situational stress, a warning that someone is suffering."[1] You already know, because of statements made in refuting some of the myths about adultery, that I do not agree fully with this quote. Every time there is an affair it is not because someone is suffering from deficiencies in the relationship—it may be that his or her expectations are unrealistic. Also, some people have affairs because of psychopathology they brought into their marriages. Some people have affairs, even though they are content with their marriages, because they want more adventure than monogamy provides.

However, with those exceptions identified, it is true that some affairs are a sign of a need for help, an indication that one spouse feels that his or her needs are not being met in the relationship. A common cause of female adultery is that a husband gives almost all his time, energy, and attention to his job, leaving nothing for his wife. To her it is almost as if he had taken a mistress (his work), and that his mistress is consuming all of his attention and affection. Wives continue to need reminders that their husbands still love them throughout marriage, not just during courtship. And in a reciprocal way men still need to know that their wives respect them, even though their wives have learned all the husbands' faults.

In some marriages, requests become demands. When a marriage partner fails to respond to requests from his or her spouse, frustration grows, and the gentle requests may be gradually replaced by angry demands. Since no one likes to be ordered around, partners may stubbornly refuse to respond to each other's demands. By this time they have become fixated on the point of contention ("You're going to do that!" "No, I'm not!") and the point of contention assumes an emotional significance out of proportion to its actual importance.

Unfulfilled requests or demands increase vulnerability. When a person fails to meet the realistic, communicated expectations of a spouse over a period of time, that marriage becomes increasingly vulnerable to an affair. The adulterer enters a liaison in an attempt, whether conscious or unconscious, to find something that is lacking in his or her marriage.

There are three kinds of affairs that can develop at this point, each one indicating something about the emotional state of the participants.

The Supplemental Affair

Christians sometimes enter a supplemental affair for friendship, or because their marriages have lost their sense of vitality. These persons are not so alienated from their partners that they want a divorce, but they want to supplement what they are not getting from their marriages by finding some of it somewhere else. While initially the person remains committed to his or her marriage, an affair that begins as a supplemental one can eventually rupture a marriage.

The Affair of Anger

The affair of anger is entered out of frustration at the faithful spouse. Often in such an affair, little holds the relationship together but bad feelings toward a spouse. Such affairs quickly disintegrate. The guilty party in an affair of anger may sometimes confess the affair, but this is often an attempt to vent anger and force the spouse to start dealing with issues that are unsatisfactory in the marriage. Because of the anger that motivates such confessions, the aftermath is likely to be very painful to everyone involved. It may, however, be the only way a spouse knows to thoroughly gain the mate's attention.

The Replacement Affair

The replacement affair is the most extreme of these three. In this type the anger has hardened into an attitude of permanent disdain. The angry person is looking for someone to psychologically and sexually replace his or her spouse. For all practical purposes, the marital relationship is dead, but the person may be hesitant to ask for a divorce for one reason or another.[2]

Sometimes a marriage partner constantly produces anger in the spouse by failing to meet that person's realistic, communicated expectations. When this happens, the anger may allow the spouse to feel justified in meeting some needs through an extramarital relationship. This anger also reduces any guilt feelings the unfaithful person may have for the affair. While theologically such persons are still guilty of adultery, psychologically they often feel at least partially justified in their behavior.

FAILURE TO MEET THE EGO NEEDS OF THE UNFAITHFUL SPOUSE

In this section I would like to develop what I call "An Ego Needs Theory of Adultery."[3] This theory consists of nine postulates.

1. We come into marriage with many ego needs, some conscious, many unconscious. These ego needs get translated into expectations, things which we believe we need from a partner in order to be happy and satisfied in marriage. This process of translating ego needs into expectations usually happens unconsciously. Some of the more well-known of these needs include the need for affection, the need to be respected, the need for attention, and the need for sexual fulfillment.

2. A person explains his feelings of attraction to someone by saying that the other person makes him feel good about himself. Translated into ego needs theory terminology, this means that he feels attracted to someone who meets his ego needs. A man is more likely to feel good about himself in the presence of a woman if he believes she finds him attractive; a woman is more likely to feel good about herself in the presence of a man if she believes he likes and respects her.[4]

3. People marry to get their ego needs met. They marry persons whom they believe will be able to make them feel good about themselves on a continuing basis. Romantic fantasies and love stories encourage people to believe that they are attracted to certain persons because they truly care about the other persons' happiness and well-being. The reality is that most individuals marry persons whom they unconsciously believe will help them feel happy, secure, attractive, and respected.

4. What keeps most couples contented in a marriage is the nurturing of each other's ego needs.

5. *The basic ego needs of males and females overlap, but the needs that are greatest for most males are different from the ego needs that are greatest for most females.* (This point will be discussed further in the following pages.)

6. *People usually stay within the boundaries of marriage if their primary needs are being adequately met there.* People are tempted to stray when their primary emotional and sexual needs are not being met through their marriage partners.[5] No matter what lofty promises a person made years before in a wedding ceremony, if any of a spouse's basic needs go unmet for a significant period of time, that person becomes vulnerable to the temptation of an affair.

7. *An affair often occurs because it meets some ego needs that aren't being met in the marriage.*

8. *In order for people to maximize the chances that their marriages will remain monogamous, they must understand how their needs differ from their partners' needs, must learn to communicate their needs to their partners, and must effectively meet the needs of their partners.*

9. *Even if a person earnestly attempts to meet the ego needs of his or her partner, the marriage may not remain monogamous if that partner has a personality disorder or is sexually addicted.* "Certain men are . . . unfaithful because of unmet needs that no woman can meet."[6]

EGO NEEDS OF MEN AND WOMEN

We will now look at postulate 5 in a little more depth. Numerous surveys and interviews have indicated that a positive friendship (companionship), good communication, and a good sex life are three of the most important ingredients in maintaining a healthy marriage. However, many of these surveys or interviews have been less helpful than they might have been because they have not clearly defined what constitutes a good relationship or good communication. Dr. Willard Harley is one psychologist who has studied this subject more carefully.[7] Harley identified ten needs that are frequently believed to be the most important needs of individuals in marriage. He then constructed a psychological test that measured the strength of these needs and found that there are significant differences in the priorities men and women give to these ten needs.

The ten needs, with a short explanation showing how Harley is defining them, are:

- Admiration: knowing that your spouse is proud of you.
- Affection: using actions and words that say to your spouse, "I love you. I'll take care of you and protect you. You are important to me and I don't want anything to happen to you."
- An attractive spouse: making yourself as attractive as you reasonably can. Includes weight control and cleanliness.
- Honesty and openness: avoiding any kind of dishonesty with our spouse. Nurturing trust by being truthful.
- Family commitment: being involved in parenting, committed to being a good parent.
- Conversation: taking time to show that you are interested in your partner's life and being willing to share your own, through conversation.
- Domestic support: handling the household and children in an organized and efficient way.
- Financial support: being involved in providing enough money to live comfortably.
- Recreational companionship: finding ways to play together that both enjoy. Avoiding any recreational activity that bothers the other.
- Sexual fulfillment: giving and receiving sexual pleasure in a pleasant way.

Women, as a group, rated their five highest needs in this order:

1. Affection
2. Conversation
3. Honesty and openness
4. Financial support
5. Family commitment

Men, as a group, rated their five highest needs in this order:

1. Sexual fulfillment
2. Recreational companionship
3. An attractive spouse

4. Domestic support

5. Admiration[8]

As you can see in comparing the lists, although men and women have many of the same needs, the importance of these needs differs for men as compared to women. Most of us, in trying to be loving to our spouses, do the things for them that we would like them to do for us. However, this approach may not produce significant results because a woman's deepest needs are not a man's deepest needs. In order to significantly improve a marriage, both partners must focus on increasing the efforts they put into meeting those needs that are most important to one another.

NUMBER ONE NEEDS FOR MEN AND WOMEN: SEXUAL FULFILLMENT VS. AFFECTION

Other studies have borne out the validity of Dr. Harley's findings. One of the most frequent reasons given by males for infidelity is infrequent and poor quality sex. A number of empirical studies* have come to this same conclusion.[9] One of the most frequent causes that women cite for their affairs is a lack of affection and of caring conversation with their spouses.[10]

Discontent often develops in the following way: A man generally comes into marriage with a strong expectation that his wife will provide sexual enjoyment whenever he desires it. A woman marries with the expectation that her future husband will continue showing the same level of affection and caring conversation as he did during the courtship period.

For most men, sex is sometimes an expression of love, and sometimes an expression of something else—release from

---

* As noted on page 5, there seem to be differences in the empirical literature about the relative importance of sexual attraction versus unmet relationship needs as contributing factors in men becoming involved in affairs. These different findings may be explained in at least two ways. One explanation is that some men may have affairs primarily because of sexual attraction, and others because of unmet relationship needs. Another explanation is that because of men's physiological and psychological makeup, these two sources of temptation may frequently comingle to such an extent that it is difficult to reliably identify which is primary.

tension, boredom, depression, or loneliness. It may even be his response to seeing an extremely sexy female earlier in the day. Women usually believe that sex should always be an expression of love—that any reason other than this degrades this most intimate of all interactions. When wives sense that their husbands are using sex to meet other needs, they begin to resent it. If, in addition, their husbands drastically reduce the amount of affection and caring conversation they are providing, wives feel doubly frustrated.

In the early part of many marriages, women may receive little satisfaction from love-play because men are often not very competent lovers initially. Most men don't know that their wives need fifteen to twenty minutes of foreplay to be physically and psychologically prepared for intercourse. They don't know the best kind of foreplay, so they generally do what they would find stimulating, which is generally not what their wives most enjoy. On the other hand, usually young wives are desperately trying to please their husbands, and may not even be aware of what they need and want. Thus they don't tell their husbands how unsatisfying the sexual experience is for them, nor ask them to do things differently. They eventually realize that sex is not the romantic experience they had believed it would be, and that they feel used rather than loved during it. They may start to show less interest in sex, or develop excuses why "this is not a good time," or use various other nonassertive ways to express their unhappiness.

At this point some husbands try to understand why their wives do not desire sex. However, they are probably a minority. A more common response is for the frustrated man to provide even less caring conversation and affection than before. He may begin to demand that his wife become more enthusiastic about sex, and quote verses from Ephesians 5 and 1 Corinthians 7 to try to persuade her. As he demands sex, either gently or harshly, his wife feels even less excited about it. Sex, which is only one part of a positive marriage, may become a focal point of contention as the sexual relationship deteriorates. The husband says the marriage would be acceptable if his wife would be more enthusiastic about sex, and she says that she would be more enthusiastic about sex if her husband would show her he really loves her.

Harley's results are also confirmed by Dick Brzeczek, (pronounced "Bree-zek") co-leader of a support group for couples who have experienced unfaithfulness in the marriage. He has written:

> When a wife has an affair, she is generally not looking for sex, but for something emotional that's missing in her marriage: romance, intimacy, or perhaps tenderness. The physical act is usually secondary. When a husband has an affair, generally it's the physical aspect that's enticing at first, then the emotional aspect comes into play.[11]

NUMBER TWO NEEDS FOR MEN AND WOMEN: RECREATIONAL COMPANIONSHIP VS. CONVERSATION

Another significant difference between men and women as groups is found in what they identify as their second most important need. Men want a companion who will participate in recreation with them: Their wives are more likely to prefer someone who will *talk* with them.

Men who have had affairs frequently indicate that they wanted someone with whom they could escape the daily round of problems and pressures; they wanted a few moments of enjoyment where no pressures could intrude. Their idea of a wife is someone who will keep the household running smoothly, and who will not give them a constant litany of problems each evening when they get home. If they cannot get such a break with their wives, they will look for it with someone else.

OTHER DIFFERENCES IN NEEDS

Wives want a relationship characterized by honesty and openness (their number 3 need). Alexandra Penney gives her opinion on why men often do not meet that need well: Men "don't want to discuss intimacy because they don't want to admit they need anything or anybody. . . . Anxiety and/or fear of appearing inadequate are at the real roots of a man's unwillingness to say what he needs. If he's inadequate, he may be rejected, so his thinking goes. Rejection can be painful, if not devastating, thus, better not to talk about such touchy issues as needs."[12]

Many husbands may not be good at meeting their wives' number 5 need (family commitment). By the time they come home from a long work day they do not want to deal with kids and broken appliances. They want their wives to have these things under control (their number 4 need: domestic support). Although wives do not generally go out and have affairs because of their husbands' lack of family commitment, this may be one of several frustrations that could eventually lead them to an "affair of anger."

Men's number 5 need is admiration or respect. When a wife's needs are not met it is normal for her frustration to cause her to focus on his weaknesses and inadequacies and to fail to see or affirm his strengths and positive efforts. When she fails to affirm him for his work and efforts for her and the family, one of his important ego needs remains unmet. The longer this situation continues the more vulnerable he becomes if some other female starts showing him the respect he is not getting at home.

THE LOVE BANK

Our relationships and feelings toward each other can be conceptualized in terms of a love bank, an emotional "bank" inside us where we have an account with each person whom we know.[13] If we have a slightly positive interaction with someone, the result is that we deposit one love unit in his or her account. A slightly more positive interaction results in a deposit of two love units; a very positive interaction, three; and an especially memorable one, four. On the same scale, a slightly negative interaction represents a withdrawal of one love unit; a more negative interaction results in a withdrawal of two units; a very negative interaction, three units; and an extremely traumatic and negative interaction, four units. The story of John and Nicki can serve to illustrate the love bank theory.

John and Nicki attend the same college. They meet during their sophomore year, but only see each other casually during that time. Their casual interactions are positive, and so with each interaction one love unit is deposited in John's bank in Nicki's name (for simplicity, I will focus only on the units deposited in John's love bank).

When they return from summer break for their junior year, something clicks in John's mind regarding Nicki, and he calls her to ask for a date early in the fall. She accepts, they go out, and find they have an amazing number of things about which to talk. At the end of a very pleasant evening, three love units are deposited in John's love bank in Nicki's account. Two more dates, one on each of the following weekends, result in the same thing happening. Then they decide to go on a weekend retreat sponsored by one of the Christian groups on campus, and find they share many of the same religious values and commitments. At the end of the weekend John deposits four love units in Nicki's account.

By Christmas vacation John and Nicki are going steady, and the thought of being away from each other seems almost impossible to bear. They write several romantic letters to each other, have two long-distance telephone calls during the break, and the net result is that John enters the New Year with twelve more love units in Nicki's account. At this point her total is 210 love units, higher than any other girl he has ever dated.

They date consistently through their junior year, and visit each other's family during spring vacation. By the end of the spring quarter Nicki's account stands at 450, and John proposes. Nicki surprises him by saying that she thinks they should spend the summer apart without a great deal of interaction, so that they can think more objectively about their relationship. John doesn't agree, and they have two or three rather unhappy discussions about this (total withdrawals of six love units from Nicki's account). John finally agrees to Nicki's proposal, and prepares for a very lonesome summer. He dates a few girls (as per their agreement), but he finds no one who interests him. His dates only serve to reinforce his belief that Nicki is the undisputed best person for him. He arrives back at college in September with feelings of both hope and fear of what Nicki has decided. Since he has had no negative interactions with Nicki, his love bank total still stands where it was when he left in the spring, much higher than for any other girl in his life.

John is relieved when Nicki tells him that her summer experience was similar to his, and that she is willing to date steadily again if he desires to do so. He readily agrees and by Thanksgiving Nicki's account in John's love bank stands at 750. After returning from Thanksgiving break, he proposes, she accepts, and they spend Christmas visiting both sets of parents and sharing the news with them. New Year's Eve, spent with John's family, is an especially memorable time, and Nicki's love bank account nears 1000. They make plans to be married in July, one month after graduation.

The next six months are spent finishing college classes, applying for jobs, getting ready for the wedding, and enjoying each other's company. By the time of the wedding their relationship is at an all-time high of 1,250 love units in Nicki's account. John never knew it was possible to love someone so much or to be so happy.

Their first home is a small, one-bedroom apartment, furnished mostly with things given them by their families. Money is tight, but that is tolerable because they are together and they know brighter days are ahead. John is working at an entry-level position in a law firm, which doesn't pay much, but he feels certain he will be promoted within a few years. By the end of their first nine months they are still very much in love, despite a few frustrating times, and Nicki's account in John's love bank stands at 1100 points.

In the tenth month of their marriage a major problem develops. Nicki discovers that she is pregnant (a birth-control accident). John is angry with Nicki for what he regards as her carelessness, and for the financial difficulties this will cause them in their next few years of marriage until he receives a promotion. Nicki is contrite, so much so that John keeps much of his anger inside, not wanting to make her feel more depressed. But the net result is that Nicki's account drops below 1000 for the first time since the Christmas before they were married.

John doesn't feel psychologically ready to be a father, but they both believe that abortion is wrong, so they rule out that option. Nicki knows that she could never give up for adoption a baby that she carried for nine months, so that alternative is ruled out. John and Nicki know they have to start preparing themselves for parenthood. It is frustrating, because they have had so little time to be married before the baby is on the way.

To make matters worse, Nicki has severe morning sickness for the first three months, so bad that she eventually has to quit work. When John gets home he does his best to be a loving husband, but the extra bills, the loss of Nicki's income, her crying spells, and her lack of desire for sex (which he can partly understand, but it doesn't make his sex drive any lower) all have made him want to scream out several times, *why weren't you more careful?* He never yells, but holding the anger in causes his interchanges with Nicki to be less positive. By their first anniversary Nicki's account in John's love bank has decreased to 750.

After her first trimester Nicki's morning sickness eases, but since she is pregnant, she can only get a temporary job which pays minimum wage. By the time she arrives home from work her feet and ankles hurt and she is exhausted. She gains thirty-five pounds in her first five months of pregnancy. She makes supper for John, goes to bed, and is often asleep by 8:30.

John is beginning to have his first misgivings about marriage to Nicki. He had felt sure, only fifteen months earlier, that she was the girl of his dreams. He had thought she was God's perfect will for his life. But now he feels so differently. He feels sorry for her more than love. He knows she is having a hard time, and that she is doing the best she can, yet he also knows how frustrated he feels that so few of his needs are being met because of this "accident." He begins to wonder if it really was an accident—yet he doesn't think Nicki would have done something like this on purpose. They aren't having any overt quarrels, but her inability to respond to his needs causes many of their interactions to result in a withdrawal of one or two points from her love bank account.

Finally something positive happens! Six and one-half months into her pregnancy John is given a promotion, meaning more income and better maternity benefits when it comes time for Nicki to deliver. He is given new responsibilities, a larger office, and a secretary designated specifically for him. John and Nicki have a special dinner with his parents at a nearby restaurant to celebrate the occasion.

Enter Barbara and Laura

The next two months are a blur of activities. Fixing a corner of their apartment to serve as a nursery until they can move into a larger apartment occupies much of their evenings. John is beginning to feel some excitement over the baby's arrival. He still feels a lot of anxiety about being a father, with all of the responsibilities that entails. His move goes smoothly at work, and his secretary, Barbara, helps him tremendously as he becomes oriented to his new job. Although the same age as John and Nicki, she has worked at the law firm since high-school graduation, and knows much of the "inside information" so necessary to John's making an efficient adjustment to his new responsibilities. John feels very grateful for her. Because she is a good secretary, and because she asks for nothing in return, she begins accumulating a small account of her own in John's love bank.

The baby comes on schedule with no complications, and John and Nicki gratefully name her Laura. Little, red-faced, with some very fine blond hair that is almost invisible, she immediately wins the hearts of her father, mother, and all the grandparents. John is given three days off from work at the law firm to spend with his new "family." The long wait and the many sacrifices seem worth it now that Laura is here. John makes several deposits in Nicki's and Laura's accounts in his love bank during those three days together. Things are looking up for them again.

Life with Nicki and Laura is totally different from life with Nicki alone. For a few weeks Laura seems to have her days and nights reversed, sleeping much of the day and crying much of the night. Nicki is nursing Laura, so John doesn't have to get up at night, but he is a light sleeper, and is awakened frequently anyway. He is sure that he never knew how exhausted a person could become before Laura arrived. Nicki is very fulfilled in her role as mother, but also is exhausted. Nicki's love bank account does not change during this time.

In a few weeks Laura begins to get her sleep schedule adjusted, and John and Nicki start to feel less fatigued. As this happens, John begins to recognize that a subtle shift has taken place. Whereas before the pregnancy Nicki's predominant wish was to make him happy, her primary energy is now devoted to taking care of Laura. John realizes it's selfish for him to feel frustrated by this change, and yet he does. The time that they had as a couple to devote totally to each other was cut short, too short, and he finds himself resenting this. He starts to spend more time watching television as an indirect way of expressing his frustration at Nicki, and in a sense, shutting her out.

Nicki senses this change and tries to talk with John about it, but he feels embarrassed to talk about feeling displaced by an infant, an infant he should love, so he tells Nicki there's nothing wrong. Each night that he spends in sullen resentment results in another love unit being withdrawn from Nicki's account.

During the daytime his life is quite different. John is able to fulfill his new responsibilities well, and is soon accepted as a valuable part of the legal team. Barbara continues to do an excellent job as his secretary, and she makes him look good and covers his occasional mistakes. While their relationship is totally professional, her consistent efforts to please him are resulting in deposits in her account in John's love bank. Her quiet efficiency and her desire to please him and to make him look good are appreciated by John. John is not looking for another woman to love, and he has no thoughts of their relationship moving in that direction.

As John continues to demonstrate his abilities, he is given more responsibilities. Eventually his workload increases to a point that he can no longer do all of his work during the daytime. He starts to work one evening a week, and then two. He is given affirmation for the quality and quantity of work he is producing. He believes he has a solid future with the law firm, and begins to invest more and more of his energy there.

John originally took his extra work home, but found it almost impossible to accomplish much there, so he talked with Nicki about his staying at the office one or two evenings a week. They both agree that this may be wise: The unspoken truth that both of them know is that having two evenings each week apart will be a relief, for they both feel the vague discomfort that has grown up between them. Meanwhile, Nicki's love bank account continues to slowly decrease, and Barbara's slowly to increase, still without any conscious awareness on John's part. Christmas is approaching, the third anniversary of announcing their engagement. But somehow the excitement in their marriage is gone, even though they have many reasons to be thankful—good health, a bubbly little girl, good job prospects for John. The marriage feels like a script played without passion: They are going through the motions of being married, but their marriage has little vitality or energy.

One evening as John prepares to spend an evening working at the office, Barbara prepares to leave. He is walking through the doorway when Barbara reaches it, and she mentions being disappointed. With only half of his attention on her statement, John asks her why she is disappointed. She points to a sprig of mistletoe that she had hung in the doorway that morning, and which apparently no one had noticed the entire day. Still half disconcerted by his other thoughts, he absent-mindedly gives her a token kiss. What he receives is much more than token. With that, she says "good-bye" and rapidly walks away.

John sits down to ponder what has just happened. That kiss! There was more life in that than he had felt from Nicki for a long, long time. And that kiss had made him consciously aware of feelings he had for Barbara that he had not recognized before. He spent most of that evening thinking about his relationship to her, not his legal work. He realized, though he would not have put it in these terms, that Barbara's account in his love bank was much higher than Nicki's.

The concept of love bank accounts for each person in our lives is an interesting one, and I think points out how easy it is, when men and women work closely together most of the day, for the accounts of co-workers easily to reach higher levels than the accounts between a husband and wife. This is particularly true if there are some unresolved problems in the marriage. In fact, if we work regularly with people of the opposite sex, and if we have limited time at home, it may take conscious efforts to keep our love bank accounts higher with our spouses than with other people.

The love bank can also be tied in with Harley's concept of the differing priorities of needs that men and women have. A husband, with limited time available, should try to make deposits in the "subaccounts" that mean the most to his wife (for example, affection, conversation, honesty and openness). And a wife, with limited time and energy available, should try to make deposits in the "subaccounts" that mean the most to him (sexual fulfillment and recreational companionship). We can make deposits in the need areas that have lower priority for our spouses, but the most rapid way to build and maintain a positive account with our partners is to invest in "high-yield" funds.

If it is true that everyone has a "hungry ego," then it would follow that the reserves in a couple's love bank account are never static, but constantly need to be replenished. Simply because a couple made a vow to each other twenty-five years ago and were nice to one another for the first twenty of those years does not mean that their relationship is invulnerable. Their feelings of attraction for each other will be related to the deposits that have been made in their individual love banks in the *recent* past. Therefore the biblical command to *keep on* loving one another (i.e., regularly meeting the ego needs of each other) is very important.

KEY IDEAS FROM CHAPTER 3

The faithful partner of an adulterer may contribute to a situation that leads to adultery through:

- Failure to meet realistic, communicated expectations of the unfaithful spouse
- Failure to meet the ego needs of the unfaithful spouse

People are likely to be drawn to each other as marital partners and remain with each other if they meet the ego needs of each other. Couples who fail to meet each other's ego needs will become more vulnerable to an affair.

The five highest ego needs of women are affection, conversation, honesty and openness, financial support, and family commitment.

The five highest ego needs of men are sexual fulfillment, recreational companionship, an attractive spouse, domestic support, and admiration.

One reason that men and women do not meet each other's ego needs is the failure to realize that the priority needs for men and women are different.

The love bank can be a helpful way of understanding the ebb and flow of human relationships.

NOTES

1. Susan Squires, "Extramarital Affair," *Glamour*, September 1980, 278.

2. Daniel Dolesh and Sherelynn Lehman, *Love Me, Love Me Not: How to Survive Infidelity* (New York: McGraw-Hill, 1985), 33–34.

3. The concept of the "hungry ego" was first articulated by Dr. John Baer Train, past president of the American Society of Psychoanalytic Physicians. The formulation into nine postulates is my own.

4. Laurel Richardson, *The New Other Woman: Contemporary Single Women in Affairs with Married Men* (New York: The Free Press, 1985), 14.

5. Alexandra Penney, *How to Keep Your Man Monogamous* (New York: Bantam, 1989), 7.

6. Penney, 99.

7. Willard F. Harley, Jr., *His Needs, Her Needs: Building An Affair-Proof Marriage* (Old Tappan, N.J.: Revell, 1986).

8. Some empirically minded psychologists might criticize Harley's study and findings on the following three grounds. (1) People's verbally stated needs may differ from their actual needs as expressed through their behavior. (2) If the test questions are the same as the questions given in the appendix of Harley's book, there is a question of whether some of his terms (e.g., domestic support) were defined well enough in the test for the results to be meaningful. (3) There is not a breakdown by age, which may be important. For example, is sexual fulfillment still the most important need for males sixty and older? However, even with these reservations, his findings do seem to be generally corroborated by a number of other studies or writers.

9. Carol Botwin, *Men Who Can't Be Faithful* (New York: Warner Books, 1988), 107.

10. Botwin, 59.

11. Richard and Elizabeth Brzeczek, *Addicted to Adultery: How We Saved Our Marriage/How You Can Save Yours* (New York: Bantam, 1989), 205.

12. Penney, 115–16.

13. The concept of the love bank was developed by Willard Harley in his book *His Needs, Her Needs* 15ff.

Chapter Four

Contributions of the Faithful Partner: Unhealthy Responses and Personal Psychopathology

We have seen that unconscious, unrealistic, or uncommunicated expectations of the *unfaithful partner* can cause frustration when those expectations are not met. Such can lead to an affair. It is equally true that unconscious, unrealistic, or uncommunicated expectations of the *faithful partner* can contribute to an affair. But the mechanism by which this happens is different.

As discussed before, the faithful partner brings to marriage many unconscious and unrealistic expectations. If these are not discussed or thought through, the fact that many of them go unmet in the relationship will lead to growing frustration. At that point the faithful partner has a choice.[1] His or her response will take one of five forms: passive, aggressive, passive-aggressive, manipulative, or assertive. A response style includes both how a person initiates action and how that person responds to someone else's initiatives. The following section describes the five response styles more fully.

THE PASSIVE RESPONSE STYLE

A man who trims himself to suit everybody will soon whittle himself away.
  —*Charles Schwab*

An appeaser is one who feeds a crocodile, hoping it will eat him last!
  —*Winston Churchill*

Passivity manifests itself in a variety of ways. People respond passively when they fail to express their disappointment, hurt, or frustration. Passivity includes saying yes when we really want to say no, permitting others to speak for us, or allowing others to make decisions about our lives with which we disagree. A passive person may try to make a point (stand up for his feelings, desires, or needs), but does it so timidly that others readily coerce or intimidate him into doing things their way.

When people are passive, they sacrifice their own wishes, feelings, and desires in order to be accepted by others. They restrain themselves from expressing personal preferences. They feel and act like victims, rather than taking responsibility for how they allow their relationships to develop. They apologize for having opinions and hold their true feelings inside. They act shy, timid, and embarrassed, and try to avoid disturbing anyone. They often lack confidence in their own judgment. In short, the passive person says, "I count you, I don't count me."[2] They maximize the importance of the other person's thoughts, feelings, and goals but minimize the importance of their own.

Passive people sometimes feel okay about themselves, at least temporarily, because they believe they are acting in a Christian manner. They are "turning the other cheek," and "returning good for evil." However, in the long run passive people often feel depressed because they don't reach their desired objectives. They may be frustrated because other people don't take their feelings into consideration when making decisions. They may feel tense, in part because they are afraid their frustrations might erupt against their will and jeopardize their relationships.

The passive stance is a powerless stance. Powerlessness and lack of control over one's life usually lead to low feelings of self-worth. If we are passive, we should recognize that others can't "put us in our place" all by themselves; we (passive people) choose to go there. If we don't accept the role another has found for us, we don't have to play it. As Eleanor Roosevelt aptly said, "No one can make you feel inferior without your consent." No one has the power to intimidate a person unless that person in some sense cooperates.

THE AGGRESSIVE RESPONSE STYLE

People are responding aggressively whenever they try to reach their goals in ways that do not respect the needs, feelings, goals, or self-esteem of other persons around them. These behaviors say, "I count me, I don't count you." Aggressive behavior can result from having a need or goal blocked by someone else's behavior. When someone blocks your goal, you feel frustrated. And if you allow your anger to show without modifying it in some way, you will usually manifest aggressive behavior. Goals that frequently get blocked by other people include:

- arriving someplace on time
- completing a task without being interrupted
- having a few minutes of peace and quiet with no demands from anyone
- being able to eat supper without telephone interruptions
- not being criticized
- not being disagreed with

Most everyone becomes aggressive, at least occasionally. Usually the purpose of our aggression is either to punish the one who has blocked us from reaching a goal or to intimidate that person into changing so that we are no longer blocked.

Aggressive responses may range from mild to severe. Included among them are name-calling, blaming others, talking at or down to people, and interrupting others. Speaking for others, railroading others to agree, and insisting on having the last word are also aggressive responses. More intense forms of aggression include intimidating others through haughtiness, snickering, glaring, or physical violence. Some teenagers and adults keep their families intimidated simply by insinuating that they may become violent if not allowed to have their way.

Aggressive behavior usually gives one an initial feeling of satisfaction, if the desired goal is achieved. However, the long-term result of continued aggressiveness is usually low self-esteem for the aggressive person. Aggressive people know that they are alienating family and friends, and they feel guilty and depressed about their behavior. They may be remorseful about the destructive effects of their aggressiveness, and attempt to cover that by a gruff and distant façade. Even when aggressive people are sorry for their behavior, their remorse may go unnoticed because other people are too busy trying to stay out of their way. Aggressive people may continue their quarrelsome behavior because they feel lonely and misunderstood.

THE PASSIVE-AGGRESSIVE RESPONSE STYLE

A third response style includes characteristics of both the passive and aggressive styles. Passive-aggression (or indirect aggression) usually begins when we allow someone to do things that bother us, or fail to tell someone when he or she isn't doing what we expect. Eventually the irritations accumulate and begin to come out in indirectly aggressive responses.

Passive-aggressiveness may manifest itself through hostile humor, sarcasm, and ridicule—the kind Archie Bunker would often use. Sarcasm and ridicule may be used either passive-aggressively or aggressively (as a form of intimidation). The difference is that aggressive sarcasm, that is used to intimidate, usually occurs during the situation, whereas passive-aggressive sarcasm or ridicule may slip out several hours or days after the situation. The recipient of passive-aggressive sarcasm may have difficulty figuring out what caused the outburst.

A type of passive-aggressiveness frequently seen is the withdrawal of attention or affection. A good-night kiss becomes perfunctory, or doesn't happen at all. The greeting, "Hello, I'm home!" is dropped, or receives no response. Family members give each other "the silent treatment." Silence in such situations doesn't simply mean that no one is talking; it is intended to send a very powerful message: "I don't like something you've done and I'm withdrawing from you to show you how much I don't like you." Christians frequently use this type of passive-aggressiveness because it seems less un-Christian than other types of passive-aggressiveness, such as ridicule, sarcasm, or hostile humor.

The passive-aggressive style can stem from a person's subconscious attitude that says, "I don't count me." This person doesn't identify his or her needs or feelings, and doesn't ask others to consider them at the time. Then later, as anger festers it erupts in behavior that screams, "I don't count you." Thus, in the passive-aggressive style, the rights and feelings of neither the initiator nor the recipient are respected.

If a person continually responds in a passive-aggressive style, his or her self-concept is eventually lowered. As mentioned earlier, *passive persons* may occasionally feel good (because they see themselves as good Christians when they let others have their own way). And *aggressive people* may occasionally feel good about getting their own way. But *passive-aggressive people* rarely feel good about themselves, for their initial passive response makes them feel powerless in social situations. As they brood over the wrongs inflicted on them, they become bitter. Their delayed, indirect responses offer little satisfaction to them and often alienate family and friends.

THE MANIPULATIVE RESPONSE STYLE

A fourth way of responding to differences in expectations between people is by manipulation. While aggressive people attempt to coerce someone to change by angry threats and intimidation, manipulative persons use more indirect, frequently psychological, means to get their way.

For example, one mother would never tell her daughter openly and directly what she wanted. But whenever the daughter would deviate very far from her mother's wishes, the mother would rush into her own bedroom, fling herself onto the bed, and cry, "I don't know what I'm going to do with you!" or "You're going to drive me crazy!" A father told his ten-year-old daughter that he would return home (the father and mother were separated) if she got straight A's in school. One mother claimed to have heart pains whenever family members or friends broached a subject she didn't want to talk about.

Aggressive people usually try to produce fear of themselves as a way of getting what they want. Manipulative people try to control others by producing a different kind of fear—the fear of the outcome (the manipulator will have a heart attack, God won't love them, other people won't respect them, etc.) if others do not give them what they want.

People who habitually manipulate others seldom feel good about themselves, even though they may feel satisfied momentarily when their manipulation achieves its desire goal. Manipulators realize how destructive their methods are to relationships. They can't respect themselves because their methods, even when successful, are unhealthy and unfair. In their more honest moments they feel guilty for the pain and hardship their self-centeredness causes others. Manipulative people seldom admit any of the above problems. Like aggressive people, they usually cover over any feelings of sadness with brusque, irritable, or self-righteous behavior.

THE ASSERTIVE RESPONSE STYLE

Assertiveness depends upon the basic skills of *relationship-enhancement* and *self-protection*.

Relationship-enhancement skills are those which have to do with the ability to initiate, maintain, and end conversations comfortably. Among them are the ability to give encouragement and compliments comfortably, and to receive compliments from others without discounting them. They also include expressing love and affection appropriately, and the ability to deepen relationships when desired.

By "self-protective" skills we mean the ability to discuss one's thoughts, feelings, and wishes without undue anxiety, even among strangers or in hostile situations. Assertive people can disagree with others without apologizing. They can comfortably refuse requests from others which conflict with their own priorities, and can defend themselves against accusations which they consider unfair or inaccurate. They can express anger or annoyance assertively—in ways that respect the feelings and self-esteem of others. Similarly, they can deal with someone else's anger comfortably and nondefensively. Finally, they can make reasonable requests of others.

Assertive people are not easily manipulated nor intimidated. They make choices about what they will do with their time, energy, or money, rather than being forced into situations by others. Assertive people are actors, not only reactors. Because they can say no, their yes means yes. Those who are usually successful at manipulating or intimidating others may dislike assertive people, but they will consciously or unconsciously respect them.

When people are assertive, they relate to others from an "I count you, I count me" frame of reference. Because they show consideration and respect for others, they do not feel guilty about how they have treated them. And when they count themselves, they maintain their own self-respect. Because they make choices about how they are going to respond to others and to life, they see themselves as actors rather than victims.

Assertiveness is not only rooted in a healthy self-esteem, but it also produces healthy self-esteem. As people feel good about themselves, they are able to count themselves and others. And as they count themselves and others, they feel good about the way they are treating themselves and others.

Many people are assertive in some situations and relationships and nonassertive in others. For example, someone may have good relationship-enhancement skills, but relatively weaker self-protective skills. Or a person may be assertive with young children, but not with teen-agers and his or her spouse.

When a man (or woman) has unconscious and/or uncommunicated expectations which are not met by his spouse (since she didn't know what they were), he may initially respond by being passive. However, as the frustrations build up over time, they almost certainly begin to come out in aggressive, passive-aggressive, or manipulative ways. (Very few come out assertively, for we have so few role models of assertiveness or situations where it is "safe" to learn to be honestly assertive.)

When frustration comes out either aggressively, passive-aggressively, or manipulatively, it builds walls between people. Those walls, if they grow thick enough and high enough, prevent a healthy relationship from continuing. A person no longer meets his or her partner's ego needs, nor is the partner able to meet his or her needs. Such a situation is fertile ground for an affair.

PSYCHOPATHOLOGY OF THE FAITHFUL PARTNER, INCLUDING CODEPENDENCY

Mental illness on the part of one marriage partner can contribute to unfaithfulness on the part of the other. The following situations illustrate some of these possibilities. We will discuss them under the headings of *individual psychopathology* and *codependency*.

INDIVIDUAL PSYCHOPATHOLOGY

Almost any extreme psychopathology can lead to marital frustration and, thus, to an affair. Don, for example, experienced rejection from the day he was born. A third child, unwanted and unexpected, he received the bulk of the family punishment even when he was totally innocent. When his father and mother were having difficulties, they often displaced their anger onto him. Don was thrown out of his family when he was thirteen and fended for himself from that time on. Understandably, he trusted no one and fought everyone.

In his early twenties Don met Linda, a person who showed him unconditional love for the first time. He was suspicious of her at first, but when he saw that she didn't change in her acceptance of him regardless of what he did, he allowed a relationship to begin to develop between them. Linda was encouraged as she saw that by loving Don he began to relax his suspiciousness and started trusting her. They were married fifteen months after they met.

Things were unremarkable for the first few weeks of marriage, but it concerned Linda when she saw how easily Don misinterpreted the meaning of other people's behavior. He was "on guard" constantly, and before long was alienated from his in-laws, even though they tried to be caring toward him. He regularly had difficulties with his co-workers. Linda tried to help him see that perhaps he was misinterpreting situations and reading rejection into relationships where it was not intended, but gradually Don turned on her also, claiming that she was always taking the other person's side. He became an angry, volatile, closed-off man. They had no real closeness anymore, and sex, when it occurred, was coarse and unloving.

Linda, at the beginning, felt hurt by Don's rejection, then depressed, then angry. After several years without genuine male companionship, Linda became friends with a man at work. For a while it was only a friendship, but eventually Linda had an affair with the man who was showing her affection. Don's psychopathology (paranoid personality disorder) definitely contributed to her vulnerability.

Marianne was the oldest child and only girl in a family of three children. Her family was not rich, but they always had one of the most attractive and well-cared-for homes in their community. Her mother worked unceasingly to keep their home looking its very best. Marianne's father was not as concerned about having things immaculate. He did take care of the yard and the home's exterior—with further help from Marianne's mother, who tidied up her husband's work after he left.

George came from a family which was more relaxed about keeping up their home. It was clean enough for everyone's health, but picking things up was not a priority with them. Consequently George's home sometimes bordered on chaos. He was attracted to Marianne by how well-organized and neat she appeared. It was sometimes a welcome relief for him to get away from the constant piles of things at his home by spending time with her. Marianne was attracted to George by his more relaxed manner about things, and hoped that she might be able to gain some of that easy-going style from him if they were married. They did marry, and things went along quite well for several months. George tried to pick up after himself, for he knew Marianne wanted that. Marianne tried to be a little less compulsive about putting away everything, for she knew George wanted that.

After a while problems began to develop. George, while he never was as sloppy as he had been in his family of origin, became less careful about picking up after himself. Marianne took this personally, believing that George's behavior of leaving things lying around the house was his way of showing he didn't care how she felt. She began scolding him, which he did not like, and they grew emotionally distant and hostile. The overt hostility grew less as they adjusted to each other, but they were no longer close.

Sex was very infrequent between them now. For Marianne (a compulsive personality disorder) to even think of lovemaking, everything had to be just right. The house had to be cleaned, the ironing done, and her hair looking good, and she had to be happy with George in every way.[3] Once they went three years without having sex. In anger and frustration, George had an affair. Marianne's compulsiveness, exacerbated by the interaction with his lack of tidiness, created an environment which increased George's vulnerability to an affair.

Tim was a quiet, mild-mannered, self-employed businessman, married to Vianne, a woman with a much stronger personality and tongue. Both were sincere Christians and wanted their family to be a good Christian home for their adopted son. One problem that continued to be difficult for them to manage was Tim's lack of organization and motivation, and Vianne's response to it. When Tim felt pressured, he would sometimes avoid going to work at all (since he was self-employed, he had some choice about this). Vianne let him know what she thought about this in no uncertain terms, for she was responsible for paying the bills. She regularly attacked his low self-esteem, which was partly responsible for his lack of organization and motivation. Tim was never strong enough to assertively tell Vianne how demeaning her scoldings were to him, but he found another way of getting back at her. Every six months or so on his way home from work he would stop at a tavern, get drunk, then pick up a girl for a one-night stand. Afterward he would return home, confess his misdeed, and revert back to his nonassertive state for the tongue-lashing he was bound to get for the next several weeks. Tim never learned to say honestly and assertively what was bothering him about Vianne's behavior, and Vianne continued her passive-aggressive behavior, never considering that her constant verbal chastising of Tim had anything to do with his intoxicated one-night affairs. Tim and Vianne eventually divorced.

CODEPENDENCY AND COADDICTION

In recent years much has been written on codependency and coaddiction, attitudes and behavior a person brings into the marriage that may unwittingly encourage a partner's infidelity and enable it to continue. Codependency refers to a set of thinking patterns and behavior which result, for example, when one grows up in an unhealthy family. At first this label was used to describe someone who grew up in a home where a parent was alcoholic. It has subsequently been found that the same traits are often seen in anyone whose childhood was spent in an unhealthy or dysfunctional family, whether or not alcohol was abused.

In an unhealthy family there are often oppressive rules, or rules that are applied inconsistently. Oppressive rules say to the child "don't be!" Inconsistent rules leave the child with chronic anxiety about whether his or her behavior is acceptable or not. Expressions of true feelings are not allowed, nor are direct discussions of family problems. As a result the child never learns to trust his or her own feelings or perceptions of what is occurring or to learn appropriate and healthy ways of interacting. In such families the only way to gain self-worth is to care for someone who is addicted (which is probably why codependents so often marry someone with an addiction or the potential of developing an addiction). Codependency develops in one's family of origin before one becomes an adult and lays the groundwork for coaddiction.

ADDICTION

As discussed in an earlier chapter, a person with an addiction develops a self-destructive relationship with either a chemical (alcohol, nicotine, drugs, etc.), food (compulsive overeating), or sexual experience. Even though the person knows that the behavior is destructive, he or she continues it. At some point such persons lose control of their ability to stop, and the habit becomes compulsive. Repetition of the addictive sequence becomes more important than relationships (marriage and family), career, and health, and the person may end up losing all three. With some addictions, including sexual ones, the person becomes habituated to the behavior, and so needs more extreme behavior to attain the same "high." The addiction (if alcohol, drugs, or sex) causes a person to violate the values or convictions he or she once held, even if previously these were held very sincerely. All addictions include two elements—a behavior disorder and a thinking disorder. The thinking disorder enables the person either to deny or rationalize the addictive behavior.[4] It is estimated that 10 percent of the men who have affairs are sexually addicted.

COADDICTION

When a person with codependent traits (usually female) marries someone who is predisposed to developing an addiction,

the codependent person may unwittingly do things that contribute to the addiction. Or the codependent may not enforce
the normal consequences that could halt a partner's developing addiction in its early stages.

Since a codependent's self-esteem is built around rescuing
someone, when a potential addict begins behaving unhealthily the codependent becomes even more focused on that
person, for now he or she has someone to save. The
codependent may join in the addiction (e.g., drinking with
the alcohol addict, or participating in group sex because this
is what the sexually addicted spouse wants). Or the
codependent may try to control the partner's addiction (e.g.,
by never refusing the spouse sexually, so that the developing
addict has no reason to go other places to satisfy sexual desire). The codependent often withdraws from outside social
life (and consequently from the healthy input this would give
them both) in his or her attempt to cure the addict or to keep
the addict's behavior from becoming a public embarrassment.
The coaddict, as does the addict, tends to resort too much to
denial and repression, ego defense mechanisms which are
designed to shield the conscious mind from a reality (or realities) that would be too frightening or painful for the
conscious mind to bear. Whether by denial or repression,
large numbers of wives claim they don't know about their
husband's sexual addiction.[5]

Having entered into a relationship with a sexual addict, a
woman is in a no-win situation. Even if she keeps herself extremely attractive and never refuses him sexually, even if she
joins him on his sexual adventures against her own judgment
and values, no matter what she does, her efforts to keep him
from straying are doomed to failure. It is the nature of his addiction to always want new experiences and to want to
conquer new women.[6]

Those who are codependent because of their home environment are primed to become sexual coaddicts. Penney
empathically describes the situation of the sexual coaddict
(wife of a sexually addicted male) in the following way:

The wife of a sexual addict is so needy that she is willing to settle for almost any mate and then convinces herself that she cannot live without that person. She is usually terrified of abandonment and does anything she can to maintain the relationship, ignoring her own feelings and needs, excusing his behavior and avoiding conflicts and confrontation. As an ironic result, she is helping to perpetuate her mate's behavior. By accepting an unacceptable situation and deliberately sidestepping a showdown, she does nothing to force her partner to acknowledge his addiction and the hurtful consequences of his behavior and seek help.[7]

The alcoholic coaddict unwittingly enables the alcoholic to continue to drink excessively by covering up, lying to the boss about his or her mate's sickness (when it's really a hangover), and hiding bruises which are inflicted during the addict's violent drinking sprees. The sexual coaddict may cover for the man's inappropriate behavior in similar ways. She doesn't question his long unexplained absences (or accepts explanations that clearly are untrue), doesn't ask for an accounting of excessive amounts of money that are spent, and doesn't demand an explanation for his sexually transmitted disease which now she shares. By covering for him, which she does out of her codependent need to be a caretaker and from fear of a solid confrontation, she fails to demand the accountability that a healthier person would require. Therefore, she unwittingly allows his addiction to grow worse with time.

In *Love Must Be Tough* James Dobson discusses this concept, although his book was written before phrases such as "sexual addiction," "codependency," and "coaddiction" were widely used. He talks in terms of the concept of respect, arguing that a Christian husband owes his wife respect, as she does him. When a partner flouts the marriage vows he or she made, it is time to call for accountability. When a codependent spouse fails to do this, he or she invites the unfaithful partner to treat him or her with disrespect. Allowing the disrespect to continue only allows the unfaithful partner's progression into sin, and deeper addiction to proceed. Chapter 5 describes recommended methods for changing this situation.

In summary, psychopathology in the faithful partner may cause that person to fail to meet his or her partner's legitimate needs. These unmet needs may increase the unfaithful partner's vulnerability to an affair. Codependency may also increase the likelihood of an affair, but through a slightly different mechanism. Codependents' absorption in the rescuing role may unwittingly encourage their partners to continue down an unhealthy path (such as sexual affairs, alcohol abuse, or drug abuse), and their failure to confront unhealthy behavior may invite their partners' disrespectful attitude.

MARITAL ARRANGEMENTS OR COLLUSIONS

Sometimes husbands and wives agree to "marital collusions."

In this context a marital collusion refers to an agreement (usually unspoken) in which one partner agrees to tolerate (and usually not even speak about) the philandering of the spouse in return for some benefit received in return. It is usually the husband who strays, and the wife who agrees to look away and not make comments in return for benefits she receives from her husband's affairs or from remaining in the marriage despite them.

What benefits could a wife possibly receive in such an arrangement? First, she may like the psychological distance such an arrangement provides: She (or both mates) may be afraid of intimacy and a marital collusion of this type allows both of them to maintain distance in the relationship.

Second, some women do not confront a husband's affairs out of fear of the consequences, including their fear of being single again. Third, sometimes a woman continues to live with a husband even though she knows of his affairs because she does not want to lose the money, prestige, power, or security of being associated with him.

Fourth, a woman may continue a marital collusion because she does not want to be bothered by having sex with her husband or may not want the variety of sexual play he desires. She may be willing to let someone else satisfy his desires. Fifth, his affairs may give her the freedom to carry on an affair of her own.[8] While the collusion may provide enough psychological benefit for both partners to sustain the outward appearance of a marriage, the lack of integrity and fidelity inevitably leaves these couples with but the hollow shell of a marriage.

KEY IDEAS FROM CHAPTER 4

The faithful partner of an adulterer may unwittingly contribute to the making of an affair through:
- Unconscious, unrealistic, or uncommunicated expectations of the faithful partner which are expressed in nonassertive ways
- Psychopathology, including codependence, of the faithful spouse
- By entering into some sort of marital collusion

Depending on the degree of frustration present, an affair may be viewed as a supplemental affair, an affair of anger, or a replacement affair.

NOTES

1. Much of the material in this section was adapted from my book entitled *Speaking Your Mind Without Stepping on Toes: A Christian Approach to Assertiveness* (Wheaton, Ill.: Victor Books, 1991), chapter 1.

2. The "I count, you count" framework is adapted from Sherod Miller, Elam Nunnally, and Daniel Wackman, *Talking Together: Couple Communication 1* (Minneapolis: Interpersonal Communication Programs, 1979), 143–58.

3. Part of this wording was adapted from Petersen, page 47, who tells of a similar incident.

4. Adapted in part from Jennifer P. Schneider, *Back from Betrayal: Recovering from His Affairs* (San Francisco: Harper and Row/Hazelden, 1988), 225.

5. Barbara Gordon, *Jennifer Fever: Older Men, Younger Women* (New York: Harper and Row, 1988), 91.

6. Schneider, 21.

7. Alexandra Penney, *How to Keep Your Man Monogamous* (New York: Bantam, 1989), 54–55.

8. Carol Botwin, *Men Who Can't Be Faithful: How to Pick Up the Pieces When He's Breaking Your Heart* (New York: Warner, Books, 1988), 142–55.

Chapter Five

How Even Committed Christians Become Involved in Affairs

Family therapist Frank Pittman believes that almost all affairs are variations on four themes.[1] We have already discussed two of them. *Philandering* is the habitual lifestyle of being involved with one or more people besides one's mate. The motivation of the philanderer is usually fear of or lust for the opposite sex. Philandering is often part of a personality disorder or sexual addiction and was discussed in chapter 1.

Marital arrangements or *collusions* are relationships in which one or both partners have another lover outside the marriage, and some agreement (usually unspoken) exists between the marital partners to keep such an arrangement hidden. Typically each partner receives some advantage from such a collusion, and so the marital arrangement may last for many years, even decades. Collusions were discussed in chapter 2.

The two kinds of affairs most likely to occur within a Christian marriage are what Pittman calls "accidental infidelities" and "romantic affairs." Accidental infidelities are those sexual encounters that "just happen" without any conscious planning, leaving everyone bewildered and disoriented. The person and his or her family are often totally surprised that such a thing could take place, and frequently plead ignorance concerning how it developed. Probably many first affairs are of this type. The response to and interpretation of such an affair by each person involved will determine whether it was only a one-time occurrence or the beginning of a lifelong pattern. People involved in an accidental infidelity sometimes go on to become habitual philanderers.

"Romantic affairs" refer to that temporary insanity called being "in love," a state in which people's minds are clouded, allowing them to forget, at least temporarily, their marriages and families. Such affairs are similar to the temporary insanity that teen-agers pass through in their first, deep, love experience. But they are much more serious and damaging because the players are adults with spouses and children who depend on them.

Some accidental infidelities are also romantic affairs, some are not. For example, some accidental infidelities develop over a period of time, and include a romantic relationship. Other accidental infidelities happen when two people find themselves together in a highly tempting situation and have a one-night fling (as, for example, the two music teachers in chapter 1 who met for two days at a music convention). With accidental infidelities there may be little or no romantic involvement afterward.

Should Christians even be tempted by an affair?

Many believers think that if a Christian is living as one ought to, temptation to or involvement in either an accidental infidelity or a romantic affair will never happen to him or her. They share the attitude of Barbara:

When I heard the rumors about an apparent affair between two people I knew, I was horrified. I had no patience with people who found themselves in immoral situations. I felt there was no way wrong could happen if you were where you should be, doing what you should be doing. Somehow I felt I was "above that sort of thing." My life centered—happily—around my husband, children, home and job.

And then a new family moved into our neighborhood. They were our kind of people, fit right into our community and church. But over the months it became clear that the husband and I shared more of the same interests than the other family members did. Still, we were merely good neighbors, good friends.

Then something changed. It was nothing tangible, but a light in his eyes seemed to reflect the growing interest and excitement I too felt. I knew that our mutual attraction could easily go one step further . . . then another. And the terrible truth was that I was tempted to go along with it. I plunged from the heights of romantic imaginings to the depths of self-condemnation. What was happening? I was a Sunday School teacher, church leader, devoted wife and mother. Why couldn't I simply banish these thoughts from my mind?

But in actual practice it was not so easy. Temptation worked like an undertow, and the harder I fought it, the more fiercely it pulled: What was so wrong about what was happening? I rationalized. Who would be hurt? Could this man and I help it if we were "meant for each other"?[2]

J. Allan Petersen, after reviewing David's affair with Bathsheba, points out some important truths. He says:

The lessons from David are obvious and apply to all of us. Underscore them in your mind and heart.

1. No one, however chosen, blessed, and used of God, is immune to an extramarital affair.

2. Anyone, regardless of how many victories he has won, can fall disastrously.[3]

As perplexing as this is, even more perplexing is the effect that becoming involved in an affair has on the Christian involved. H. Norman Wright says:

Even though the majority of people I have seen involved in affairs are committed Christians and know what the Word of God says about adultery, appealing to this knowledge does not usually cause them to stop the involvement. Appeals to family, mother, church, or even job security also have negligible effects.[4]

My goals for this chapter are that by the time you have completed reading it you will be able to understand the psychological processes and behavioral progression that lead people into an affair. I also hope that you will be able to understand the psychological changes that can cause even a committed Christian wife or husband to become willing to sacrifice spouse, children, church relationships, and sometimes even one's job, in order to continue the affair.

A TYPICAL PROGRESSION OF AN AFFAIR

We will begin by following a Christian couple through a fairly common kind of affair. In doing this, I wish to acknowledge, in the text of the tables which follow, my use and adaptation of material from James Dobson's book *Love Must Be Tough* and Charles Mylander's volume *Running the Red Lights.*[5]

Stage 1	Wife's Perspective	Husband's Perspective
	This woman is in a state of emotional need. She is lonely, suffers from low self-esteem, and has had difficulty making female friends. She reaches for the emotional involvement of her husband but he fails to notice. She resorts to nagging and complaining, which puts greater distance between them.	Her husband has made business commitments that he must meet. He's in a highly competitive and satisfying position, and his emotional energies are drained by the time he comes home. He loves his wife but doesn't have much time or energy to "carry her," psychologically.

Comment: Husband fails to recognize his wife's legitimate emotional needs.

Stage 2   Wife's perspective   Husband's perspective

She experiences greater frustration and depression, which gradually gives way to anger. She begins to "bludgeon" her bewildered husband for his lack of involvement in the home.

He makes some feeble attempts to relate to his wife, especially after emotional explosions have occurred between them. But this leopard finds it difficult to change his spots. He is still overcommitted at work, whether he likes it or not, and he constantly falls back into familiar patterns.

Comment: Unmet ego needs lead to increased vulnerability to meeting those needs outside the marriage.

Stage 3   Wife's perspective   Husband's perspective

This needy woman is now in a dangerous position. She is vulnerable to any attractive, available man who comes into her life. Inevitably, it seems, such an encounter occurs. A casual introduction to a flirtatious man sets the wheels in motion, and he quickly becomes the object of her fantasies, hopes and dreams. He appears to be so com-

The husband continues in ignorance of what his wife is experiencing. His mind is elsewhere. He wishes she would be happier because he does love her and the children, but he has no idea how her unhappiness relates to him.

passionate compared to her husband, so much more dignified, so much more in touch with her feelings, so much more worthy of respect. Nothing illicit has occurred at this point, but she's spending a great deal of time thinking about an affair with this specific man.

Comment: Someone outside the marriage starts meeting those needs. The wife and her "friend" talk and meet more frequently. She feels like she has found someone at last who truly cares about her feelings. "Innocent" touching begins.

Stage 4	Wife's perspective	Husband's perspective
	An extramarital relationship gradually begins to heat up. It's no sudden romp in the grass. Rather, the affair grows slowly, with more secret meetings and an escalating friendship. She feels guilty, of course, but the excitement is incredible. Anyway, her husband doesn't seem to care.	The man of the house is still not aware of any unfaithfulness. He may notice some coolness and a lessened demand for his attention, but his suspicions are not aroused. Her hostility to him may increase during this time, but he has already become accustomed to that attitude in her.

Comment: Enjoyment of "innocent" touching causes couple to want more. They spend as much time together as possible. She becomes aware of very intense feelings on her part, but rationalizes that this is not adultery because they haven't slept together.

Stage 5   Wife's perspective   Husband's perspective

Finally, it happens: a sexual experience occurs. In the following weeks more illicit sexual activity transpires, with all the guilt, fear and raw passions that accompany this way of life. Her spiritual life rapidly deteriorates, as she lies and rationalizes and lives a double standard. It is a tough assignment to play-act the role of a faithful wife when she's giving herself to someone else. Bible reading and church attendance become less frequent or even nonexistent. She loses all sexual interest in her husband.

The man may now begin to worry about the deteriorating relationship for the first time. He doesn't yet have much evidence on which to base his suspicions, but he knows intuitively that something has changed. His reaction is still one of confusion at this stage.

Comment: As the adultery continues, one's spiritual commitments tend to decline rapidly, even though they may continue to be affirmed verbally.

UNDERSTANDING THE TEMPTATION PROCESS: BIBLICAL PERSPECTIVES

THE GENESIS 3 NARRATIVE

A helpful framework for understanding the process of temptation toward any sort of sin can be drawn from the story in Genesis 3:1–6, which recounts the first temptation. The text reads:

> Now the serpent was more crafty than any of the wild animals the Lord God had made. He said to the woman, "Did God really say, 'You must not eat from any tree in the garden'?"
>
> The woman said to the serpent, "We may eat fruit from the trees in the garden, but God did say, 'You must not eat fruit from the tree that is in the middle of the garden, and you must not touch it, or you will die.'"
>
> "You will not surely die," the serpent said to the woman. "For God knows that when you eat of it your eyes will be opened, and you will be like God, knowing good and evil."
>
> When the woman saw that the fruit of the tree was good for food and pleasing to the eye, and also desirable for gaining wisdom, she took some and ate it. She also gave some to her husband, who was with her, and he ate it.

Significance of the Actions

Satan's temptation of Eve can be conceptualized in six steps—steps that can be seen in Satan's temptations of believers today. Step 1 is found in the first verse.[6]

The Hebrew may be paraphrased in the following way: "Now the serpent was more crafty than any wild creature that the Lord God had made. He said to the woman: 'Is it really a fact that God has prohibited you from eating of all the trees of the garden?'"

What is the dynamic here? Why did Satan ask this question? He obviously knew what God had said to Adam and Eve, or he would not have been able to ask what he did. Furthermore, he deliberately distorted what God had said. "Is it really a fact that God has prohibited you from eating of *all* the trees of the garden?" Satan's ploy is rather obvious: he was enticing Eve to take her eyes off all the things God had given her to enjoy, and to focus on the one thing that God had forbidden. There were probably a thousand pleasurable things Eve could have done in the garden, but now all her attention was focused on the one thing she could not do. We might call this first step *maximizing the restriction*.

Eve was now psychologically prepared for Satan's next step. In response to Eve's statement that God had said that eating of the fruit of the one tree would result in death, Satan boldly declared: "You will not surely die." The results of such and such an action, he countered, won't really be as bad as God said. He was *minimizing the consequences* of sin. Satan minimized sin's consequences in two ways: first, by telling Eve that the consequences of her action would not be as bad as they had been stated to be; and second, by eventually focusing her attention so completely on the tree that she forgot about the consequences entirely (v. 6).

The third step Satan took could be called *mislabeling the action*. In verse 5 he said: "'For God knows that when you eat of it your eyes will be opened, and you will be like God, knowing good and evil.'" Here Satan planted the suspicion in Eve's mind that it was not because the fruit would injure her that God had forbidden her to eat it, but because he did not wish her to be like himself. Satan deftly removed his temptation from the category of "sin" by relabeling it. In this particular instance, partaking of the fruit was relabeled as a way of expanding her consciousness. She would become a more complete person if she tried it once. Before this time Eve had thought of the forbidden action as disobedience; now she sees it as a necessity if she is to become a complete and mature person.

Satan then quickly added another aspect to his temptation, *mixing good and evil*. Verse 6 reads: "The woman saw that the fruit of the tree was good for food. . . ." C. S. Lewis has commented that evil is often a perversion of something good which God created. In this instance Satan added potency to his temptation by mixing good with evil: Eve saw that the fruit on the tree was good for eating.

The fifth aspect of Eve's temptation is found in the middle part of verse 6: She "saw that the fruit of the tree was . . .

pleasing to the eye." This was *mixing sin with beauty*. Temptation often comes wrapped in the form of something beautiful, something that appeals to our senses and desires. It is often necessary to think twice before we are able to recognize that a beautiful object or goal may be sin in disguise. In this incident Eve failed to discriminate between the beautiful package and the sin which she would commit by taking that package.

Finally Eve took a sixth step: The narrative tells us that "she saw that the fruit of the tree was . . . desirable for gaining wisdom. . . ." In essence she swallowed the devil's lie. This step might be called *misunderstanding the implications*. Although this may seem like a less significant point in the temptation process, it is perhaps the most crucial. In effect, by accepting Satan's statement Eve was calling God a liar, even though she might not have recognized that in her action. She accepted Satan as the truth-teller and God as the prevaricator. By partaking of the fruit she was implying that Satan was more interested in her welfare than God. Yielding to the temptation implied that she accepted Satan's analysis of the situation instead of God's.

APPLICATION TO EXTRAMARITAL TEMPTATION

These six steps of the temptation process can often be found today in the temptation to an extramarital affair. In an office setting, for example, while surrounded by others who combine the security of a marriage with the adventure and excitement of an affair, it may seem confining to a Christian to be the only one apparently not participating. The moral guidelines of biblical Christianity begin to feel very confining (*maximizing the restriction*).

Then, too, we see those around us who are carrying on "discreet affairs"—they seem to be enjoying the pleasure of both the marital and extramarital worlds, without experiencing any negative repercussions. Allowing us to see those who are "having it both ways" and who seem to be enjoying life to the full may be one of Satan's ways of subtly *minimizing the consequences* of sin. Another approach Satan sometimes tries is to convince us, usually at an unconscious level, that the rules apply to everyone but us. Because of our intelligence, our ability to be discreet, and from what we have learned by watching others make mistakes, the usual bad things that happen to other people won't happen to us—or so we think.

Sometimes two people are in a positive relationship which is inexorably heading toward the sexual. However, if they were to admit this to themselves, they would have to break off their relationship in order to remain true to their convictions. They might be strongly tempted to deny the sexual orientation of their relationship, saying, "it's only a friendship," and thus *mislabel the action.*

The relationship is not all bad; some good has come out of it. A Christian friendship may have been instrumental in helping someone get through a difficult situation, perhaps even preventing a suicide attempt. It is quite possible that one or both persons' self-esteem has been bolstered as a result of the friendship. A life situation that once had seemed depressing and hopeless now sparkles with new-found energy and life. One or both parties may feel like new energies have been discovered to take back to the spouse and children. Satan has been successful in *mixing good with evil.*

The relationship that has developed seems like a beautiful thing. Certainly the risk of sexual involvement is there, but the "friends" have kept clear of that. Theirs is only a very beautiful Christian friendship. They have never even kissed; yet they have a relationship that is as beautiful as any they have experienced. Satan has succeeded in *mixing sin with beauty.*

And then it happened. They were alone for a few hours undetected. It was unplanned. It had seemed to happen so naturally. It was a beautiful experience. They had never believed they could experience such joy and ecstasy. Nothing as beautiful as this could really be wrong, could it?

They have taken the sixth step. By believing and acting on Satan's lies, they have implicitly expressed (through their behavior) that they believe that God, who would call their action adultery—a bad and sinful behavior—was less truthful than Satan, who affirmed their action as good. If pressed to state this verbally, neither one would have felt comfortable doing so, but they have, through their actions, acted as if Satan were the truth-teller and God the prevaricator (*misunderstanding the implications*).

METAPHORS OF LIGHT AND DARKNESS

In the Bible the words "light" and "darkness" are often used metaphorically. Light refers to that which is good, as well as that which reveals the true nature of good and evil. Darkness refers to what is evil and what conceals reality. Satan is the one who blinds the eyes of those who wish to be deceived (John 3:19–21; 2 Cor. 4:4). God is identified as the bringer of light, the One who reveals what truly is (Luke 2:32; John 1:4–9; 12:46; 2 Cor. 4:6; 1 John 1:5).

As we close our eyes to God's truth, we become less able to see it. We see things through the distorted lens that Satan provides, and move deeper into sin. We shall see later in this chapter that what Scripture alludes to as "having the understanding darkened" correlates well with a description of how ego defenses work in keeping anxiety-producing truth out of our conscious awareness.

METAPHORS OF FREEDOM AND SLAVERY

Scripture asserts that as we yield ourselves to sin we become increasingly enslaved to it (John 8:34; Rom. 6:15–18; 7:14–23; 2 Pet. 2:18–19). We are no longer free to do as we choose, because we progressively lose that freedom as we continue the practice of sin.

The biblical metaphor of slavery also has its counterpart in the psychological field, in the term *addiction*. By definition persons are addicted when they have lost the ability to respond voluntarily to a stimulus. One can see how sexually addicted people, by giving in to sinful temptation, gradually lose their ability to make voluntary choices.

I believe that a related kind of slavery applies to all who become involved in extramarital affairs. They do not necessarily have a sexual addiction, but they do have a relationship addiction. Such a person believes he or she cannot survive without contact with the lover. As an affair continues, he or she finds increasingly that the focus of life is on the next opportunity to meet with the illicit party, much as the alcohol or drug addict increasingly builds life around the drug. Their lives are no longer free in the sense of their being able to choose how to find happiness; they have become enslaved to the mistaken belief that their only route to happiness is by way of the affair.

There is another troubling point of resemblance between the alcohol or drug addict and the person addicted to an illicit lover. All three kinds of addicts will continue the relationship to their particular "fix" even though, by so doing, they endanger their health, families, or careers. They have become slaves of their "fix," unable to change on their own, and often so psychologically blinded to reality that they think their bondage is their best option.

UNDERSTANDING THE TEMPTATION PROCESS: PSYCHOLOGICAL PERSPECTIVES

PREDISPOSING FACTORS THAT ARE CULTURE-WIDE

In previous chapters we have discussed several cultural factors which make marriages more vulnerable today, and we will note them briefly again here. Opportunities for men and women to work together or interact for extended periods of time have increased. Opportunities for adult males and females to be alone together have grown. Our expectations about what we want out of marriage have increased. The time and energy we believe we have available for our spouses has decreased. Our sense of entitlement to emotional happiness and sexual fulfillment has increased, while the social consequences of going outside marriage to meet those needs have decreased.

PREDISPOSING FACTORS THAT MAY
AFFECT CHRISTIANS (MORE THAN OTHERS)

Several predisposing factors may make Christians *more* vulnerable to affairs than non-Christians, at least relative to the factors alone. The factors have to do with ego defense mechanisms.[7] Although many readers of this book will be familiar with these, I will include a brief discussion of them for those to whom they may be less familiar.

Among those parts of Freudian theory which many psychologists have accepted, even though they may strongly disagree with Freud on other things, are his theories about ego defense mechanisms. Freud believed that we all experience unwanted thoughts, feelings, and impulses that are unacceptable to the superego (roughly equivalent to the conscience). If we were to experience all these thoughts, feelings, or impulses consciously we would become anxious, maladaptively so.

Ego defense mechanisms serve an adaptive function by keeping such unacceptable thoughts, feelings, and impulses in our unconscious mind. This is not a conscious process. Suppression, for example, is a conscious activity and is therefore not an ego defense mechanism. Ego defenses operate below the level of conscious awareness. They produce a kind of psychological dishonesty in that they shelter us from experiencing mental events with which we are uncomfortable. The better known of the ego defenses include repression, denial, projection, rationalization, intellectualization, dissociation, reaction formation, displacement, identification, and sublimation.

Repression and denial. The three ego defenses that are of the greatest interest to us in the discussion of Christians and affairs are repression, denial, and rationalization. *Repression* refers to the exclusion from conscious awareness of troubling psychic contents. *Denial* involves refusing to admit into awareness that which comes from the environment. These two terms are sometimes used interchangeably, but there is a technical difference. Denial involves refusing to admit things that come to us from the external environment. For example, the dependent (or codependent) wife who refuses to admit into her conscious awareness all the data that suggest that her husband is having an affair. Repression is refusing to admit into conscious awareness things that are happening within one's own psyche, for example, a man's refusal to recognize that he is developing romantic feelings for someone other than his spouse.

Rationalization. Rationalization is the process of generating justifications for ourselves. Again, this is not, at least within orthodox Freudian thought, a conscious process. Instead it is done unconsciously as we come up with plausible (but untrue) reasons for our behavior. For example, if we start to recognize that we are spending an inordinate amount of time with a certain person (somebody to whom we are not married), we may rationalize this in terms of the depth of the person's needs, or the "fact" that no one else can do it.

REPRESSING AWARENESS OF ONE'S FRUSTRATIONS

Everyone employs defense mechanisms at times in order to deal with the complexities of life. Ego defenses become unhealthy when we overuse them, or when we depend on them rather than deal with important personal issues. The Christian may use ego defenses in several ways which increase one's vulnerability to an affair. First, he or she may repress the awareness of certain emotions, such as frustration, so as not to recognize how irritated he or she has become about unmet ego needs in the marriage. Because a wife, for example, is uncomfortable admitting that she is angry, she may repress angry feelings about unresolved issues. She may also deny the input from her environment that indicates that there is little intimacy in the marriage. Many Christians exist in emotionally hollow marriages, managing to repress and deny the evidence that shows this, because at a conscious level they are committed to permanence in marriage. A non-Christian may be much more willing to admit the lack of intimacy in his or her marriage because he or she does not feel the necessity of striving for marital permanence. These emotionally hollow marriages make a believer highly vulnerable when someone outside the marriage starts to satisfy unmet needs.

REPRESSING AWARENESS OF GROWING ROMANTIC FEELINGS

When a Christian starts to become emotionally involved with someone outside of marriage, he or she may repress the awareness of those feelings because of biblical convictions that are held. A man, for instance, may believe he should only have such feelings toward his wife. Thus, he may begin to become romantically involved with another woman but only be dimly aware of it because of repression. A non-Christian, who may have fewer inhibitions about going outside his marriage, may be much more consciously aware of what is happening inside him than the Christian.

RATIONALIZING EXTRAMARITAL INVOLVEMENT

Third, we as Christians can become adept at behaving in ways that meet our ego needs, and then rationalizing our behavior through spiritual-sounding phrases. I am convinced that most of us, even as committed Christians, choose to do what we believe will meet our ego needs and then offer a spiritual-sounding rationalization (this may be wholly or partially unconscious). Only in our more honest moments do we recognize our real reasons for doing things.

Rationalization can occur in an affair in its early stages. Typically, one person may be going through a difficult time, and the other is only "showing Christian love." Prayer sometimes is used in a genuine way to comfort and support the other person during the early part of the relationship. As the relationship continues, however, prayer may come to be less spiritually motivated and become more a psychological method. The two people enjoy the intimacy which occurs when they pray together, and that intimacy, rather than talking to God, becomes the more important motivation (this awareness is usually repressed).

Prayer may serve a second function as well: At a time when the two should be concerned about where their relationship is heading, they feel less anxiety about it because they pray together regularly. And they tell themselves that anything that is bathed in prayer couldn't possibly be sinful.

Committed Christians can be more vulnerable than nonbelievers for another reason. Most believers try to shelter themselves from the more tawdry aspects of the world. They don't subscribe to the Playboy channel, go to R- or X-rated movies, or purchase sexually explicit novels or magazines. Some have even removed television from their homes, or view it only on a very selective basis. These actions are probably well and good as a part of separating themselves from a sinful world. But a disadvantage of doing those things is that the individual Christian may be innocent and naive when a nonbeliever tries to involve him or her in an affair. Because of a sheltered life the Christian may be totally unprepared for some of the devices of the Evil One. I don't think the answer is immersing ourselves in the above-mentioned things; but it will be some help to read books such as the present one, and others listed in the Bibliography (Appendix A), so that vicariously we may be prepared for the ways in which a person of the opposite sex may try to initiate a wrong relationship.

PRECIPITATING FACTORS THAT MAY AFFECT CHRISTIANS (MORE THAN OTHERS)

There is not a qualitative difference between what I have labeled "predisposing factors" and those called "precipitating factors." The difference is in timing and direction. Predisposing factors are those which are all around us, and which make us vulnerable in a general way to an extramarital affair. Precipitating factors are those which serve to move us toward a specific person at a specific time. I will identify four important precipitating factors.

The drivenness which comes from unmet ego needs and expectations. People often describe an affair as something that happened to them, rather than something in which they were a primary actor. They felt propelled into it, rather than having consciously and volitionally chosen it. This is so because a large part of the psychological process which moves people toward an affair happens unconsciously.

When people come into marriage they usually have expectations. Unconsciously, these expectations are changed into "needs." Not only is the process of translating them from expectations into needs an unconscious thing, many expectations and needs themselves are unconscious. When these are not met, frustration often builds. But this may be repressed in a Christian's marriage due to wrong beliefs about anger and the couple's desire for harmony (thus one or both may not be consciously aware of how frustrated he or she is that certain needs are not being met). When someone outside the marriage begins to meet the needs of the man, for example, he may feel powerfully attracted to that person. Because so much of the above process is occurring below the level of conscious awareness, this Christian man (the same is true for non-Christians) may not feel like he is making any choices. He may believe that the experience of falling helplessly in love is something that just happened to him, rather than something he chose of his own free will.

The coercive power of unrecognized feelings and drives. This second psychological factor is related to the one mentioned above, and to the ego defenses discussed earlier. In trying to be biblical Christians, people sometimes repress their awareness of feelings which they consider unbiblical so that they are not aware of what they are actually feeling. Just as repressed frustration may push such a person toward an affair, repressed awareness of sexual feelings may keep him or her from becoming aware of the growing intensity of romantic and sexual feelings within a relationship. These unrecognized feelings may precipitate an affair because the person is actually unaware of his or her true feelings. A point is reached where the individual no longer wants to change those feelings.

The blinding effects of yielding to sinful temptation. As discussed earlier, in Scripture God is identified as the bringer of light (the One who helps us see reality clearly), and Satan is the one who tries to blind our eyes from that reality. This blindness reveals itself in a number of ways when Christians "fall" into affairs. Satan blinds the eyes of the players to the fact that he is moving them toward adultery. He also blinds them to each other's faults: They see each other in a highly idealized manner. They are blind as well to the difficult decisions they will have to make before too long—either to leave a spouse and children or break off the affair. Satan blinds them to the tremendous pain the affair will create for the spouse, not to mention the pain and anger the children will experience when they learn the truth, and the anguish transmitted to future generations should those children follow their example of marital infidelity. And that is not all. Satan blinds them to the possible public humiliation their family may endure before the church, their friends, and in the workplace. They are unable to see the damage that will be done to their Christian testimony and to the name of Christ by an affair. And, finally, Satan blinds them to the pain their sin causes God.

The propulsive power of lust. An extramarital relationship that has gotten to the point of "innocent touching" rarely stays there. Why is a relationship unlikely to stay at that point? An anonymous article written by a pastor and printed in *Leadership* magazine a few years ago said:

> I learned quickly that lust, like physical sex, points in only one direction. You cannot go back to a lower level and stay satisfied. Always you want more. I've experienced enough of the unquenchable nature of sex to frighten me for good. Lust does not satisfy: it stirs up.[8]

It seems that a common denominator for all illicit sex, whether it be fornication, adultery, pornography, or sexual addiction, is that the person involved always wants more. The previous experience no longer satisfies; the person or couple involved want more powerful experiences.[9] For this reason affairs almost always move toward a sexual consummation.

WHY DON'T CHRISTIAN CONVICTIONS
FORM A STRONGER BARRIER?

It is a matter of distress to many that Christian convictions, Christian moral standards, don't serve as a stronger barrier for many believers. When it comes to a question of meeting one's ego needs or obedient biblical living, a distressingly high number of Christians choose to meet their ego needs. Why is this so? Are our convictions just a charade which would be exposed in all of us if the right temptation came along?

Some believers do obey their convictions rather than act on their ego needs. Not everyone whose ego needs come into conflict with their convictions chooses to abandon his or her convictions. Barbara, the woman quoted early in this chapter, is an example. After recognizing the incongruity between her convictions and the romantic feelings she was beginning to experience, she said no to the romantic feelings. We have no idea of how many potential affairs have never developed because Christians chose to honor their convictions rather than meet their ego needs through an affair.

Convictions are conscious; impulses are often repressed into the unconscious. I think there are two other ways in which Satan can work in conjunction with our ego defenses to tempt us to violate our convictions. First, he allows/causes us to experience an ego need unconsciously (e.g., loneliness for someone to care for us), and then moves us through the early stages of a relationship without our becoming aware of the deep needs within us that are being met or of the potential direction the new relationship is taking. Because our convictions operate primarily—not totally—in the conscious mind, we may not be consciously aware of the potential conflict between our convictions and the meeting of our ego needs until the relationship has developed substantially. The more we utilize repression in our daily lives, the later that recognition is likely to occur.

Second, by the time that recognition occurs, another psychological mechanism has already become operative—one called *cognitive dissonance.* This mechanism has the ability to alter our convictions or change our relationship to them.

COGNITIVE DISSONANCE

One of the most productive theories developed by social psychologists to explain human behavior is the theory of cognitive dissonance, first developed by Leon Festinger.[10] Festinger taught that individuals attempt to achieve consistency among the various opinions, attitudes, and values they hold. When there is disagreement between one or more of these elements (cognitive dissonance), pressure is created to change one or more of the opinions, attitudes, or values.

The amount of pressure toward change will depend on the amount of dissonance that exists. Dissonance acts like a drive or a need: Its presence leads to actions that can reduce it. Dissonance can be resolved or reduced by changing one of the cognitive elements involved, by adding new elements, or by decreasing the importance of one or more elements.[11] (If the theory of cognitive dissonance is unfamiliar to you and this preceding section seems unclear, the examples below should make it more understandable.)

How does a person maintain cognitive consonance, especially in view of the fact that we are continuously exposed to new information, values, or opinions that may conflict with those we already hold? Heider and Newcomb have developed theories which explain how cognitive balance is achieved.[12] To

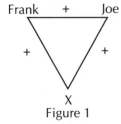

Figure 1

illustrate, the apexes of the triangle above indicate Frank, Joe, and their attitude toward a certain object. If Frank likes Joe (represented by a plus sign between Frank and Joe), and both Frank and Joe like X, this is a balanced system.

If Frank likes Joe, and both of them dislike X (represented by minus signs) this will also be a balanced system.

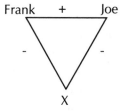

Figure 2

If Frank likes Joe and also likes X, but Joe dislikes X, this will be an unbalanced system.

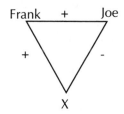

Figure 3

Frank may attempt to produce cognitive balance by convincing Joe that he really ought to like X, or Frank may change his own mind and begin disliking X, or he may decide that a person's attitude toward X is not a very important matter anyway (decreasing the dissonance by decreasing the importance of the elements which are dissonant).

Applying this to the situation of extramarital affairs, John, who has been raised in the church, loves God, and accepts God's teaching that extramarital affairs are wrong, as pictured below.

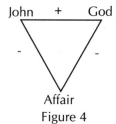

Figure 4

However, in the course of time John, who is married to Andrea, meets Sally. They develop a friendship, and eventually the friendship deepens. The implications of the deepening friendship are only dimly apparent to John because of the action of his ego defenses—denial, repression, and rationalization. Suddenly John realizes one day that he is very deeply in love with Sally, and that he feels unfulfilled with Andrea. His state at that moment could be diagrammed as:

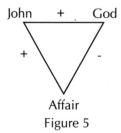

John   +   God

Affair

Figure 5

This is a state of imbalance or dissonance, and John will feel some pressure to reduce this dissonance. There are several ways he can do this. If John recognizes what is happening early (or if someone confronts him early about what is happening), he might decide to give up the affair. This would achieve balance, returning him to the state pictured in Figure 4.

John might, especially if he is of a more liberal theological persuasion, attempt to redefine what God meant by adultery and conclude that God is not describing the same thing as his relationship to Sally. For example, since there is a deep commitment between the two of them and he perceives no exploitation (his "redefinition" of adultery), this is not really adultery.

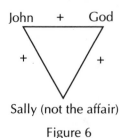

John   +   God

Sally (not the affair)

Figure 6

If John's relationship with Sally has gone on a long while before he is confronted, a number of other attitudes, thoughts, and opinions have undergone change so as to be consistent with the relationship he has with Sally. If many of John's most important ego needs are being met by Sally, and he sees no way that those could be met by Andrea, he may make the decision to continue with Andrea and minimize the dissonance he feels theologically by placing more distance between himself and God. He may deal with his fear of disobedience to God by telling himself that God is a forgiving God and that he will not remember his wrath forever. Thus John's decision looks like the following:

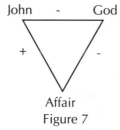

Figure 7

We would predict from this diagram that John will experience difficulty in his spiritual life, and probably withdraw from many of the Christian activities in which he has been active. Another implication of cognitive dissonance theory is that the earlier John is confronted, before he has made significant shifts in many of the attitudes surrounding and supportive of his relationship to Sally, the more likely he is to resolve the dissonance by leaving the affair.

Thus, the changes that happen within Christians as they become involved in affairs and gradually leave the close walk they once had with God can be described in both spiritual and psychological terms. Spiritually we see that Satan tempts believers by maximizing God's restrictions, minimizing the consequences of sin, mislabeling the action (notice how uncomfortable it is to use the words *adulterer* and *adultery* today), mixing good with evil, mixing sin with beauty, and causing us to misunderstand the implications of our behavior. The believer progressively loses sight of true spiritual realities and becomes enslaved to the idea that he or she must have a certain person in order to be happy.

The psychological descriptions of what is happening within this same believer include the overuse of the ego defense mechanisms of denial, repression, and rationalization, the drivenness that comes from unmet ego needs and expectations, the coercive power of unrecognized (i.e., unconscious) feelings or drives, and the value-changing impact of cognitive dissonance.

KEY IDEAS FROM CHAPTER 5

The two kinds of affairs most likely to occur in Christian marriages are what Pittman calls "accidental infidelities" and "romantic affairs."

A progression that can easily lead a Christian into an accidental infidelity or a romantic affair is the following:

- A person fails to recognize marital partner's legitimate emotional needs.
- Unmet ego needs lead to increased vulnerability (temptation) to meet those needs outside the marriage.
- Someone outside the marriage starts to satisfy those needs. The marital partner and his or her "friend" gradually begin to talk and meet more frequently. The Christian believes that here at last is someone who truly cares about his or her feelings. "Innocent" touching begins.
- Enjoyment of "innocent touching" causes the couple to want more. They spend as much time together as possible. The involved couple become aware of very intense feelings on their part, but rationalize that this is not adultery because they haven't slept together.
- Intercourse occurs. As it is repeated, the unfaithful couple's spiritual commitments and involvements tend to decline rapidly, even though they may continue to verbally affirm their Christian beliefs.

There is a strong correlation between the spiritual processes described in Scripture and the psychological processes described by contemporary psychology.

As Christians yield to Satan's temptation in an extramarital affair, they become progressively blind to true reality. As they yield further to sin, they gradually lose the ability to choose right.

Believers' ego defenses keep anxiety-producing thoughts out of their conscious awareness, and thus they are frequently unaware of (blind to) the changes occurring within them. They enter a relationship addiction, where their entire life begins to revolve around the lover. They experience loss of control over what they do in that relationship, and may violate values that they have strongly believed for many years.

When Christians involved in an affair finally recognize that they must make a choice, cognitive dissonance pushes them in the direction that will cause them to have the least incongruence with the other values, opinions, and thoughts that they hold at that time. Because they have altered many of their values, opinions, and thoughts as a result of the affair, the decision that leads to less cognitive dissonance at that point may be very different from the decision that they would have made several months earlier.

For those reasons, the earlier point at which believers recognize that an improper relationship is developing, and the earlier they confront it (either in themselves or in someone they love), the more likely is the problem to be resolved in ways consistent with previous biblical convictions.

NOTES

1. Frank Pittman, *Private Lies: Infidelity and the Betrayal of Intimacy* (New York: Norton, 1989), 133.

2. Told in Charles Mylander, *Running the Red Lights: Putting the Brakes on Sexual Temptation* (Ventura, Calif.: Regal, 1986), 33–34.

3. J. Allan Petersen, *The Myth of the Greener Grass* (Wheaton, Ill.: Tyndale House, 1983), 32.

4. H. Norman Wright, *Seasons of a Marriage* (Ventura, Calif.: Regal, 1982), 122–23.

5. James Dobson, *Love Must Be Tough: New Hope for Families in Crisis* (Waco: Word, 1983), 135–37 and Mylander, 32–33.

6. This section offering an analysis of the temptation process is taken from my book *Hermeneutics: Principles and Processes of Biblical Interpretation* (Grand Rapids: Baker, 1981), 217–20. Used with permission of the publisher.

7. Much of the following discussion on ego defense mechanisms and their definitions is adapted from C. W. McLemore, "Defense Mechanisms," in the *Baker Encyclopedia of Psychology* (Grand Rapids: Baker, 1985), 286–88.

8. A quotation from *Leadership*, xx, 1982, cited in Mylander, 150.

9. Mylander, 150–51.

10. Leon Festinger, *A Theory of Cognitive Dissonance* (Evanston, Ill.: Row, Peterson, 1957) and Leon Festinger, *Conflict, Decision, and Dissonance* (Stanford: Stanford University Press, 1964)

11. Henry Lindgren, *An Introduction to Social Psychology* (New York: Wiley, 1969), 115.

12. Fritz Heider, *The Psychology of Interpersonal Relations* (New York: Wiley, 1958) and Theodore Newcomb, *The Acquaintanceship Process* (New York: Holt, Rinehart and Winston, 1961).

PART TWO

Counseling Christians After an Affair

Chapter Six

Individual Counseling with the Unfaithful Partner

Every Christian counselor or pastor today can expect many times during his or her career to be called on to help individuals or couples trapped in affairs. This chapter presents a model for helping such individuals or couples. Although I believe this model has been used of God to bring healing for many Christian couples, it is far from a finished product, and certainly needs refining through dialogue with other Christian counselors. It is my hope that the model offered here will serve as a stimulus to others to develop and articulate their own models for working with this increasingly common problem, so that together we might increase our effectiveness in helping couples work through this very difficult experience.

When a person or couple first comes for counseling he or she may come in one of three ways: The transgressor comes alone, the faithful partner comes alone, or they come together. Later in this chapter and the next we will consider counseling with one mate alone, but let us begin with a discussion of the couple who come together.

THE INITIAL SESSION

When a couple comes for counseling, several things can be done during the first session. At this time it is of primary importance that the counselor establish a caring relationship with *both* people. One of the easiest ways to do this is through the use of empathy statements. By the end of the session both husband and wife should know that their counselor cares about them, that the counselor understands the depth of their pain, and that they will receive help in deciding where they want to go with their marriage.

In addition, it is important for the counselor to obtain a full understanding of what they both know concerning the affair, and provide time for each partner to express his or her feelings about it. Each partner should be given an opportunity to express his or her desires for the marriage. The counselor may also wish to identify other problem areas needing attention in the marriage.

In this first session, it is helpful for the couple to spend the last few minutes reflecting on the strengths in their marriage and some reasons why it is worthwhile for them to try to rebuild it. I ask them to recount two or more memories of happier times in their relationship (one from each person). This can ease the couple's pain, at least momentarily, and remind them that they have shared good times together in the past. It gently raises the hope that, since they have been happy in the past, perhaps they can be happy once again.

I then ask the couple to take a personality inventory, explaining that this will assist me in getting to know them more quickly. Since the first session may be quite emotionally draining because of the newness of therapy, I give them the choice of either completing the personality inventory immediately after the first session or before or after the second session. I prefer the Personality Research Form, because it addresses so many of the basic ego needs that are important in a marriage.[1] At a later session I will plot the husband's and wife's scores on the same graph, and discuss how their needs and traits complement or fail to complement one another. I usually spend two hours (two sessions) giving this feedback, and many couples have remarked that this was one of the most helpful experiences of the marriage counseling. The session(s) in which the feedback is given depends on the needs of the couple.

During the last few minutes of the first session I tell the couple that usually I have found it helpful to see each person alone for a few sessions, and so I schedule separate appointments for them. If I sense during the session that it will be important to see one of them privately before the other because he or she may think that I am going to side with the other mate I schedule that person first. Otherwise I let them make the decision about when each will see me.

THE RATIONALE FOR SEPARATE SESSIONS

I schedule separate sessions for the husband and wife because initially each person has different therapy needs. The person involved in the affair needs to decide if he or she wants to stay with the affair partner or return to the marriage partner. Obviously he or she cannot discuss this struggle comfortably when the spouse is present and probably will not do so. Also, if it did occur, it would be quite painful for the spouse to sit in on such a discussion.

Many counselees at this stage have not definitely decided to end the affair, so this issue must be discussed. Even if the partner having the affair has decided to leave his or her lover, he or she probably will have some grieving to do. This person will usually have periods of ambivalence during the process of letting go. At times during the letting-go process he or she may have difficulty forgetting the lover. He or she is unlikely to bring up or discuss these issues in the presence of the spouse.

You as the counselor may have some goals for these individual sessions that could not be met if the couple were together. You may want to ascertain what the guilty partner's *true* goal is in coming for counseling: Is it to deliver the spouse

to a counselor before exiting the marriage? Is he or she seeking help because of being "torn between two lovers"? Is the
person trying to decide whether or not to stay in the marriage?[2]
You may want to know how this affair fits into one's life pattern: Is it the first and only one, or is it one of many? Is there
evidence of a personality disorder expressing itself, either in a
relationship addiction or a sexual addiction? You are not likely
to get accurate answers about one's sexual history unless you
meet each person alone and promise confidentiality about the
material revealed.

Another counseling goal will be to understand the *meaning*
of the affair. What does it say about the needs that are not being met in the marriage? This will be important information to
be used later in marital counseling. But helping the guilty
partner identify this in the presence of the faithful one may
make the faithful spouse think you are helping the unfaithful
partner find justifications for the affair.

The *faithful* marital partner also needs private therapy time.
He or she has just received some of the most painful news one
will ever hear. Despite the fact that affairs are occurring with
increasing frequency, it is always a major crisis for the person
who has tried to build a lasting marriage. The offended partner needs to be able to grieve over the loss of his or her
partner's faithfulness.

The grieving process usually takes portions of several sessions and is likely to include elements of denial, rage at the
spouse, rage at the spouse's lover, thoughts of vengeance toward either one, self-doubt ("what's wrong with me that
caused him to stray?"), and depression. Frequently this emotional catharsis will be repeated several times before the
wounded partner has adequately vented these emotions.

If the counselor allows this repeated catharsis in the presence of the guilty party, that spouse may believe that it is being
done to punish him or her, and may become resentful. The
grief work of the faithful partner is best done in the presence
of the counselor rather than his or her spouse so that the faithful partner is free to grieve as needed without damaging the

chances of reconciliation. It is important for the faithful partner to express the full intensity of the grief, anger, and pain to the other partner, to feel that he or she has been fully heard *at least once*. Repeated ventings probably are done best with the counselor.

Can couples sort out the powerful emotions that are stirred up by an affair and make the difficult decisions necessary on their own? It is clear that some people do. However, when I read the stories of those who have gone through the trauma of an affair without the benefit of consistent professional counseling (e.g., Kuhne[3]) I am certain that such people suffer much longer and deeper than they would have if they had gone through the process with the assistance of a caring, skilled helper. I agree with both James Dobson and Frank Pittman that the depth of need and the increased likelihood of successful reconciliation warrant the help of a trained counselor.[4]

In this chapter we will discuss what a counselor may hope to accomplish during individual sessions with the unfaithful partner alone. In chapters 7, 8, and 9 we will examine the issues to be covered with the faithful partner.

INDIVIDUAL COUNSELING WITH THE UNFAITHFUL PARTNER

All interpersonal behavior makes a statement of some sort. One of the first things to be done in counseling those who are affected by an affair is to discover *what the affair means*. The counselor asks why this affair occurred. Here, a review of the possible causes of affairs, discussed in chapters 1 and 2, can provide a cognitive map as the counselor and client attempt to answer this together. Usually more than one factor contributes to an affair. The categories and reasons for affairs discussed in chapters 1 and 2 do not constitute an exhaustive list; rather, they are representative of the most common ones.

Sometimes the unfaithful partner may not be motivated to look at what caused the marriage's demise; he or she is enjoying the blissful experience of romantic love and has no desire to look back. The present relationship is all that seems important now. Nancy Duvall has suggested one powerful motivator that may cause such a person to reexamine what happened in his or her marriage. If people do not understand what steps led the marriage to its present state, there is no way to protect a future relationship from the same fate.[5]

Some people can come to understand the meaning of their past affairs best through the medium of writing. Especially if there has been more than one affair, it can be useful for the person involved to write about each affair in the order in which it occurred. He or she should try to identify the multiple factors involved, since few affairs are caused by a single one. The written content can then become the basis for further discussion in the counseling session. In a case of multiple affairs, it is important to look for common themes (such as marital situations, life situations of the unfaithful partner, or self-talk) that might have made the person vulnerable to an affair at that time. Precautions should be taken so that such writings are not discovered by the faithful spouse or anyone else.

THE EMPATHIC-SOCRATIC METHOD

When Christians are involved in affairs they often come to counseling knowing that they have sinned; these people feel depressed, guilty, and trapped by the situation. As long as the counselor comes alongside them gently and in a noncondemning way, the guilt feelings will remain attached to the counselees' sinful behavior. However, these feelings can quickly change if the counselor confronts them with their sinfulness. In confrontation the negative feelings counselees had about their own behavior become displaced onto the counselor's confrontation, building a wall between counselor and counselee.

A similar process can happen when a Christian counselor attempts to confront a person who is in the early stages of an affair, and may be experiencing more pleasure than pain. We have seen in an earlier chapter how sin activates one's ego defenses; by denying or repressing or rationalizing what is happening, the unfaithful person's ego attempts to minimize the amount of guilt the person would otherwise experience. When a pastor or counselor confronts such a person with his or her sin, that person's ego defenses constrict, and they close out the anxiety-producing material (and usually the confronter as well). In both of the above situations confrontation regarding sin, while theologically justified, produces a psychological barrier between the unfaithful partner and the pastor or counselor who is trying to help the person.

For this reason I believe empathy is more helpful than condemnation of the believer's sin. What the person is doing *is* sin; however, reiterating it in a combative or confrontational fashion is likely to build a wall between the unfaithful person and the counselor which will decrease or terminate that counselor's ability to minister to him or her. Empathizing with the pain and sense of entrapment the counselee is feeling, or allowing the counselee to confront his own behavior, is more likely to encourage that person to open up and share the struggle more fully.

An affair, even if it is not so at the moment, eventually becomes torment for the Christian involved. Through empathy the counselor can build a bridge to the very lonely island where the guilty partner now lives. We do this by being a friend rather than a critic. I am not suggesting that we become moral relativists, but that in the counseling session we respond with empathy so that the guilty person knows that we understand the pain he or she is feeling and the difficult situation he or she is in.

Confrontation has the right biblical goal, but the wrong method of reaching that goal. To fully help these people we need to provide an environment where they can be comfortable in talking about how they became involved in the affair in the first place. They need to be able to identify what factors were a part of their marriage that made them vulnerable to an affair, and to say if they are ambivalent about leaving the affair. Eventually we will want to help them look at possible mistaken beliefs, their lack of communication skills, or other factors which they brought (and the spouse brought) to the marriage. We will want them to look at the high cost of continuing an affair—for the spouse, their children, and for themselves. However, they will only listen to us if we have listened to them first. Empathy is what keeps us in the listening mode, and what encourages them to talk. While early confrontation may seem like the quickest way to move the person toward biblical obedience, it is actually a less effective way. If we cause our client or parishioner to close his or her ears to what we have to say because of the way we say it, we have lost that person.

The empathic-Socratic method combines the use of empathy statements with the method of teaching that Socrates used so effectively. Socrates taught by asking his students questions that helped them discover new truths or new relationships between ideas themselves. His teaching style is incorporated into modern education in the form of experiential learning. His teaching principle is this: *Truth that is discovered by students themselves will have a more lasting and powerful impact than truth imparted by a teacher* (in this case, a counselor). Modern social psychology has also shown that truth discovered through discussion is more likely to produce behavioral change in the student's life than truth delivered by lecture.

I believe that a combination of empathy and the Socratic method can produce a powerful Christian counseling technique. Empathy allows the clients' ego defenses to relax so that they can look honestly and deeply at themselves. The Socratic method, when carefully used, can help them probe even deeper. When blended with the right amount of caring empathy, the Socratic method can help clients begin to recognize the mistaken beliefs to which they have subscribed. It can help counselees begin to think about discrepancies between their values and their behavior. And eventually, it can help them to reaffirm biblical obedience as their standard for living.

When should a counselee be asked to look at the situation from God's perspective, or from the perspective of his or her spouse or children? An empathic stance affirms that we should start by understanding the situation from the counselee's perspective, and only gradually refocus the person's perspective to look at things from these other' viewpoints. The reason for this is that forcing the person to consider the situation from the viewpoints of others before they are ready to has the same impact as confrontation—it causes the person's ego defenses to become more rigid. There is a time, as Christian counselors, when we must ask the person to look at the situation from God's perspective and that of the individual's loved ones, but this needs to be done with a careful sense of timing and only after the client knows surely that the counselor cares.

REASONS TO LEAVE AN AFFAIR

For Christian counselors and pastors, God's teaching on adultery provides enough reason to encourage our client or parishioner to leave an affair. Even among secular mental health professionals there are few who believe that affairs are psychologically healthy. However, the most important person to convince in the counseling situation is not the counselor or pastor or other mental health professionals. It is the client. Theological arguments may be effective with a few, but probably the majority of those who become deeply involved in affairs will be unmoved by scriptural arguments. The reasons for this have been discussed in chapter 5.

For a confrontation to be most effective, it must come from within the person. By careful listening and the use of empathy statements, the counselor can often find a number of ways in which the affair is producing dissonance and pain rather than pleasure. Each of these may become a motivation eventually to leave the affair. The following are only a few of the many ways in which affairs produce pain for the unfaithful person.

The person is likely to be experiencing tremendous psychological pressure because of the number of lies he or she has told to cover the affair. After a while, it becomes impossible to remember the lie used in each situation so that it is increasingly difficult to lie in ways that are consistent. The guilt that a formerly honest person feels about the lies he or she is telling adds to the anxiety that is felt about being found out. The anxiety caused by needing to remain consistent with the lies one has already told can be a related motivator.

Since relating to others now involves deception, the affairee withdraws from others to escape the pressure of always having to keep up a deceptive front. Fewer needs are being met by the person's circle of friends, family, and acquaintances—people who customarily meet such needs—so he or she becomes almost entirely dependent on the affair partner to meet those emotional needs. Such a state is unhealthy even in a marriage, and much less so in an affair, because guilt, anxiety, and limited contact with one's lover often mean that one's needs are not met adequately.[6]

When women have an important relationship developing, they like to talk about it with other women. But in an affair, this important avenue of processing a relationship usually does not occur. Men generally talk about their relationships less than women, but they do talk at least sometimes with other men about frustrations they are feeling. A Christian man is not likely to share his developing infidelity with another Christian man, and so neither sex has an opportunity to gain realistic feedback or emotional release concerning the "new person in my life" by talking with same-sex peers.

Another frustration that arises, particularly in the life of a Christian single woman involved in an affair with a man, is that because of psychological inequities between the sexes she gradually loses her identity. Whereas before the affair she may have experienced a healthy balance of work, recreational, and spiritual activities, she gradually stops many of these activities so she can be free when her lover is free to see her. She may also have had a healthy emotional support system, but she gradually gives that up as she drops out of the activities. As she loses the positive reflected appraisals from her friends, as well as the activities and friendships themselves, her sense of identity decreases. Her whole emotional life centers around, and becomes unduly dependent upon, her affair partner.

When a woman becomes involved with a married man, other frustrations may develop as well. Richardson describes them well:

> She has low priority and few privileges. She cannot count on him, and she has less power in the relationship than he. As a result, in time, almost invariably the single woman finds herself disillusioned with her married lover and disappointed in herself. . . .
>
> Something as basic as determining the frequency and extent of time spent together becomes a source of pain and resentment. The single woman loses control over how her time is spent because it is his free time which determines when and for how long they can be together.[7]

A man in this kind of relationship usually feels free to interrupt a woman, but often she does not feel comfortable interrupting him. Richardson goes on to describe the frustration this causes, and then quotes the words of a woman in this situation:

> Being unsure whether one will be summoned or dismissed keeps one emotionally and psychologically off balance. . . .
>
> "I don't like the aspect of getting worked in [to his schedule] and then you get cancelled a lot and that's tough. I'm never sure when he can go and when he will cancel out. And there are times [when I feel] like I can't go on. I can't put up with any more, but I just feel so strongly toward him."[8]

Another motivator for leaving an affair for the woman involved in an adulterous relationship is this: After all is said and done, a majority of husbands end up staying with their wives. When such a man does divorce, he generally does not marry the woman with whom he was having an affair, but someone else.[9]

Another motivator, one with increasingly frightening consequences, is the possibility of contracting an incurable or even life-threatening disease. For younger women, the possibility of contracting a disease that could cause sterility can be a very

powerful motivator. The list of possible motivators could go
on. The point here is that if we listen empathically and long
enough so that persons involved in affairs can become
honest with us (and also with themselves), a number of possible motivations to leave the affair will be verbalized by the
counselee. By gentle Socratic questioning we can also help
them recognize factors that are they are denying, repressing,
or rationalizing, and thereby also increase the dissonance involved in remaining in the affair.

DISCOVERING THE LEVEL OF COMMITMENT TO THE MARRIAGE

After understanding what the affair means, a second step in
counseling with the unfaithful partner is to find out his or her
level of commitment to the marriage. If the person is not committed, the counselor will want to assess how willing he or she
is to reconsider that level of commitment.

While this is listed as a second step, much of this will have
been done during the first step. If the person has kept his or
her ego defenses high, and has remained unwilling to look at
any possible problems with the affair or any possible strengths
in the marriage despite the counselor's attempts to be empathic, there is little likelihood that counseling will result in
marital reconciliation. If there is some ambivalence (i.e., the
person wants both the affair and the marriage to continue),
counseling can possibly result in reconciliation.

UNDERSTANDING THE DIFFERENCES:
INFATUATION, OR MATURE, COMMITTED LOVE?

If there is a willingness to reconsider, a third important step
in counseling the unfaithful partner may be taken. This is
to help the person develop a realistic understanding of the
differences between infatuation-stage love and mature
love, and between infatuation-stage love and a neglected marriage.

As discussed in chapter 2, infatuation-stage love (or romantic love) is a specific psychological phenomenon that is
characteristic of the early stages of certain relationships. The

persons involved believe they have finally found ultimate happiness, revealed through another human being (a modest delusion). Being "in love," they believe they are finally complete, having found the perfect person for themselves. It is important that they not know each other well, so that the excitement of gradually revealing more of one's inner self to the other person, and having him or her do the same, can continue. The scariness of not knowing how the other person will respond when something new is shared, the anxiety of not knowing the other person fully, a certain unpredictability—these must all be there, for all of this adds adventure to the relationship. Also, barriers to the relationship must exist, such as a need for secrecy, and limited time available to see each other. The need for secrecy, the drama, and the intrigue all heighten the tension within the relationship and raise it above the normal and mundane.

It is important that the counselee realize that this specific state of being "in love" is a developmental stage in a normal heterosexual relationship, and that once two people know one another well and barriers to their relationship have been removed, the romantic high of that relationship will decrease as predictably as the sun rises each day. If each no longer feels a romantic high for the marriage partner of five years, that does not mean that they have fallen out of love: It may mean that their love has matured into something we might call "commitment love" or "companionship love," where they continue to show caring as an act of the will and out of genuine regard for each other. Other components of mature love have replaced the romantic high they once experienced.

It may be that what the counselee is experiencing in the marriage is not the contrast between romantic love and commitment love, but between romantic love and an impoverished marriage. Probably most people enter marriage with the illusion that a love relationship will continue forever with very little effort or conscious activity needed to keep it strong and healthy. The counselee may be discovering that a marriage untended becomes impoverished. On the other hand, the act of doing loving things for a person generally makes us feel closer to that person. The degree of love one feels for someone is directly related to the time and energy one has invested in that relationship. If a spouse has given little of one's self other than finances for several years, then there may be very little love, either romantic or mature, left in the relationship.

If this is the case, then the counselee or parishioner needs to realize that it is unfair and invalid to compare the emotional intensity of the affair with the lack of feelings in an impoverished marriage. The present affair will become as lackluster as the marriage in a few years unless this person changes how he or she relates to the other partner.

When a person says that his or her relationship to the lover is much more harmonious than his or her relationship to the spouse, a clarification may be in order. What may actually be true is that the relationship to the lover is *untested*; he or she never has had to work out decisions concerning budgets, child rearing, or countless other issues with the lover.[10] If forced to deal with all the issues of married life, he or she might find that the same difficulties arise with one's lover that are now present with one's spouse. The solution is not to leave the marriage partner, but to learn how to resolve differences effectively.

LOOKING REALISTICALLY AT THE COST OF DIVORCE

Another important step in counseling the unfaithful partner is to help him or her look realistically at the disadvantages of divorce—for himself or herself, and for the family. An increasing number of counselors, even non-Christians, have begun to do just that. They are willing to state in print that they believe it is better to preserve and strengthen the marriage when possible rather than replace it with a new relationship.[11] Diane Medved summarizes this point of view:

> In my private practice as a marriage counselor and psychologist, I've helped plenty of struggling couples through separation and "liberation." I originally thought that staying together in turmoil was more traumatic than making the

break, that striking down taboos about divorce was part of modern enlightenment.

I was wrong. As I shifted my professional focus to divorced individuals, the truth was difficult to avoid: Treating divorce as "morally neutral"—an option no better or worse than staying married—was irreparably damaging to the very people I wanted to help.

Often in tears, the divorced people I talked with described fantasies of an ex-spouse returning or confessed guilt over abandoning a devoted mate. They spoke of being uprooted from their homes, of splitting possessions, of children changed from innocents to confidants or scapegoats. And they mourned a part of their life never to be recaptured—the family unit now destroyed.

I'd ask, "Looking back, do you think you could have made it work?"

Women would respond, "He was not romantic. He thought only of himself and his career." Men might say, "She took all my money, and then wouldn't trust me when I was away overnight." But each side would then conclude: "Knowing what I know now, yes, we could have made it work."

Divorce is so disastrous to body, mind and spirit that in an overwhelming number of cases the cure is worse than the disease. Of course, there are exceptions. Divorce may be the only recourse in cases of drug or alcohol addiction, physical abuse, severe emotional cruelty or permanent abandonment. But on balance, people could spare themselves enormous suffering if they scotched their permissive acceptance of divorce and viewed marriage as a lifelong commitment not to be entered into—or wriggled out of—lightly.[12]

Most of the time, a married person in the midst of a romantic affair greatly underestimates the problems that result when divorce occurs, especially if children are involved. Divorce often causes both partners (and their children) to lose the family home because there is not enough money to maintain it. Objects that had deep sentimental value sometimes go to the other spouse. Children are angry about being uprooted from their home and friends. Everyone resents the lowered standard of living. Children may not want to visit their noncustodial parent every other weekend, as is often the plan of the divorcing parents, even when a room is set aside for them, because so many of their toys, their clothes, and their friends are not there. Frequently there are temper outbursts and episodes of serious rebellion and acting out toward both parents. Custody battles and fights over visitation and child-support payments can keep the anger between the parents intense for many years after the divorce. Divorce is very expensive—financially, emotionally, interpersonally—for everyone involved.

And is a divorce over an affair worth it? Professional educator Dr. Barbara Matthews found that only one in twenty affair relationships were viable for more than eighteen months. In four of five cases, the husband ultimately wants his wife back.

Providing Mediation If Divorce Is Inevitable

Even after discussing the above issues, the unfaithful partner may remain committed to divorce. If this is so, the counselor need not automatically think his or her ability to help a couple is over. The marriage partners will need to work out as fair a divorce as possible. If the man and woman are willing to be honest and fair with each other, divorce mediation—with the aid of the counselor or a specially trained divorce mediator—is usually a better alternative than the antagonistic legal process that normally accompanies a divorce. Even at this stage there is still hope for a reconciliation: Sometimes when people see how much they will lose in a divorce, they are willing to try to work on the marriage somewhat longer.

One other situation that may still cause an unfaithful partner to reconsider staying in the marriage is the time when the children are told that their parents are filing for divorce. Usually the unfaithful partner will want the other spouse to break this news to the children. I think it is best that the spouse who has chosen to leave the family tell the children himself or herself.

Often, seeing the intensity of children's grief at such news will be enough to cause the unfaithful partner to reconsider.

HELPING THE AMBIVALENT COUNSELEE

If this partner is still ambivalent about leaving the affair, the counselor may need to help him or her clarify certain issues. One of these is whether behavior and feelings can be changed. People try a number of ways to say, "I can't stop the powerful feelings I have for this other person." A woman in an affair may make a decision to end it; but then as she remembers the good times she has had, she makes another telephone call, sets up another rendezvous, and becomes reinvolved. Or she may find that her thoughts keep returning to her affair partner, seemingly against her will. She thinks that it is impossible to end the relationship. In part this may be the normal process of grieving over a relationship that is ending, but it also may reflect the fact that she has not made a definite decision to end the relationship.

Part of therapy at this point involves helping her recognize that her "I can't end it" really means "I won't make the decision to permanently end it." We will look at the behavioral dimension of this ambivalence first, and then the cognitive dimension.

If a counselee contends that he or she cannot stop the adulterous behavior, it may be useful for the counselor to ask, "If you and your lover were preparing for a sexual encounter, and the Lord, or your mate, entered the room, would you be able to keep from carrying out your love-making?" If the answer is yes, the point should be clear: The counselee has the ability to say no to temptation, but is not choosing to do so.

If the person says that certain thoughts cannot be kept from coming to mind, the counselor can remind him or her that having thoughts of a former lover is a normal part of grieving whenever a relationship must end. The difference between conquering wrong thoughts and giving in to them depends on how the person responds to the thoughts. He or she can encourage them, and keep the fantasy alive and well in the mind, or force the affair relationship to become more and more peripheral in the thought life. What the counselor is doing here is gently encouraging the counselee to recognize that "I can't end it" often means "I haven't fully made up my mind that I want to end it."

Biblical Reframing

The struggle in the counselee's mind often is focused on comparing one's mate and the affair partner—a comparison in which the mate usually appears less desirable than the new partner. As Christian counselors we can help people reframe this situation, and there is biblical warrant for doing so. Our most important question to our counselees at this point is: "Are you willing to obey God in this matter, or are you going to purposely disobey his clear commands?" They may say that they are going to disobey—adding that "God is a loving Father and will eventually forgive." Such people need, at that point, to know that God has left a message in his Word specifically for anyone who chooses flagrantly to disobey him.

We can ask such counselees, "Do you know what that message is? Would you like to see it for yourself?"

If the counselee answers yes to these questions (and most will if convinced that the counselor genuinely cares), the counselee can be asked to read 1 Thessalonians 4:3–6 and explain what he or she thinks the passage means in his or her situation. The same can be done with Hebrews 13:4.

If the counselee responds by saying that the happiness that has been experienced in the affair cannot be found with the mate, a series of three questions may be gently asked:

- "Have you ever deliberately disobeyed God and ended up finding more happiness than you would have through obedience?"
- "Have you ever seen anyone flout God's laws and end up truly happy?"
- "Have you ever seen anyone disobey God's laws and end up miserably?"

As Christian counselors we have a responsibility to help all who seek us out—but to fellow Christians we are particularly responsible to help them recognize the spiritual dimensions of their interpersonal choices, for Satan will try to minimize the consequences of sin. We need to use our best judgment in deciding the most appropriate time to confront them when we believe they are making unhealthy or sinful choices. After we have done that, their decision becomes their responsibility.

PRACTICAL HELP FOR COUNSELEES WISHING TO END AFFAIRS

Therapy groups. The precise form of helping will depend on the psychological state of the individual as well as the theoretical framework of the therapist or counselor. If there is evidence of a sexual addiction or of a personality disorder which causes the person to use sex in a neurotic way, group therapy similar to that practiced in Alcoholics Anonymous— but which focuses on sexual addiction—may be helpful. In most larger cities, groups such as Sexual Addicts Anonymous or Sexaholics Anonymous (see Appendix B for more details) are available. For those with either a sexual addiction or a personality disorder that results in sexual acting out, long-term counseling will probably be appropriate. However, the crisis of the moment centers on stopping the acting out, which becomes the initial focus in therapy.

Emotionally unhooking from the affair. The first step in counseling is to help the person emotionally "unhook" from the affair. The beginning of this process should already have been accomplished by this time. By providing an environment in which he or she can tell the entire story of the affair, and by helping the person begin to see the ego needs that perhaps were not being met in the marriage—but were being met in the affair—the counselor can enable him or her to start making sense of why the affair happened.

By bringing unconscious material into the conscious, and by becoming aware of the processes in which the affections turn toward someone outside the marriage, the counselee can begin to understand his or her powerful feelings which previously were thought to be uncontrollable. And that is not all. He or she also is helped by learning why feelings could be so strong for a new partner and so weak for the marital partner.

As a result, hopefully, the counselee no longer conceptualizes the situation as being "I am totally in love with my affair partner" and "I am totally out of love with my mate." If the marriage relationship has been taken for granted and neglected for several years, the counselee may begin to see why he or she has few positive feelings for the marital partner. The goals of counseling at this point are that counselees will understand why they feel the way they do toward their spouses and their affair partners, will understand the huge price the family will pay if they divorce, and will recognize the serious spiritual implications of choosing to disobey God in this matter. With these understandings as the foundation for further work, counselor and counselee are ready to proceed toward breaking the romantic attachment of the affair.

A total break is necessary. Writers and counselors are unanimous in this: The affair relationship has to be broken completely if the marriage is to have a chance of surviving. (Usually the other mate, if he or she knows of the affair, will insist on this.) In treating alcoholism, relapses can more successfully be avoided if the client chooses total abstinence rather than "controlled drinking." Similarly, the complexities of romantic love require that a person stay as far away from temptation—the affair partner—as possible. It may be helpful in some instances for the counselor to discuss the love bank analogy from chapter 2 in order to show how it is impossible emotionally to close down an account if one continues making deposits in it.

This raises a problem for those who work in the same setting as the affair partner. In such instances it may not be possible to insist on absolutely no contact with the other person because to do so could jeopardize the job of one or both individuals. While the faithful partner will not be happy with such a situation, the best that may be done in certain settings is to have the unfaithful partner agree to have no *unnecessary* contact with the former lover, nor any *secretive* or *romantic* contacts.

Use of Scripture. Another way to help break the emotional relationship between the two lovers is for counselors to suggest Scripture meditation. I suggest that Christian clients find verses related to marital fidelity and infidelity and copy them on 3 x 5 cards so they can memorize them. Then I ask them to meditate on one or more verses for ten minutes each day, and bring such verses to mind in times of temptation. (Some verses frequently used include Proverbs 2:11, 16–18; 5:15–23; 6:25–32; 9:13–18; Malachi 2:15; 1 Corinthians 6:18–20; 1 Thessalonians 4:3–8, and Hebrews 13:4. It is best to let counselees or clients research and find these themselves.) Clients can also motivate themselves by thinking on verses that tell of the Lord's love and of the fear of the Lord.

Some people, when trying to end a relationship of this nature, speak of feeling almost like they are demonically oppressed by tempting thoughts. I would agree with Mylander when he says:

> Much more research is needed in the relationship between demon activity and any kind of sexual sin. The danger remains great enough, however, that anyone wanting release from any compulsive sex sin . . . should constantly pray a warfare prayer [i.e., a prayer that renounces any inroad Satan may have made into the person's life and any kind of demonic oppression affecting him or her, and claims Christ's victory over Satan based on Christ's atoning work on the Cross.][13]

Mylander recounts a time when, almost by accident, he prayed a brief warfare prayer ("Lord Jesus, protect me by your blood") when he was dealing with strong sexual temptation in his own life. Here is his own description of what happened:

> God honored it and a strange thing happened. The temptation did not just vaporize, but its power was broken. When I prayed, something like an invisible curtain came down between me and the lustful thought. It was not a solid curtain,

but one that blocked enough of the tempting sight that I was able to resist it if I so chose.[14]

Use of Rational-Emotive Therapy concepts. Another method that may be helpful in changing a person's thought processes is the A-B-C-D-E theory of emotion, also known as Rational-Emotive Therapy (RET). For those unfamiliar with this model, it is sometimes diagramed the following way:

A	+	B	———>	C
Activating event	+	Belief	———>	Emotional consequence

The activating event (A) is the affair. Because of what the counselee is saying to himself or herself about the affair relationship (B), he or she feels attracted to it (C). For example, a female counselee may be saying to herself at B, "I've never been so happy as when I'm with George." At C she experiences blissful feelings when she thinks of George.

To change those feelings, she must change what she is saying to herself and dispute (D) the self-talk that is causing her to feel attracted to the affair (B). This will lead to a new emotional consequence (E) about the affair partner.

A	+	D	———>	E
Activating Event	+	Dispute	———>	New emotional consequence

An example of disputing self-talk might be: "It's not true that I've never been so happy as when I'm with George. When I fell in love with Ray and Tom (two fellows she had dated during early adulthood) I remember feeling the same way. That probably means this happiness is a common occurrence whenever you're in the early stages of falling in love."

This model can be used at this point in counseling by asking a person to identify the self-talk he or she is using that could be causing feelings of attraction to the affair partner. The counselee may need help in devising disputing statements to defuse that attraction.

The counselee may also be engaging in negative self-talk regarding the marriage partner, such as, "He'll never change," or "If he changed it wouldn't be genuine." It can be helpful to show this person that the negative feelings that are harbored toward the marriage partner are a result of his or her conscious and subconscious self-talk. The counselee can be taught cognitive-behavioral techniques of thought-stopping and thought-replacement to use throughout the week.[15]

Fantasy modification. A person involved in an affair probably fantasizes—creating pleasant and romantic images about the lover, and unpleasant, painful, boring, or lonely images in relation to the marriage partner. If such a counselee wants to end the relationship with a lover, the pleasant, romantic fantasies about the lover must be stopped (thought-stopping can be used with fantasies as well as with self-talk). If the counselee finds that the romantic fantasy comes back repeatedly, he or she can be taught to focus on something interesting that blocks out the ability to recall the romantic fantasy. Or prayer—for strength to refocus one's attention, or even to command Satan to go—may be prescribed. Then the positive fantasy concerning the lover can be substituted with a neutral thought or a negative fantasy about him or her.

As a part of fantasy modification, the individual can fantasize his or her own family doing positive things together. These fantasies can include memories of positive experiences from the past as well as hopeful fantasies for the future. He or she can be encouraged to develop negative fantasies about the lover (e.g., to be discovered with the lover by the Lord, or by his or her pastor). By using both RET and fantasy modification, the counselor can assist the person on both cognitive and experiential levels. The counselee can begin to associate pleasant things with one's family (rather than just with the affair partner) and negative things with the affair partner (rather than just associating negative things with one's family).

It is important to encourage this person to realize that cognitive restructuring and fantasy replacement are *process techniques*—that is, if practiced over time they will *gradually* change one's thoughts and feelings. Jim, who had sexual fantasies about his lover twenty or thirty times a day when he was involved with her, practiced these techniques for several months. By the end of that time he found that he only thought about her a few times a month.

Learn from relapses. It is not unusual for the person attempting to leave an affair to fall back into the relationship once or twice. The relapse may be anything from giving in to the temptation to call the affair partner to becoming sexually involved again. The counselor can treat such a situation in a way similar to that which a substance abuse counselor might use for the relapse of a recovering alcoholic.

Usually a progressive series of thoughts and behaviors led to the eventual relapse. The counselor can try to help the person identify the thoughts and behaviors which became steps toward failure, and aid him or her in developing alternative self-talk or behavior to use if the temptation reoccurs. The earlier the counselee stops the harmful chain of cognitions and behaviors, the easier it is for him or her to say no. And conversely, the further he or she moves along the cognitive-behavioral chain before stopping, the more difficult it is. The secret is to move back along the cognitive-behavioral chain to a point where the person can easily say no.

Richard and Elizabeth Brzeczek have pioneered a program in Chicago named WESOM (for We Saved Our Marriage). The group uses the twelve steps of AA, replacing alcohol with infidelity. Spouses of those involved in infidelity use an approach similar to Al-Anon for guidance about their behavior and thinking. At this writing the WESOM approach is confined to groups which the Brzeczeks have started in Chicago. WESOM sounds like a healthy supplement to therapy, and perhaps even a substitute for therapy when that is not available. The approach, which is too detailed to discuss adequately here, is described thoroughly in their book, *Addicted to Adultery.*

The sponsor. When an individual is at the stage of leaving a relationship, the counselor can further help him or her by asking that one person or a couple be identified as a "sponsor"—someone who can be called upon to pray for and lend support to the person when tempted. This sponsor need not have been involved in an affair, but should be a Christian whom the counselee knows well and respects. The sponsor should be willing to be readily available when needed. If the counselee is tempted to contact the affair partner again, he or she can call the sponsor instead. This person then provides companionship, a listening ear, and helps the person develop an action plan to deal with that specific situation.

Substitution. Another method for helping those who want to terminate affairs could be called *sublimation* (or *substitution*), since it operates more in one's consciousness than does an ego defense. This involves finding a healthy replacement for the energy and time that were given to the affair. Optimally the person should substitute activities for and with the marriage partner and their children for the time spent in the affair. If that is not feasible (or they are not married), something else can be substituted. What is important is that the person find someone or something to invest his or her time in that gives a sense of fulfillment and happiness while keeping the mind occupied on something other than the affair.

REPENTANCE AND CONFESSION

Once a person has gone through the difficult experience of giving up a lover, he or she often is emotionally unprepared for the times that lie ahead if (and when) one's spouse learns of the infidelity. (Sometimes the faithful partner already knows.) For unfaithful partners, what they consider the most important action has been taken—they have made the decision to stop the affair and have put it behind them. There seems little reason to review it again and again. They now want to move on with life and usually have little awareness of how traumatic their infidelity has been to the other marriage partner.

Something that can help prepare the unfaithful spouse for what lies ahead is the development of an appropriate sense of repentance. This can be done in a number of ways; first, through an *anticipatory empathy rehearsal.* For example, if a wife was unfaithful, the counselor can ask her to imagine being told that her husband had been unfaithful *to her*. The counselor can use empathy statements to help her understand what becoming aware of the infidelity is like or will be like for her husband.

She might be asked to imagine how she would feel upon learning that her husband had lain in bed naked with someone else, or what she would think if she knew that he had shared intimate thoughts with that person. Further, the counselor can ask her how she would feel about trusting her husband again, after having been deceived by lies or half-truths. He or she can ask her to think about the feelings of betrayal, outrage, and embarrassment she would experience. This anticipatory empathy rehearsal can perform two important functions. First, it can prepare the unfaithful spouse to recognize the traumatic impact knowledge of an affair can have on the faithful partner, and why he will need weeks and months to recover from it. Second, it can lay the groundwork for developing an adequate sense of repentance and contrition, both toward God and toward her husband.

An important part of becoming contrite about one's infidelity relates to what Hession has called "the sin of multiplied duplicities." This refers to "the multiplied duplicities to which a person has to resort [in order] to hide what he or she has done or is doing. It is what the Bible calls 'adding sin to sin.' To the sin of the actual sexual misbehavior . . . [have] to be added the further sins of lies, deception, giving false impressions, play-acting, subterfuge, all to hide what has taken place or is still going on."[16]

Another means of helping the person develop an adequate sense of contrition includes helping him or her become aware of the emotional pain inflicted on the *affair partner*. A man needs to see, for example, the damage done to the other person through the affair, such as the raising of her expectations that he would leave the marriage and continue to be her lover. Yet there was no way he could continue to meet the woman's emotional needs without destroying his own marriage. Further, he may have given the affair partner a more debased picture of what it means to be a Christian, and may have contributed to further promiscuity on her part.

A sense of contrition can also be developed by helping the guilty partner realize that he probably has damaged the name of Christ before unbelievers, for it is rare that those around such a man are unaware of what is happening even when he thinks he has successfully covered up the sin. If a younger Christian has become aware of the infidelity, he or she may be weakened by it and made more susceptible to temptation in the future.

If the partner in an affair was married, that marriage was definitely damaged. The affair partner has inevitably fallen into the trap of making unfavorable comparisons between his or her mate and the lover. Because the intensity of infatuation love is so much greater than that of mature committed love, the affair partner may hereafter view normal marital feelings as boring and dull, and may never be satisfied with his or her marriage again. In addition, an affair causes a person to be a poorer marriage partner. In the case of the man who is unfaithful, he gives the best of his time, attention, and energy to someone other than his own wife and family.

The man or woman who has been unfaithful to the marriage partner has also been unfaithful to God. Second Samuel 12:7–14 recounts what God said to David after his infidelity with Bathsheba, and much of that applies to any believer who willingly sins in any area of life. God had richly showered David with his blessings, but in return David had forgotten him. If he had asked, God would have blessed him even more fully; instead, he chose to go outside God's will, and bring shame on God's name. Believers who become involved in adultery do likewise.

Some mental health professionals believe it is unhealthy to experience guilt feelings, and certainly it would be wrong for a mental health professional to foster them. I agree with psychiatrist Willard Gaylin of Columbia University's College of Physicians and Surgeons when he said:

> When you have actually done something wrong it is always good to experience guilt—always. We do not [not] knock

down old ladies to beat them to cabs merely because it is against the law to do so but because most of us, feeling that we had violated our own standards of decency, would feel guilty and ashamed. The kind of person who does not experience guilt in that situation is not a specimen to be admired in our society.

When we examine either the behavior on our public streets or the moral behavior of many of our public officials, we begin to sense that the problem of our time is not an overwhelming sense of guilt but an underdeveloped one. When you do bad, feel guilty. It is good for you and for the rest of us who share your environment.[17]

Should Infidelity Be Confessed to One's Partner?

When the unfaithful partner's spouse already knows about the infidelity, the question of confessing it is not an issue. But if the faithful partner does not know, should the person confess? Counselors and pastors differ in their opinions.

Arguments for not confessing. Several reasons can be proposed for not confessing a marital affair. First, such a confession initiates an emotional crisis that is rarely relieved in less than six months' time at best. Second, if the innocent partner is emotionally unhealthy, the infidelity may never be forgiven and forgotten. Third, the confession may precipitate a divorce, breaking up the family unit. And fourth, confessing may be a self-centered way for the unfaithful person to get rid of the pain (guilt for the adultery and guilt for harboring unconfessed sin), a method that dumps the pain on the faithful partner.[18]

Arguments for confessing. On the other hand, reasons can be given in support of making a confession to one's spouse. First of all, a true confession, even though it precipitates an emotional crisis that may take several months to resolve, can serve as a catalyst for the marriage. It often causes a couple to take a careful look at their relationship and make changes that significantly improve the marriage. Without confession, the guilty party still holds an awful secret in the heart, and the unhealthy marriage that may have contributed to the affair in the first place is unchanged.

Second, keeping a "secret" in what is supposed to be the most intimate of all relationships can only harm that relationship. If the heart of a good marriage is a good friendship, the heart of a good friendship is being open and honest in that friendship. A secret regarding disloyalty to one's closest friend inevitably changes that friendship. To live as if one has been loyal to one's deepest friend when, in fact, he or she has been disloyal is living a lie. Alexandra Penney, on the basis of her interviews with several hundred men, writes that even for a man who commits adultery only once and never confesses it, something happens that continues to affect the man's marriage for years afterward.[19]

Third, even when a person believes his or her partner knows nothing of the affair, that may not be the case. Very often women know or strongly suspect that an affair has occurred, but they do not confront their husbands for a number of reasons. They may fear the consequences, or they not be certain of the evidence, or they may have promised the sources of their evidence confidentiality. In such a situation an unconfessed affair continues to live on in the consciousness of both marital partners and never is confessed and worked through.

A fourth argument for confessing an affair is that the faithful partner may happen to learn of it months or years later—through a slip of the tongue, finding a receipt from a financial transaction, or from a neighbor, co-worker, relative, or even the aggrieved affair partner. While such news is hard for anyone to receive from any source, hearing it from a repentant marriage partner is better for future reconciliation than knowing that partner lived a lie for months or years, and hearing about it from someone else.

A fifth reason is the dissonance that is created when one marriage partner fails to be honest with the other. Those who have affairs usually tell a multitude of lies, half-truths, and statements that encourage the partner to believe something that is not true—even though the other person did not actually tell an untruth. This causes dissonance for the faithful partner, for example, the wife: What she is experiencing and what she hears from her husband does not add up. At times she faces the awful possibility that he is being unfaithful; at other times she believes that her perceptions are causing the dissonance and wonders if she is going crazy. Only when her partner makes a full confession are the two of them able to gain some closure on the situation. Then she is able to feel relieved.

Although there are risks involved in making a confession, and although a time of emotional turmoil will inevitably follow, I believe it is usually better to confess than to keep an affair a secret. A possible exception might be when, in a relatively happy marriage, one partner has an unplanned one-night fling that remains absolutely unknown to the other partner, and with no continuing relationship to the third party. In such a case it may be wisest for the offender to confess the sin to God, and to use his or her guilt feelings as motivation to make the marriage as healthy as it can be.

How much to tell. Marriage partners differ in their desire to know about a partner's affair: Some want full disclosure, and others want to know nothing or as little as possible. Based on conversations with the faithful partner, the counselor may be able to suggest how much should be confessed. A spouse's initial reaction to a general confession can also serve as a gauge as to how much more specific detail is wanted. If in response to a general confession the faithful partner indicates that no more details are wanted—or can be borne—those feelings should always be respected.

PREPARING A CONFESSION

If a confession is to be made, how should that be carried out? It is important that the confessor look carefully at his or her motives for the confession. If the subconscious motive (in having an affair or confessing it) is to get revenge on the other partner for something he or she did or didn't do, the confession will backfire. If the confession is a way to get the other partner into marriage counseling, this again is not healthy.

Marital counseling may be the eventual result of the confession, but that should not be its purpose.

I believe the healthiest confession will include the following components. It is one in which a person has carefully examined the multitude of wrongs he or she has done to the marriage partner, to God, to their children, and to the affair partner as well (as discussed earlier in this section). Having done this, the individual should offer a contrite apology that recognizes the multiplicity of the wrongs. It should contain no hidden agenda; the unfaithful one confesses disloyalty and asks for forgiveness. He or she is willing to answer the spouse's questions. There should be, at the time of confession, a recognition by the offending spouse that the other partner may be angry and may not desire reconciliation, and may need a little distance at first, which should be granted. The unfaithful partner should indicate a willingness to work to rebuild the trust that has been shattered, recognizing that this process may take a substantial amount of time.

It is normally helpful for the confessor to write out what is to be confessed and to go over this material with a trusted friend, pastor, or counselor before actually making the confession. The listener can help the confessor remove statements which sound self-serving or blame the other. At this "practice" session, a decision can be made regarding the best place for the confession to occur. Some people prefer the privacy of one's home, although if the wife has been the unfaithful partner and her husband has shown a tendency to become violent, she would probably want to select another, safer place to make the confession. A public place, such as a restaurant, is sometimes chosen in the hope that the social environment there will serve as an emotional safety net to keep the partner's initial reaction in check. The counseling setting is, I believe, an optimal one for the confession to take place. There a trained person is present to help the couple if needed. In the event that the counseling office is used, it is wise for the counselor to schedule a follow-up session with the faithful partner within forty-eight hours, and help the couple develop a few guidelines (e.g., who to talk to, keeping knowledge of the affair within defined boundaries, etc.) to give direction during the first week after the confession is made.

DEALING WITH CRISIS RESPONSES FROM THE SPOUSE

After a confession or the discovery of an affair, the faithful partner may feel the need to get away from the other partner for a few days. Allowing him or her to take an emergency "vacation" with a close, confidential friend can be helpful. Sometimes the person will choose not to use this avenue, but knowing that it is an option—even if it is not chosen—means staying with one's mate becomes a *choice.*

It is helpful for the guilty partner (and the counselor) to acknowledge the faithful partner's anger or right to be angry. This anger may show itself in such a marked degree that the other partner becomes quite concerned. The best cure for such rage is for the guilty partner to listen fully and quietly to it. This affirms the validity of the partner's anger. It is important not to become defensive or to begin to offer excuses for the affair. That will only prolong or even intensify the rage.

Don-David Lusterman says in this regard:

When the affair has just been discovered, the victim feels infuriated and betrayed. By simply admitting the affair the infidel [unfaithful one] rarely satisfies the victim's need for some kind of emotional catharsis. The infidel may say, in effect, "Yes, I did this, but now it's over and let's get on with our lives." But the victim wants much more: she wants clear and repeated statements of remorse, and needs to know that he is aware of the pain and feelings of craziness that his dishonesty and unfaithfulness have caused her. She experiences wildly ambivalent emotions about the unfaithful partner, venting intense rage at one moment, experiencing a deep sense of closeness at another, often including passionate sexual longing. The victim may want to spend a great deal of time with the infidel, usually much more than has ever been the couple's normal habit. This period of wild emotional swings can be frightening and disorienting for the infidel, who had never imagined that the affair could generate such *Sturm und Drang* [fury and distress]. . . .[20]

Sometimes a faithful partner has known of an affair for some time, and has been quite loving while the unfaithful partner made his or her decision whether to remain in the marriage. Once the unfaithful partner has made the decision to stay in the marriage and broken off the affair, the spouse may erupt in anger. The anger was held in check for fear of alienating the ambivalent spouse. Once that danger appears to have passed the suppressed and repressed anger may come flooding out.

Angry spouses have been known to pack their partners' bags and tell them to leave. If this happens it may be wise to do so for a few days, staying with a family friend who is able to keep the matter confidential. The departing mate should let the other one know of his or her whereabouts, for often he or she will be invited back within a few days.

The faithful spouse may engage in search missions during this time and in the months following. It is well if the guilty party has carefully gone through his or her property and destroyed any incriminating material. Even if such material is related to incidents that have been confessed, finding it seems to intensify the faithful partner's rage (the faithful partner reasons that the material has been kept because the memories of the affair are still cherished).

These search missions may irritate the guilty partner because his or her privacy is being invaded. It is not uncommon, several weeks after the confession, for the faithful party to fear that the affair is continuing, and to initiate searches at that time. These search missions understandably cause irritation because the guilty partner believes he or she is not being trusted. To reduce that partner's frustration about such search missions, it is sometimes helpful to tell him or her that the partner is desperately hoping to find nothing (which is usually true). Each search mission that ends without finding any damaging evidence represents one more small step in rebuilding trust within the relationship.[21]

It may help the unfaithful partner to develop sympathy for the spouse's behavior by likening this to a grieving process. Until this time his or her spouse had nurtured the idea that theirs was a marriage of fidelity. Losing that grieves the partner as deeply as losing a cherished friend. The spouse's angry depression may be intense for a season, but with the passage of time, with love from his or her mate and help from the counselor and from God, this acute state usually passes within a few weeks.

Key Ideas from Chapter 6

Professional Christian counseling is recommended for Christian couples where an affair has been confessed or discovered, both because of the deep emotional needs of the partners and the increased chance of successful reconciliation.

Immediately after the discovery or confession of an affair there is value in separate therapy for the husband and the wife because each person has different therapy needs.

A possible model for working with the unfaithful partner in such a situation would include the following steps:

- Helping the counselee understand what the affair means
- Assessing his or her level of commitment to the marriage and, if the person is not committed, assessing the willingness to reconsider the level of commitment
- Helping the unfaithful partner develop a realistic understanding of the differences between infatuation-stage love and mature love, and between infatuation-stage love and a neglected marriage
- Helping the unfaithful partner look realistically at the cost of divorce—for self and for the family
- If the unfaithful partner is committed to divorce, assisting the couple in working out the healthiest and fairest divorce possible
- If the unfaithful partner is still ambivalent, helping him or her understand the issues causing the ambivalence
- Providing practical help if the unfaithful partner decides to end the extramarital relationship

- Helping the counselee emotionally "unhook" from the affair partner
- Helping him or her understand the necessity of a total break from the affair partner
- Using relevant Scriptures in counseling
- Teaching the counselee thought-stopping and thought-replacement methods
- Teaching the use of fantasy modification
- Helping the counselee learn from relapses
- Having the counselee find a sponsor
- Employing the concept of substitution
- Helping the person develop an appropriate sense of repentance and assisting in the making of a confession
- Helping the unfaithful partner handle the partner's crisis responses

This chapter has been primarily devoted to the counsel of the unfaithful partner. Now we turn to the subject of counseling the faithful partner.

NOTES

1. Available to clinicians from Psychological Assessment Resources, P.O. Box 998, Odessa, Florida 33556 or by calling 1–800–331–8378.

2. Dale Doty, "Treating Marriages Recovering from an Affair," a paper presented at the International Congress on Christian Counseling, Atlanta, Georgia, 1988.

3. Karen Kuhne, *A Healing Season: A True Story of Adultery and Reconciliation* (Grand Rapids: Zondervan, 1984). Karen and her husband received counseling from Charles Solomon twice during their ordeal, counseling which apparently was quite helpful. What I am referring to is professional counseling received on a consistent, regular (i.e., weekly) basis.

4. James Dobson, *Love Must Be Tough: New Hope for Families in Crisis* (Waco: Word, 1983), 78; Frank Pittman, *Private Lies: Infidelity and the Betrayal of Intimacy* (New York: Norton, 1989), 51.

5. This idea was shared by Dr. Nancy Duvall in a practicum class she led at the Psychological Studies Institute, 1976.

6. Laurel Richardson, *The New Other Woman: Contemporary Single Women in Affairs with Married Men* (New York: The Free Press, 1985), 77.

7. Richardson, 108.

8. Richardson, 110.

9. Richardson, 124.

10. Richardson, 147.

11. For example, Daniel Dolesh and Sherelynn Lehman, *Love Me, Love Me Not: How to Survive Infidelity;* Diane Medved, *The Case Against Divorce;* Frank Pittman, *Private Lies: Infidelity and the Betrayal of Intimacy;* Eric Weber and Steven Simring, *How to Win Back the One You Love.*

12. Diane Medved, "The Trouble With Divorce," *Reader's Digest*, May, 1989.

13. Charles Mylander, *Running the Red Lights: Putting the Brakes on Sexual Temptation* (Ventura, Calif.: Regal, 1986), 178.

14. Mylander, 17–18.

15. Thought-stopping and thought-replacement can be used in conjunction with one another. When a person recognizes that he or she is thinking a thought that produces pleasant feelings toward the affair partner (a Belief), this thought can be terminated by saying "Stop!" very firmly to oneself. Then a more appropriate thought (a Dispute) can be used to replace the B.

16. Roy Hession, *Forgotten Factors: An Aid to Deeper Repentance of the Forgotten Factors of Sexual Misbehavior* (Fort Washington, Pa.: Christian Literature Crusade, 1976), 36.

17. Willard Gaylin, "The Emotion of Guilt Has Been Given a Bum Rap," *U.S. News and World Report* (April 30, 1984), 84.

18. This fourth point is from Dr. Selma Miller, past president of the New York Association for Marriage and Family Therapy. Cited by Susan Jacoby, "Marriages That Survive a Wife's Affair," in *McCall's*, July 1984, 41.

19. Alexandra Penney, *How to Keep Your Man Monogamous* (New York: Bantam, 1989), throughout book, p. 60.

20. Don-David Lusterman, "Marriage at the Turning Point," in *The Family Therapy Networker*, May/June, 1989, 48.

21. Don-David Lusterman, 48.

Chapter Seven

Preparing the Faithful Partner for a Confrontation

ALTHOUGH MUCH HAS BEEN WRITTEN about those who have affairs, considerably less is available to help their spouses
respond to such a crisis. Several books have attempted to make
up for this lack recently, including a few written especially for
Christians.[1]

Sometimes when the spouse of an unfaithful partner seeks
the help of a pastor or counselor, the question is, *Is my husband
(wife) having an affair?* The partner may genuinely not know.
Or he or she may be trying to deny that an affair is occurring,
even when substantial evidence exists to indicate that it is, because to acknowledge the truth would produce intense
anxiety. Such a person may need help with objectively looking at the evidence available and accepting the possibility that
an affair exists.

Lipstick on a husband's collar, an anonymous telephone call,
a friend seeing one's mate with someone else—these are

sometimes ways an affair is discovered, but they are not the usual ones.[2] The most common way an affair is detected is when changes occur in the partner's habits or established patterns. He or she may begin staying late at the office or become less available for telephone calls. When the spouse attempts to call his or her mate on the office direct line, the answer is given more and more frequently that Joe or Mary is "away from the desk," or "doing research."

Some people conduct their affairs wholly around the lunch hour in order to escape detection. If one's spouse begins taking longer lunch hours consistently, it may be wise to inquire about this. The same is true when a spouse suddenly begins traveling on weekends for "business" when this had not been required before, or when he or she takes a day longer than was expected to accomplish out-of-town "business."

People in affairs, both males and females, may take a renewed interest in their appearance, purchasing new and more stylish clothing, losing weight, beginning to work out at the health spa. They may begin wearing bikini underwear or sexy lingerie for no apparent marital reason.

There are likely to be changes in sexual behavior as well. The unfaithful man may become impotent, or either partner may be sexually uninterested. An unfaithful woman may cry after intercourse with her husband, and either mate who is unfaithful may not lie as close to the other partner while sleeping. The unfaithful mate may take renewed interest in sex, and introduce new techniques to the marital love-play. However, such increased interest is usually a temporary thing, and reverts to avoidance after a time.

An unfaithful spouse is likely to have mood swings, be quarrelsome, show less caring or affection, and interact less with the other spouse. A man may begin to act like a self-absorbed "zombie," watching television rather than retiring with his wife, and a woman may become dreamy or distracted or chronically late, contrary to her normal pattern.

When he arrives home from work, an unfaithful man may go first to the bathroom to wash up before greeting his wife.

He may encourage his spouse to begin taking trips or vacations by herself. There may be accidental slips, such as calling the spouse by the wrong name, or leaving telephone numbers or addresses in view. There are likely to be unexplained credit card charges and difficulties balancing the family checkbook. If the affairee is a co-worker, the unfaithful partner is likely to make enough comments about that person to raise suspicions.

The partner of an unfaithful spouse may begin receiving signals from other people that something is amiss. Friends may ask, "How are the two of you getting along?" (A good comeback to this is, "All right, but would you please tell me why you asked?") There may be an increase in telephone hang-ups and "wrong numbers."

More important than information that might be gained from friends and neighbors is that which comes from one's own intuition. The faithful spouse almost inevitably senses a withering of intimacy with his or her partner, and may feel strongly that something fundamental is changing for the worse in the relationship. One may sense that the house has been occupied while he or she was away (e.g., the towels are folded the wrong way). While it is not wise to conclude, merely on the basis of these clues, that an affair is occurring, if several bits of evidence are present it is certainly wise to increase one's vigilance. Most people in affairs will eventually produce some incriminating evidence if the spouse is looking for it and not trying to deny or rationalize it away.

Should the spouse become a private detective?

Most counselors recommend not, for quite a bit of skill is required, as this wife found out:

Jack told me he was going to be home late on Wednesday night because he was having an evening meeting with some clients from out of town. He said they were going to meet at the Hilton and he might just as well stay overnight because they could go very late. A likely story, I thought. A business meeting at night! And at the Hilton, no less! Who did he think he was kidding?

I figured I would snoop and catch him. Half an hour before his meeting was to start, I positioned myself in an inconspicuous seat in the lobby and held a newspaper up in front of my face. I had just enough room to look around the edge of the paper.

Sure enough, about five minutes before the meeting was to begin, he strolled through the lobby with his secretary. Young enough to be his daughter, and really cute. Aha, I thought, I'm right. I've got you now, you [scoundrel].

Well, feeling terribly cunning and clever, I already had a plan worked out. After they passed, I followed and watched which room they went into. Then I went into the hotel bar and had two vodkas on the rocks. My insides were churning. I waited about half an hour and went back to the room I had seen them enter earlier. I tiptoed to the door and knocked softly. When someone began to open the door I pushed it open as hard as I could, knocking over the person who opened it, and leapt into the room. "Aha!" I yelled. There was my husband, frozen and stunned, sitting at a table with five other persons, notes and briefcases spread out around them. Fortunately, my husband kept his job, and the following month he began to speak to me again.[3]

There are pros and cons to hiring a professional private detective to shadow one's spouse. The primary advantage is that if an affair is going on, a private detective can provide evidence that would stand up in court or that could be used for leverage in a divorce proceeding or to encourage the spouse to seek counseling. The major disadvantages are the cost and the inevitable anger of a spouse when one finds that the mate employed a private detective to spy on him or her.

If an individual is strongly considering employing a private detective, a lawyer whom he or she trusts can often provide recommendations. Before employing a detective it is important to check the detective's references, discuss fees, and review the methods he or she will use to ensure their acceptability.

WHEN THE MARRIAGE PARTNER IS AFRAID
TO CONFRONT AN UNFAITHFUL MATE

Not infrequently a person will consult a pastor or counselor because he or she is fairly certain that the other spouse is being unfaithful—but the counselee is afraid of a confrontation. The counselor can help such a person evaluate the evidence. If the evidence is questionable, or if it consists only of a single item, it often is wiser for the counselee to present the evidence in question and ask for an explanation rather than make an accusation.

For example, Rod and Tina were seeing a marriage counselor because both were dissatisfied with the marriage and both had questions about each other's fidelity. Tina had formed a close friendship with two co-workers, Jim and Sandy, and Rod had asserted that Tina was having a sexual relationship with Jim. Tina denied this, saying that the three of them were friends and that if there was any sexual activity, which she doubted, it was between Jim and Sandy.

Rod had to be out of town for a work assignment one weekend. When he called Tina Friday night around 9:30, he heard voices in the background and asked Tina who was there. When she replied that Jim and Sandy were visiting, Rod hung up in an angry huff.

When Rod came home and was emptying the garbage the following Monday, he found a used condom in the wastebasket in his and Tina's bathroom. He was ready to explode in anger at Tina immediately, but called his counselor first. His counselor recommended he wait and discuss this during a session and ask for an explanation rather than making an accusation. Rod did so, and Tina expressed surprise and ignorance of how the condom could have gotten into their wastebasket. She denied any sexual activity with Jim or anyone else over the weekend. She did say that she had been very tired Friday night, and had gone to bed while Jim and Tina were still there. She offered to call her friends with Rod listening on an extension, explain to them what had been found, and ask if they knew how the condom had gotten there. A subsequent call revealed that Jim and Sandy had made love in the guest room after Tina had gone to sleep, and then because they did not want to leave the used condom in that rarely used room, had deposited it in Tina's bathroom. Thus an accusation and an angry fight were averted by asking for an explanation.

IDENTIFYING—AND WORKING THROUGH—A SPOUSE'S FEARS

When fairly strong evidence points to an affair, it is often necessary to help a person work through the fears he or she has about confronting the other person. Frequently a woman will fear that a confrontation would cause her husband to leave, and she may doubt her ability to handle the loneliness and the changes which would result. She may not think herself capable of coping emotionally if a divorce ensued. Thus she waits in silence, hoping the affair will end by itself. A typical comment of such a woman is:

> "I think we all become blind when something like this happens. We twist our insides around to keep from facing the conclusions. I knew it, deep down I knew it, but I just could not bring myself to accept what was going on. All the little signs were there."[4]

Husbands and wives, particularly wives, ignore the data that is there because change induces fear. People sense that their world is changing, but they are not certain why and they don't know how to regain control of their lives.[5] As a defense, denial is used to keep anxiety-producing material from intruding into conscious awareness.

This denial, in the case of a woman, is not only because she doubts her ability to cope with change. In some instances a woman has several children to raise, and she wants them to be able to attend college. Knowing she could not do that without her husband's financial support, she chooses to leave her suspicions unspoken.

Many women fear confrontation because they assume that a confrontation would result in divorce. Is this assumption justified? "No," answers Carol Botwin, who has perhaps studied this issue as much or more than any other writer. She states:

> [I believe] that a good number of women, particularly those who have been married for many years, are mistaken when they adopt the tactic of keeping quiet and looking the other way, year after year, because they feel they have no other choice. My interviews with unfaithful husbands reveal that many of them value their family lives enough that if their wives got tough instead, putting their foot firmly down and insisting they give up other women, these men would do it. Never underestimate the strength of men's attachments to their homes and families, no matter where their libidos lead them. This is as true of the chronic philanderer as it is of the occasional cheat.[6]

WINNING THEM BACK THROUGH UNCONDITIONAL LOVE: CAN IT BE DONE?

It is sometimes argued that, since God loves us unconditionally and marital love is to be patterned after God's love, we should try to win our straying partners back through unconditional love. No matter what they do, we should return good for evil, and gently coax them back through this means. James Dobson has some excellent thoughts in this regard. He says:

> I certainly believe in the validity of unconditional love, and in fact, the mutual accountability I have recommended is an expression of that love! For example, if a husband is behaving in ways that will harm himself, his children, his marriage, and the family of the "other woman," then confrontation with him becomes an act of love. The easiest response by the innocent partner would be to look the other way and pretend she doesn't notice. But from my perspective, that is tantamount to a parent's refusing to confront a fourteen year old who comes home drunk at 4 A.M. That mother or father has an obligation to create a crisis in response to destructive behavior. I'm trying to say that unconditional love is not synonymous with permissiveness,

passivity, and weakness. Sometimes it requires toughness and discipline and accountability.[7]

In another context Dobson argues that marriages deteriorate when one or both partners loses respect for the other. Partners invite disrespect by being passive, permissive, or weak when their mates are unfaithful. This is not to say that passivity and unconditional acceptance are *never* successful in bringing an errant partner back to fidelity. Again Dobson says:

> We must acknowledge that there are occasions when "unconditional acceptance" . . . can be successful in winning back a wayward spouse. I have seen women who permitted their husbands to abuse them, betray them, deprive them and insult them, yet who returned such love and kindness that the marriage was saved. It does occur. The personality and temperament of the abusing partner is the critical factor here, of course.
>
> Nevertheless, I must report the facts as I see them. A passive approach often leads to the dissolution of the relationship. It is especially destructive in marriages where the unfaithful partner is desperate to escape from the wife he thoroughly disrespects, yet who won't let him go and instead announces her intention of [staying with him] . . . no matter what he does to gain his freedom.[8]

Although Dobson was writing before the concepts of codependency and coaddiction became well-known, his arguments anticipate the development of the codependency literature well. While we have said earlier that only 10 to 15 percent of unfaithful men are sexual addicts, it is likely that a large number of the remaining 85 to 90 percent could accurately be described as relationship addicts; that is, they are addicted to the high that an extramarital romance brings to their lives, and purposely remain unaware of the damaging effects such behavior could have on themselves, their careers, and their closest loved ones, not unlike those who are addicted to alcohol.

Their spouses, if they take a passive, permissive position, become coaddicts. A coaddict is a loved one or friend who becomes so involved in the life of an addict that he or she starts to participate in the same impaired mental processes of the addict. Coaddictive behavior is behavior that the coaddict uses to attempt to change the addict, but that in reality contributes to the addiction.[9] Such behavior is often called "enabling behavior" because it enables the unfaithful partner to continue the affair without experiencing the negative consequences that normally should follow such disloyalty.

Enabling behavior of a coaddictive wife can include "understanding," ignoring, or forgiving the affair that is occurring without making any demands that it stop. She often will beg for, plead for, and accept any kind of abuse in order to keep her partner from leaving. By finding "excuses" for her unfaithful partner, she allows the disloyal behavior to go unchecked. She may assume that she is responsible for the affair rather than expect her husband to change his behavior. She may conceal the affair in order to protect her partner's reputation and in order to allow him to continue it without the pressures he would otherwise experience from children, parents, fellow Christians, and family friends. He also does not experience other unpleasant results of his infidelity, such as having to move into different and inconvenient living quarters, losing sexual privileges with his wife (he can now have it both ways), or having to bear the costs of a marriage counselor and the support of two households plus attorney fees.[10]

The coaddictive wife continues her permissive approach to her unfaithful partner because of at least four sets of irrational beliefs (the B's in Albert Ellis's Rational-Emotive Therapy). Jennifer Schneider, a physician who struggled with coaddiction in her own life, identified these as:

1. The belief that she is not a worthwhile person, and therefore needs to acquire her worth from outside (e.g., by being loved and validated by a man).

2. The belief that no one would love her for herself, therefore she must earn her love from the addict. The person with the potential to become a coaddict is drawn to a man who is

needy, and whom she believes needs "fixing." And she makes herself indispensable to him. Believing that the more she can do for him, the less likely he is to leave her, she assumes increasing responsibility for his life.

A coaddict is terrified of abandonment and will do anything to keep this man in a relationship. To this end she excuses his behavior, avoids conflict, and overuses denial and repression.

3. The belief that she can control other people's behavior through nagging, prodding, and pleading. Therefore she encourages family members to be irresponsible and to depend on her.

4. The belief that sex is the most important sign of love. This mistaken belief causes her to confuse sex with love. One of the results of this is that she may desperately try to keep her husband sexually involved with her, even when he is exhibiting profound disrespect by continuing his affair in an obvious way.[11]

To those women who recognize themselves in one or more of these four paragraphs, David Wilkerson says:

> Step out of your bondage of living your life only through others. God never intended that you find happiness only through your husband or your children. I'm not suggesting that you forsake them—only that you forsake your degrading bondage to the idea that your happiness depends only on other people. God wants you to discover a life of true happiness and contentment based only on what you are as a person and not on the moods and whims of people around you.[12]

Will and Marguerite Beecher make the relationship between the irresponsible partner and the enabling behavior of the codependent spouse clearer when they say:

> A person may have a problem or be one. The person who is a problem does not feel that he has one. He gets along splendidly, exploiting and taking from others who put up with him. The person who puts up with him is the person

who has the problem—the problem of providing support for the one who is the problem. In short, it takes both of them to make it possible for the one to fail.[13]

DISPUTING CODEPENDENT THINKING

A husband or wife may not be assertive in confronting an unfaithful mate for any of several reasons. As mentioned in the previous paragraphs, such a person may be afraid of the results of the confrontation—divorce, loneliness, financial problems, or other undesirable possibilities. The individual may have developed a codependent personality style in his or her family of origin, and brought it into the marriage. He or she may believe that his or her deficiencies are the cause of the affair, or that it is biblical to be submissive and turn the other cheek. The partner may not know how to be assertive, so being passive, aggressive, or passive-aggressive are their only choices. The partner vacillates. Counselors may wish to help such people see the unhealthiness of remaining codependent, aided by some the following points.

First, fearing a confrontation because it could possibly lead to divorce. As we have seen in the quotations above from Botwin and Dobson, failure to confront a spouse leads to a breakdown in marital respect, and therefore is *more* likely to eventually lead to a divorce than is a reasonably presented confrontation. Many men, when they know they must make a choice between marriage, family, and home versus lover, will leave the lover.

Second, developing a codependent personality style in one's family of origin, and believing one cannot change. One can obtain a number of books, discover support groups through which he or she can gain information and support or enter personal therapy and move out of a codependent lifestyle.[14]

Third, believing one's deficiencies are causing the infidelity. This is typical codependent thinking, but not correct. It may be true that some of the faithful partner's behavior needs to be changed, but the faithful partner does not *cause* the unfaithful partner's infidelity. Each person is responsible for his or her own behavior.

Fourth, turning the other cheek is biblical. However, God's relationship to the nation of Israel (or to the New Testament church) is often looked upon as a model for Christian marriage relationships. This is appropriate, for God drew this parallel himself in his Word. How did God respond when his people committed spiritual adultery? Did he remain passive, hoping that someday they would turn from their adultery? No! In each case he strongly confronted. He said he was a jealous God, not willing for them to consort with lovers. Thus God's model for us is that we take an assertive stance in demanding that the unfaithful marital partner turn from his or her infidelity and be faithful to us.

Fifth, vacillating between being passive, aggressive, and passive-aggressive behavior because "I don't know how to be assertive." Dr. Dobson says: "Simply becoming angry and throwing temper tantrums is no more effective with a spouse than it is with a rebellious teenager. Screaming and accusing and berating are rarely successful in changing the behavior of human beings at any age. What is required is a course of action—an ultimatum that demands a specific response and results in a consequence."[15] A counselor can help a nonassertive mate develop assertive responses appropriate to the situation. Books such as *Your Perfect Right* by Alberti and Emmons, and *Speaking Your Mind Without Stepping on Toes* by the present author can provide further training in this area.

IS "SETTING LIMITS" AN ATTEMPT TO CONTROL ONE'S PARTNER?

When a woman, for example (the same is true for a man), fails to set limits on what she will accept regarding her partner's sexual behavior, she loses his respect. However, many marriage partners are uncomfortable setting such limits lest they appear to be trying to control the partner or give ultimatums. Jessica, a nurse, clarifies this distinctive:

> When I first learned about my husband's affairs, I went through a great deal of emotional pain and a terrible loss of

trust in him. I don't ever want to experience such pain again or to share him sexually with anyone else. I told him that if he has another affair I can't continue in our marriage. One of my friends said, "I, too, have given my husband ultimatums. But isn't that trying to control him? Doesn't the [Al-Anon] program teach us that we cannot control another person's behavior?"

I explained to her that I'm not trying to control [all of] his behavior. What I'm doing is setting boundaries of behaviors that are acceptable to me and those that aren't. My husband can choose how to behave, and I can choose whether or not to live with that behavior. My husband's "first drink" is not sexual intercourse: it's making that first connection with a new woman. Several deliberate decisions then lead to the "tenth drink," the bedroom. He can choose to risk the "first" or the "second drink"; but if he proceeds to the "tenth drink," I will no longer be there for him. This is my boundary; it is not an ultimatum.[16]

Trying to control a partner's behavior refers to attempts to regulate behavior that should be left to the individual; it is therefore unhealthy. In this context, setting limits refers to stating consequences for *clearly unacceptable* behavior, such as infidelity; this is healthy.

The belief that many unfaithful spouses have fallen for is that they would be happy and satisfied if they could just have the marriage *and* a lover. The faithful spouse must assertively state that he or she has to make a choice—one cannot have both the marriage and a lover. And it is often important to lovingly but firmly remind the spouse of all of the other things that he or she will lose by persisting in the affair. The errant spouse often breaks off the affair when it is made crystal clear that almost everything of value to him or her—home, children, marriage partner, reputation—is slipping away.[17]

Another fear that some spouses have about confronting the unfaithful mate is that they will ruin any possibility of saving the marriage. They think their marriage might be one of the few in which patient submission rather than assertive confrontation will win back the straying partner. One reply to this is that by the term *assertive confrontation* we do not mean being harsh or unloving. Rather, it is firm love focusing on the choice that is in the best interests of both marital partners. If the choices were between an aggressive confrontation and patient submission, there might be more reason to lean toward passive submission; but an assertive confrontation really involves "speaking the truth in love." If that kind of encounter results in the spouse's departure, then, as Dobson says, "the relationship was already in the coffin."

Another thought that should encourage the wavering spouse to be assertive as soon as a developing affair is discovered is the fact that most affairs develop *gradually*. The earlier the confrontation the less emotional involvement will have developed. This makes the recovery period shorter for both marital partners and decreases the chances that the illicit relationship will become a serious competitor to the marriage relationship.

RECOGNIZING THE FAITHFUL PARTNER'S OPTIONS

Before attempting an assertive confrontation it is important for the faithful partner to identify the options which he or she has. From this group, the partner needs to identify which options he or she is willing to follow through on if the other mate will not leave the affair. The choices open to the faithful mate can be summarized in five categories:

1. He or she can decide to stay with the spouse, allow sexual intercourse as before, and purposely focus on the positive things in the relationship.

2. He or she can decide to stay with the spouse, and purposely focus on the positive things in the relationship, but disallow sexual intercourse with the spouse until he or she has made a commitment to fidelity.

3. He or she can ask the spouse to make a decision to continue or discontinue the affair within the next month (or some other designated time). If he or she will not make such a commitment by that time, the faithful partner will expect the

spouse to find another place to live so that he or she can experience (in a temporary setting) the losses that would be suffered permanently if the marriage ended.

4. The faithful partner can try, if his or her mate is a Christian, to ask their church's aid in a biblical confrontation.

5. He or she can divorce the unfaithful spouse (I am basing this on the traditional evangelical understanding that Jesus' words in Matthew 5:31–32 and Matthew 19:3–9 mean that when a person's mate has been sexually unfaithful, the faithful partner is free to divorce and remarry).

A counselor or pastor can discuss each of these options with the faithful partner so that he or she can become aware of the choices available. Whichever choice is made will have to be communicated to the other spouse. For purposes of illustration, I will use choice 3 in the following pages.

EMBARKING UPON AN OPTION

One model of assertiveness suggests that an assertive statement has three parts—Affirmation, Assertion, and Action.[18] The Affirmation component includes one or more sentences that try to convey care and affirmation of the person, so that that individual realizes that the speaker—the faithful partner, in this case—is not rejecting him or her, but is rejecting unacceptable behavior. The Assertion component identifies the *behavior* that the speaker finds objectionable and describes why it is objectionable, if that is not evident. The Action component describes what specific behavioral change the speaker is requesting.

In our example let us suppose that Jim, a Christian, has become involved in an affair with a family friend, Kay, and that Joyce, Jim's wife, has found out about the affair and has confronted Jim. Jim says he needs some time to sort out his feelings. He is continuing to see Kay a few times a week, but lives at home. An assertive letter might go like this:

Dear Jim,

It is very difficult to write this letter to you, for our marriage has been the center of my life and happiness for these last ten years. Because of the common faith we share, I had believed that infidelity was something that would never darken our marriage, and I have found reassurance in the active spiritual leadership you have provided for our family through most of these years. It is my hope that we will be able to work through this crisis successfully, make our marriage stronger, and enjoy our relationship as long as we both live. I am willing to be involved in marriage counseling to examine any part I may have played in you becoming dissatisfied with our relationship, and I am willing to try to make those changes we both agree on (AFFIRMATION).

I was devastated when I discovered that you had become emotionally and sexually involved with Kay, our mutual friend. The pain was greater because I felt betrayed by two people whom I had counted as my closest friends. I don't understand how affairs develop or why they develop even among Christians, and I am willing to learn more, because on rare occasions I too have felt the temptation to let a relationship develop beyond a friendship, but never have. As I try to understand you, I ask that you try also to understand my feelings. There is no pain that has ever hurt worse than the pain I have experienced these last two weeks. I know that I cannot live with such pain for long: We must do something to bring some direction to our relationship (ASSERTION).

What I am asking you to do is this. First, I would like you to start seeing a Christian counselor to help you sort through your thoughts and feelings, as I will do also. Secondly, I ask that you make a decision to end your relationship with Kay within one month, and that if you are unable or unwilling to make a full commitment to me by that time, that you find a place to stay temporarily until you make your final decision. I am asking you to do this so that you can have time to experience what life would be like without your home, without your children, and without our relationship, before you make your final decision. I am also asking this because it is too painful for me to live as if we were a normal, happy family when I know that you are being intimate with Kay two or three times every week.

I am not willing to continue our own sexual relationship until I have a commitment from you that your relationship with Kay has ended. This is not intended to punish you: It is simply too painful for me to continue to be intimate with you when I know that you are also sharing yourself with Kay (ACTION).

I hope that our marriage relationship can be restored and even made stronger through this crisis.

> With love,
> Joyce

A message like the above can be sent as a letter, or it can be read and later given to Jim. This can be done with or without witnesses. The witness could be a pastor, a pastor and his wife, a counselor, or trusted family friends. Especially if there has been a history of violence (or threat of violence) in the relationship, it is important to have impartial observers present. It can be helpful to have someone there who has some authority with the couple (a pastor or counselor) and who can feel comfortable asking them to make promises or commitments to each other. In light of the complexities of family relationships, it is usually best that this arbiter not be related to either partner.

To summarize, after helping the faithful partner decide which option he or she will pursue, the counselor can help frame an assertive message and help decide how and when the message will be delivered and who will be present to help process the response to the message.

NOTES

1. Excellent Christian books that are available include James Dobson's *Love Must Be Tough*, J. Allan Petersen's *The Myth of the Greener Grass*, Sally Conway's *You and Your Husband's Midlife Crisis*, Charles Mylander's *Running the Red Lights*, and Les Carter's *The Prodigal Spouse*. H. Norman Wright also has an excellent chapter on affairs in his book *Seasons of a Marriage*.

2. The following ways are compiled from the author's own experience and from Daniel Dolesh and Sherelynn Lehman, *Love Me, Love Me Not: How*

to Survive Infidelity (New York: McGraw-Hill, 1985), 17; Carol Botwin, *Men Who Can't Be Faithful* (New York: Warner Books, 1988), 20–34; and Audrey Chapman, *Man Sharing: Dilemma or Choice?* (New York: Morrow and Company, 1986), 79.

3. Dolesh and Lehman, 24.

4. Quotation from a client in Dolesh and Lehman, p. 8.

5. Dolesh and Lehman, 14.

6. Botwin, 223.

7. Dobson, 81.

8. Dobson, 54–55.

9. Patrick Carnes, *Out of the Shadows: Understanding Sexual Addiction* (Minneapolis: CompCare Publishers, 1983), 92.

10. Dobson, 121–22.

11. Jennifer Schneider, *Back from Betrayal: Recovering from His Affairs* (New York: Harper and Row/Hazelden, 1988), 28–37.

12. David Wilkerson, *Have You Felt Like Giving Up Lately?* (Old Tappan, N.J.: Revell, 1980), 36.

13. Willard and Marguerite Beecher, *Beyond Success and Failure* (New York: Julian Press, 1966), 213.

14. For example, books include *Codependent No More* by Melody Beattie, *Back from Betrayal* by Jennifer Schneider, and *Love Must Be Tough* by James Dobson. Support groups include Al-Anon groups, especially those for adult children of alcoholics, which are available in most communities.

15. Dobson, 123.

16. Quoted in Schneider, 188.

17. Dobson, 59–60.

18. See my book *Speaking Your Mind Without Stepping on Toes: A Christian Approach to Assertiveness* (Wheaton, Ill.: Victor Books, 1991) for a fuller description of assertiveness and for the rationale of the three-part assertive statement.

Chapter Eight

The Faithful Partner: What *Not* to Do

LEARNING OR RECOGNIZING THAT ONE'S MARRIAGE PARTNER has been unfaithful is emotionally devastating. Among those people who have experienced both the death of a spouse and a spouse's affair, the consistent finding is that losing a partner through adultery is more painful than losing a partner through death. When the mate dies, there is usually no sense of shame or humiliation.[1]

Daniel Dolesh and Sherelynn Lehman, who conducted extensive interviews with a large number of people whose partners had been unfaithful, reported that practically everyone they interviewed described the discovery of an affair as the worst experience of his or her life.[2] It was not uncommon for grown men to sob in agony when learning of a wife's affair. Women did likewise. The phrase "it hurts so bad" was heard repeatedly. This betrayal of trust caused emotional anguish which the faithful partner likened to being slashed open with a knife.[3]

A number of writers, researchers, and therapists agree on one point: The stronger the emotional pain of the faithful partner, the more likely that he or she has a marriage that is worth fighting for. If a man or woman doesn't react strongly to news of a partner's affair, the relationship has already probably decayed. Botwin says in this regard:

> If a woman discovers her man's secret [affair] and doesn't get upset, it is generally a sign that something, apart from infidelity, has already rotted away the relationship in her eyes.
>
> Phillip Blumstein and Pepper Schwartz concluded from the results of their survey that the wives who did not react to a husband's affair as a catastrophe felt that the relationship was doomed anyway. David Moultrap, a marriage therapist and expert on affairs, feels that a cool reaction to infidelity bodes poorly for the future of the couple—the less anxiety a spouse feels in reaction to an affair, the higher the probability that the marriage will be terminated.[4]

Nothing can take away the intense pain of discovering a partner has been involved in an affair, and the counselor should not try to hurry a person through this pain. As with any severe pain, it is most helpful if the counselor, through empathy statements and patient listening, allows him or her to deal with the agony, not moving on in the counseling process until the person is ready. At some time in the empathizing stage it may be helpful for the counselor to reframe positively the pain by stating what has been mentioned above, that is, that the presence of pain indicates that there is still something left in the marriage that is worth fighting for. If there were little or no pain, it would be an indication that the relationship was already dead.[5]

COUNSELING INTERVENTIONS

An important part of counseling for an affair is preventing the couple from reacting unwisely. The shock of the affair is so difficult that many people act out in ways that are destructive to the future of the marriage. For that reason it may help to consider the early part of counseling, especially counseling with the faithful spouse, as crisis intervention counseling, to be followed by a period of individual and then marital therapy.

These immediate interventions can be discussed as a list of things which the person is encouraged *not* to do, and a second list of things which he or she is encouraged *to do*. People in crisis, particularly if it is the first crisis of this kind they have ever experienced, frequently appreciate practical guidance on how to respond. If the counselor has allowed the faithful spouse adequate time to express pain over the affair, he or she can usually proceed with guidance, which, as crisis intervention experts have shown, tends to stabilize the counselee.

Sometimes the faithful partner believes he or she can do little to affect the future of the relationship. This is not true. This partner will often feel uncertain about the best plan of action during the weeks that follow, but once the initial emotional crisis has subsided, he or she may be in a much healthier place psychologically (not less painful, but healthier) than the unfaithful spouse. Thus the faithful partner may be able to provide healthier input into the marriage system than the other spouse. The following list of suggestions can guide this partner in doing so. They are written as if addressing the counselee in order to facilitate their use in counseling. The text that follows contains the rationale for the various suggestions, so, whenever possible, it is helpful for counselees to read the chapter itself.

What *Not* to Do

Don't let the present crisis destroy your perspective of the total marriage, with its past positives and future potentials.[6] When a crisis as emotion-laden as an affair hits you, you often forget the rest of your marriage history, and see only this one disaster. You may question the validity of your earlier happiness and wonder whether all of the past loving deeds of your partner were phony. One wife, as she attempted to develop a balanced perspective on her marriage experience, wrote about it this way:

We recognized our marriage had been good. This was easier for my husband to affirm than for me. I had a tendency to discount the entire fabric of our years together because of one spot, as though something that had occurred in the present could negate the goodness of the past. We began to recall those years both in the heat of our arguments and in our more quiet times. Our life together had a rich history of shared experiences, three children, and a little grandchild. All of this was put on one side of the scale. It far outweighed the unhappiness of the past year.[7]

Don't let the present crisis destroy your perspective of your total life; that is, don't seriously contemplate suicide. Probably everyone who has experienced the pain of a partner's affair considers suicide at some time: The pain is so intense that a person feels that he or she needs some relief. But this pain, like others, will diminish in intensity over the coming weeks and months. Suicide is a permanent solution to a temporary problem. Whatever problems a person and one's family are presently facing will be made more complicated, not less, by a suicide attempt, whether the attempt is successful or not. A husband who wants freedom from a marriage will not be pulled back into it permanently by a suicide attempt which says, "I can't live without you." Such dependency decreases rather than increases his respect for his wife.

Don't rail at and denounce your partner.[8] Once the initial shock has worn off, it is normal to be very angry with your spouse. The great bard has said, "Hell hath no fury as a woman scorned." While anger is normal, if the railing and denunciation continue very long, it is likely to push a guilty party even further from the faithful partner.

Don't tell more people than absolutely necessary.[9] Telling others is usually an attempt to pay the guilty spouse back for the hurt that has been caused. It is tempting to pay your partner back. However, if you broadcast your partner's affair to the church family, for example, and the affair eventually ends, he or she may feel humiliated because the affair is common knowledge in the church. Your mate may feel too uncomfortable to return to a church where everyone knows of his infidelity. The same applies to telling parents. You will need one or two friends to talk with regularly, but you should make certain that what is shared will be kept in confidence. Reconciliation and eventual reintegration into your church or family will be easiest if few people know, and if what is known is minimal.

Don't ask others to straighten out the unfaithful partner. This usually only provokes defensiveness and anger. In addition, it does not fit the biblical guidelines of first going to the offending party alone, and then taking another person with you if the first conversation proves unsuccessful.

The first person to confront and ask for a renewed commitment to the marriage should be you, the marriage partner. Then if there is a need to involve a counselor or minister, do so as a second step in the process. (There usually is such a need, for the trauma of discovering an affair and the process of uncovering the reasons for it are too painful and too involved for most couples to sort through themselves. The best way to prevent another affair is clearly to understand how this one happened, and then to build safeguards into your marriage to reduce the likelihood of a recurrence. This is an almost impossible task for a couple alone.)

Don't become hostile without explaining why. This only confirms your partner's belief that there is nothing left to the marriage and that the other relationship is the only place where his or her needs will be met.

Don't collapse into helpless dependency—"I can't survive without you." Sometimes the faithful partner truly believes that he or she cannot survive without the other spouse. At other times this may be a manipulative (although subconscious) strategy to cause the unfaithful spouse to remain in the marital relationship. However, counselors and writers are in unanimous agreement that this strategy almost always backfires. Whenever persons seem to need us much more than we need them, we usually feel an impulse to flee. Few people are attracted to weakness; almost no one to utter desperation.[10] Writers and therapists agree that if a person is sure that he or she wants to leave, the best thing a partner can do is to allow it. Pleading, bargaining, threatening, or groveling won't help if your mate is determined, and such demeaning efforts injure your self-esteem and lower your partner's respect for you.[11]

Dobson recommends that if the unfaithful partner desires to be free of the marriage, he or she should be given the freedom to leave. When this is done, three things are likely to happen:

> 1. The trapped partner no longer feels it necessary to fight off the other, and their relationship improves. It is not that the love affair is rekindled, necessarily, but the strain between the two partners is often eased.
>
> 2. As the cool spouse [i.e., the one who wants to leave] begins to feel free again, the question he has been asking himself changes. After having wondered for weeks or months, "How can I get out of this mess?" He now asks, "Do I really want to go?" Just knowing that he can have his way often makes him less anxious to achieve it. Sometimes it turns him around 180 degrees and brings him back home!
>
> 3. The third change occurs . . . in the mind of the vulnerable one [the one who was begging]. Incredibly, he feels better—somehow more in control of the situation. There is no greater agony than journeying through a vale of tears, waiting in vain for the phone to ring or for a miracle to occur. Instead, the person [who gives his partner permission to leave] has begun to respect himself and receive small evidences of respect in return.[12]

Don't apologize for not being a good enough mate. There is a difference between recognizing that you may have contributed to a situation in which your partner became involved in an affair, and taking responsibility for the affair. The first is healthy, the second is codependent. If there is anything an adulterer does not need it is a partner who takes responsibility for his or her adultery.

Don't go to the other woman (or man) and plead with her (or him), or physically or verbally attack that person. A female client of mine, upon learning that her husband's lover was the receptionist at the town bank in a small southern town, prepared a list of Bible verses. Then in the middle of the banking day (in the center of the bank) she confronted the woman, screaming that she had always wanted to see what a whore looked like. She then proceeded to read a list of verses from the Bible about whores and harlots!

The wife's behavior did almost get the receptionist fired. However, as with most such retaliatory behavior, it caused her husband to feel sorry for the humiliation of the lover, and actually put more distance between the husband and wife. Dolesh and Lehman tell of a similar instance:

> We know of an instance where a woman, after learning that her husband was having an affair, went with her girl friend to the suspected lover's apartment and physically beat her, tearing out large clumps of her hair. The betrayed woman's husband, upon learning of his spouse's violent retaliation, became disgusted and angry. He cared deeply for his lover, even though he had no intention of leaving his wife for her, and was devastated by his wife's violence. When they discussed the incident, he became so angry that he spit in her [his wife's] face, spun on his heel, and walked out of the door never to return. The wife's violent action not only landed her in court but drove her husband away permanently.[13]

Don't panic over a separation, even if your spouse moves in with his or her lover. There are several reasons why your mate's moving in with the lover may actually increase the chances of his or her eventual return. First, it removes the secrecy of the affair; virtually all researchers agree that the secret aspect adds emotional intensity to the relationship. Second, your spouse will begin to see the lover as he or she really is. It is possible to maintain an artificially pleasant front if all one does is see another person a few hours per week. However, by living together two people are likely to begin to experience each other as they really are. Many if not most affairs are neurotic relationships

that self-destruct quite rapidly once two people start living together. Third, the affair partner may start to apply pressure for
a commitment, and the commitment he or she wants or the
methods used in pushing for that may make the lover less attractive to your partner. Finally, your marital partner may start
to miss you and the children. Therefore, don't panic if your partner moves out, or even moves in with the lover.[14]

Don't let your partner play mind-games on you. For example, an
unfaithful partner will often define your justified jealousy (of
the relationship with the lover) as craziness on your part in
order to protect himself or herself from the anger that would
result if the affair were called what it really is.[15] This ploy has
the usual result of causing you, the faithful partner, to begin to
doubt your own perceptions and your own sanity. Your partner may use the same response ("you're crazy!") to questions
you have when the stories he or she has told you do not line
up with reality. Unless you have a history of being overly suspicious when there was no cause to be, your suspicions and
your jealousy are likely to be justified, and you shouldn't let
your partner define away your perceptions as craziness.[16]

Don't play games. When you are very emotional, it may be
tempting to play games as a means of obtaining your partner's
sympathy or taking revenge. Sally Conway tells the following
story which illustrates how games can backfire:

> Marian decided she was going to make her husband, Ted,
> pay for leaving her and living alone in an apartment while
> he tried to think things through. He still came home fre-
> quently to be with her and the children, and they sometimes
> had sexual intercourse while he was at home, but he would
> always leave without staying overnight. She decided she
> was making things too easy for him by allowing him to have
> both the intimacy of family life and the privacy of his own
> apartment. She hastily decided to take the children and
> move out of state so they wouldn't be so convenient for Ted.
> They are now legally separated, and Ted is spending eve-
> nings and weekends with another woman and her children.
> Marian had really hoped Ted would beg her not to move

and would promise to come home permanently. Many men have eventually returned home to stay, and marriages have been stronger than ever, when wives have been patient and have waited for them to be ready to come back. Marian's game went too far.[17]

Don't try to retaliate through a revenge affair or in other ways. In one study, 40 percent of those having affairs cited revenge as their motive.[18] Since the motive for revenge affairs is usually anger, hurt, malice, and the need to prove that you are still attractive in the face of your mate's straying, these affairs are generally unsatisfying themselves and leave the perpetrator feeling somewhat sick.[19]

Christian women sometimes get revenge, not with a dagger or pistol or a revenge affair, but with a checkbook and credit card.[20] Needless to say, all forms of revenge are unbiblical, are usually unsatisfying, and only make the problem worse.

Don't expect to accomplish miracles by cosmetics or a new suit or attempted diets.[21] The reason for this is that your partner is likely to be much more aware of the affair partner than he or she is of you. On the other hand, it is good to make the best of your appearance, even though in your depression you may not feel like doing so. Looking good enhances your self-esteem and self-respect. It also should be apparent that your competition will be looking his or her best. If a husband has to choose between his lover, who looks terrific, and his wife, who has "let herself go" because she is so depressed, it will be hard for him to be attracted to his wife.

Don't try to manipulate your mate to remain in the marriage because of marriage vows. While it is true that your spouse made a vow before God to be true to you for life, emphasizing this point probably won't work. More effective than that is encouraging your mate to come back by showing that he or she would be happier that way.

In a similar vein it is not wise to overemphasize your rights or those of the children; few people are motivated by having others demand their rights, especially if they are alienated from those making the demands. If you have financial needs, discuss those needs objectively, rather than making demands.[22]

Don't issue an ultimatum that forces your partner or yourself to take hasty action that could make it impossible or much more difficult to repair the marriage. Don't take any action that slams the door shut on possible reconciliation before both partners have explored the reasons for the infidelity and the initial anger has cooled.[23]

A man was having an affair with someone at his office. His wife told him to either leave the job or she would leave him. He told her that he would stop the affair, but that he could not leave the job because he had worked there seven years and was in line for a major promotion. He did what he said he would (terminated the affair), but his wife felt that she had to leave him in order to save face. Fortunately for her, he was still waiting for her when she decided to come back.[24]

Don't accept an adulterous situation. Many spouses, particularly women, provide tacit acceptance of an affair out of fear or insecurity. They may believe that half a relationship is better than none. There are differences of opinion as to whether "not accepting an adulterous situation" includes allowing the betrayer to continue to live with the family. Some of the arguments for allowing that person to remain with the family are that this situation allows him or her to have continued positive interactions with the spouse and children, permits the couple to communicate about the needs that led to the affair, and gives opportunity to them to try to make changes in their family and marital life. Further, such a choice does not force the partner out of the home with the attendant possibility that he or she may go live with the lover.

Arguments for making the unfaithful partner leave are that it removes the faithful spouse from the "craziness" of trying to live with a partner who also has a lover, it makes the unfaithful partner face the consequences of the infidelity, and it causes him or her to experience all the things that would be lost should the choice be to leave his marriage. By letting him live at home, a wife is allowing him to have all the benefits of his home and marriage, and the added adventure of a lover as well. I agree with other therapists who have said that there are certain times when the faithful spouse should force the other partner to make a choice. Richard and Elizabeth Brzeczek echo this advice:

> In a great many cases when a wife tells her husband she won't tolerate this behavior and then goes ahead and files for divorce, the husband will break off his affair. When a husband realizes he is going to be forced to face the consequences of his actions, and those consequences are the loss of his home and family, he generally breaks off his affair.
>
> Most men who are involved with another woman don't really want a divorce, they just want a wife *and* a mistress. But the wife must make it clear that this is an unacceptable solution. When the offenders realize they can't have both relationships because their wives will not tolerate another woman in the picture, most men are forced to put their priorities in order.
>
> If a man does not break off his affair, though, the wife must let her husband go, but let him go with love.[25]

There is probably not one right answer for all families regarding whether the husband should be asked or forced to move out. Matthew 5 and 19 teach that adultery is a biblical ground for divorce. By virtue of this, continuing adultery would certainly be sufficient grounds for marital separation. This much is probably clear and could be agreed upon by all:

1. Whatever action is taken regarding separation should be done out of firmness and love, not as an angry reaction to learning of the affair.

2. If the unfaithful partner is expected to leave, it should be clear that this is done, not as an act to punish him or her, but as an opportunity for him or her to experience temporarily the loss of family relationships and other positive benefits which will be lost permanently if the affair continues.

3. Separation is a forceful way of saying to the offending partner that he or she has to make a choice. He or she will not

be able to continue indefinitely enjoying the benefits of a marriage and family and also a lover.

4. Separation says to the children, if they are aware of the situation, which they usually are, that infidelity is a very serious infraction of the marital relationship, and one that is not allowed to continue in healthy Christian families.

The decision concerning whether or not to force the unfaithful partner to leave the family home needs to be made on a case-by-case basis. It is dependent upon that partner's response to the other mate's demand that a decision be made. For example, if an unfaithful man is involved in counseling and is making headway in the process of understanding himself and the affair, and if he has begun emotionally to let go of the affair relationship, it may be advisable to allow him to remain in the home. If he is rebelliously flaunting God's laws and his own promises, or if he gets stuck and becomes ambivalent about ending the relationship, the added dimension of experiencing the loss of family may be enough to motivate him to leave the affair.

Don't make changes in your sexual relationship with your mate without careful thought. In this area there are also a variety of opinions as to the proper course to take. Some writers and counselors suggest that you make an all-out effort to be sexually available, thereby showing your mate that you can provide as good or better sex than the lover. By doing so you also can hope that your partner's sexual needs are satisfied, giving him or her less reason to seek satisfaction elsewhere.

Others suggest that you not be sexual with your errant partner until the affair is broken off and a commitment to fidelity is made. The reasoning behind this approach is that if you try to compete with the lover, or even if you continue to be sexual while your mate is unfaithful, you sacrifice not only your self-respect but any respect he or she might have for you. Being sexual with your mate when the affair continues says that you are so desperate or dependent on your mate's love that you will sacrifice your own self-esteem in order to woo the partner back.

For some faithful partners, such a theoretical discussion is a moot point. They find that the emotional trauma of the infidelity makes them completely unable to be sexually involved with their marriage partners. If this is so, it is best for such a spouse to tell this to the marriage partner in a nonvindictive way, and promise to resume normal sexual relations if he or she leaves the affair. If sexual problems are part of the reason for the affair, it is good for the faithful mate to indicate a willingness to become involved in joint counseling on sexual issues if the partner recommits to the marriage.

For other marriage partners, this issue should be decided on the basis of what sexual involvement will mean to both of them at this point in their relationship. If such involvement by the faithful partner will be part of a desperate attempt to regain his or her mate, then it will only cause loss of self-respect and loss of respect in the partner's eyes. If it can be part of rebuilding the good in a relationship that had deteriorated from a lack of effort by both partners, and if it can take place within an atmosphere that maintains the self-respect of them both, then perhaps it will be beneficial. If a faithful partner is willing to be involved sexually with his or her mate during this time, the couple should receive guidance from a physician concerning how to reduce the possibility of the transfer of disease. Too many Christian wives, particularly, have been left with permanent and sometimes life-threatening diseases because their husbands transferred a disease to them for which the men were asymptomatic.

Don't repeatedly ask for details of the affair, but do try to understand the reasons for it. When you ask for details of the affair, the unconscious motive often is to try to find out what the lover has that you don't have. A better way to accomplish this goal is to ask the reasons for the affair, not for details. J. Allan Petersen gives this excellent advice to women, but it could just as aptly be applied to both sexes.

Once you get the honest facts you must explore the reasons for the infidelity—reasons that will help you understand the causes and how you are involved. Why has your husband turned to another woman? What are his struggles? In almost every instance of marital infidelity, the "other woman" is providing something the wife is not giving. Your motive must be to learn and comprehend, not to defend yourself or assign blame.

You may feel unjustly criticized. But bite your lip, wipe away the tears, and listen—listen! No belittling, no moralizing, no sermons, no Bible verses.[26]

Another reason it is unhealthy to repeatedly ask for details is that one's spouse usually feels guilty and defensive about what occurred. A single confession is painful, but he or she can understand its necessity. Repeated requests for the same information are likely only to produce anger and defensiveness.

A third reason that it is unwise to ask repeatedly for detailed descriptions of what occurred relates to your own healing process. If you have very accurate, detailed word pictures of what happened between your spouse and the lover, when your mind is free of other responsibilities it becomes very tempting to picture graphically the verbal descriptions you have been given. Doing this for even a few moments can cause you to become furious. One client used to do this frequently while her husband was at work. By evening she would be so enraged that she would pull all her husband's clothes out of his drawers and closets and dump them in the apartment hallway for him to pick up and pack into suitcases when he got home. At other times she would become so inflamed that she would launch into an hours-long tirade when he got home. Sometimes she would physically attack him when he opened the door or throw lamps at him. Knowing too many details of the activity of the betrayer and the lover can be damaging for everyone involved and can slow the healing process.

Don't try to control your partner's behavior. Like the wife of an alcoholic who tries to control the alcoholic's drinking, if the wife of an unfaithful spouse tries to control the betrayer's behavior, both their lives soon get emotionally out of control. Control your own behavior. You may want to set limits on what you will accept from your marriage partner. But do not try to control the partner. Not only does trying to control a partner's behavior cause your behavior to go out of control; each attempt to stop an ongoing affair seems only to strengthen it.[27]

Don't let a Carpman triangle continue. A Carpman triangle is a three-person relationship in which one person plays the role of persecutor, another the role of rescuer, and a third the role of victim.

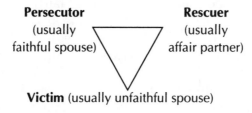

Persecutor   **Rescuer**

(usually   (usually

faithful spouse)   affair partner)

Victim (usually unfaithful spouse)

Figure 8

It sometimes happens that when a marriage is unhealthy, one spouse (the persecutor) becomes critical of the other spouse (the victim). At this point a concerned, opposite-sex friend of the victim enters the picture and begins meeting some of the victim's needs for nurture. This is "the rescuer." An affair gradually develops between rescuer and victim, and this is strengthened as long as the faithful mate remains in the persecutor role.

If the affair is discovered, the faithful spouse's role as persecutor may increase even more, driving the victim into a closer relationship with the rescuer. As is apparent by now, if the marriage is ever to survive, the faithful spouse must get out of the Carpman triangle by refusing to take the role of persecutor any more and forcing the betrayer and the lover to relate directly with each other. A therapist and client can discuss the specifics of how to remove oneself from a Carpman triangle.

There is another reason for removing oneself from this triangle. Assume for the sake of this illustration that the husband is having an affair. The wife is in the persecutor role, and the other woman, realizing she has competition, strives to always be on her best behavior. She makes few if any demands on the unfaithful partner, cooking his favorite meals, constantly adapting her schedule to his, and so forth.

If the faithful woman removes herself from the triangle, the lover now begins to feel more confident. The favorite meals are offered less frequently, she becomes less willing to adapt her schedule to the man's, and she will eventually start placing demands on him. As she does so, the affair begins to lose some of its romantic bliss, and if the lover has an aggressive way of stating demands, the affair can self-destruct fairly rapidly.

Don't use the telephone to maintain unhealthy dependency. Especially if the faithful partner has tendencies toward an unhealthy dependency, the telephone may become an instrument for expressing that dependency. Dependent behavior expressed over the telephone wires has the same result as dependency expressed in person—it tends to make the unfaithful partner want to withdraw from the marriage relationship even more.

If your goal is to develop or redevelop a friendship, face-to-face meetings are much more effective than telephone conversations. Use the telephone to *schedule* relationship times, but insist that those times be in person. Otherwise it is best not to call unless you have some specific business to discuss. Do this quickly, politely, and then hang up. Don't use the telephone to express dependency needs or to carry on fights.

Don't let attorneys make a situation worse. Weber and Simring make the following statements about employing divorce attorneys while there is still some hope of reconciliation.

> Unfortunately, the adversarial process encourages people to act out their most vengeful instincts, and divorce attorneys not infrequently fuel the aggression. If the spouses are angry before litigation, they are usually irreconcilable after it. . . .
>
> An attorney can create untold hardship if he plays upon his clients' fears and provokes a marital war. Whoever drops the first bomb can be certain that the other side will soon retaliate in force.
>
> Avoid divorce attorneys unless there is absolutely no choice, because they usually make matters worse. Lawyers

like to fight—they are trained to fight—and they can be very expensive.

If your spouse is threatening to leave, attempt to arrive at an interim pact. "If you don't retain an attorney, I won't either. Even if we can't save our marriage, let's work out the issues face to face. . . . If we absolutely cannot agree, we can always call in the lawyers later on."[28]

If your hope is reconciliation if at all possible, the above advice is probably wise, except in the case where there is significant property and you fear that your spouse might make unfair financial changes unilaterally. It can also be helpful if you can find a competent Christian attorney who understands your desire for reconciliation and will respect it in the way he or she conducts the divorce process. Since divorce papers are often written in adversarial language, it may reduce tension if you call your partner a few days before he or she receives papers, let him or her know what is coming, and explain the meaning of the papers in nonadversarial language.

This chapter has included a number of suggestions for what the faithful partner should not do upon discovering the affair. In the next chapter we give a number of suggestions regarding practical things *to do*.

NOTES

1. Barbara Gordon, *Jennifer Fever: Older Men, Younger Women* (New York: Harper Row, 1988), 110–11.

2. Daniel Dolesh and Sherelynn Lehman, *Love Me, Love Me Not: How to Survive Infidelity* (New York: McGraw-Hill, 1985), 43.

3. Charles Mylander, *Running the Red Lights: Putting the Brakes on Sexual Temptation* (Ventura, Calif.: Regal, 1986), 91.

4. Carol Botwin, *Men Who Can't Be Faithful: How to Pick Up the Pieces When He's Breaking Your Heart* (New York, Warner Books, 1988), 16.

5. There are two caveats to this generalization. First, the depth of one's pain is not the same as the amount of one's hystrionic acting out. The level of histrionic acting out is not related to the healthiness of the marriage, and in fact the two may be negatively correlated. Histrionic acting out is probably correlated with those who are unhealthily dependent on others for their self-esteem, and such unhealthy dependency, particularly if coupled with a tendency to hysteria, may bode ill for the future of the marriage. Therefore

the counselor should seek to differentiate the level of genuine pain from histrionic acting out capacity. Genuine pain may indicate there is some vitality left in the relationship. In contrast, when a person displays a high capacity for histrionic acting out (something which superficially may look quite similar to genuine pain), this does not necessarily indicate anything about the vitality of the marriage. Second, the level of pain may not be immediately apparent in those clients who tend to overuse repression to deal with life stressors. Only by careful and patient listening can the level of pain in this type of person be ascertained.

6. J. Allan Petersen, *The Myth of the Greener Grass* (Wheaton, Ill.: Tyndale House, 1983), 127.

7. Ellen Williams, "The Day the Fairy Tale Died," *Today's Christian Woman* (Winter 1981–82), 49–51.

8. H. Norman Wright, *Seasons of a Marriage* (Ventura, Calif.: Regal, 1982), 124.

9. Ibid.

10. Eric Weber and Steven Simring, *How to Win Back the One You Love* (New York: Macmillan, 1983), 137.

11. Botwin, 220.

12. James Dobson, *Love Must Be Tough* (Waco, Tex.: Word, 1983), 48–49.

13. Dolesh and Lehman, 77.

14. Botwin, 220–21.

15. Frank Pittman, *Private Lies: Infidelity and the Betrayal of Intimacy* (New York: Norton, 1989), 83.

16. The one major exception to this occurs when you are being unfaithful yourself. In this situation, your own guilt about your unfaithfulness and dishonesty is likely to be projected onto your spouse's behavior, often inappropriately so (cf. Matt. 7:1–5).

17. Sally Conway, *You and Your Husband's Midlife Crisis* (Elgin, Ill.: David C. Cook, 1980), 70.

18. Bernard Greene, Ronald Lee, and Noel Lustig, "Conscious and Unconscious Factors in Marital Infidelity," in *Medical Aspects of Human Sexuality*, September 1974, 87–111.

19. Botwin, 110.

20. Gordon, 129.

21. Botwin, 220.

22. Conway, 84–85.

23. Petersen, 123.

24. Cited in Susan Jacoby, "After His Affair," *McCall's* (February 1982), 120–22.

25. Richard and Elizabeth Brzeczek, *Addicted to Adultery: How We Saved Our Marriage/How You Can Save Yours* (New York: Bantam, 1989), 170.

26. Petersen, 131–32.

27. Pittman, 47.

28. Weber and Simring, 163–65.

Chapter Nine

The Faithful Partner: What *To* Do

If you, the reader, have recently discovered that your mate has been unfaithful, and if you have just read chapter 8, you may realize that you have done several things that have been suggested as what *not* to do. And now you may fear that you have destroyed any chances of reconciliation. Let me encourage you with three observations.

First, most of the responses listed in chapter 8 are normal responses when one discovers the other partner has been unfaithful. If you did one or more of them this indicates nothing more than that you are a normal person reacting to a personal trauma in a normal way.

Second, if you have attempted to be a caring, loving, faithful mate throughout your marriage, your partner should be able to view your crisis-initiated responses in the context of years of faithful and loving behavior. This is even more true if you are willing to apologize for any behavior of your own which, after reflection, you recognize was not the wisest response you could have made.

Third, even if your behavior *before* your partner's affair was not all you wish it had been, and even if you have made several mistakes in your initial responses, God delights in helping couples bring healing and new life into marriages which, from a human standpoint, seem either dead or hopelessly damaged. If both of you are open to God's grace, there is no relationship that is irreparable. Even if only one person is open to God's grace at this moment, God may be able to use that person's willingness to bring new life into a marriage.

With these thoughts in mind, let us look at some positive things we can do in response to learning of a partner's unfaithfulness.

Realize this doesn't have to be the end of the marriage. Like any other personal crisis, a marital affair is one of a series of life experiences that make up the whole. With counseling, the majority of marriages survive an affair and even become stronger because of the insights gained through the experience and the subsequent counseling.

Take time before you take action. Dr. Rita Rogers, clinical professor of psychiatry at the University of California at Los Angeles advises: "The most important thing to do immediately is nothing. Don't flee into action, but rather retreat into reflection."[1]

Decide whether you are willing to work on the marriage. Some people feel that adultery is such a fundamental abrogation of the marriage contract that it makes continuing the marriage untenable.[2] The majority of evangelical Bible scholars believe that Scripture teaches that adultery is a biblical ground for divorce and remarriage, if you so choose to exercise that option.[3] If this is your partner's first affair, and there is a willingness to repent, it is probably best to forgive. If your partner has had a series of affairs with little change in lifestyle or evidence of *genuine* remorse, it is probably best to assertively confront that lifestyle. Botwin, writing to women, suggests a number of questions a woman can ask herself in making an intelligent decision. A partial list of her questions, adapted to apply to men also, follows:

1. Is he or she committed to the relationship?

2. Are there things that bond the two of you besides legal and financial ties?
3. Is he or she willing to change?
4. Does your partner value monogamy even if not always practicing it?
5. Is your spouse willing to see things from your perspective as well as his or her own?
6. Is your partner capable of admitting that he or she is sometimes wrong?
7. Is your spouse willing to listen to you?
8. Is your partner willing to look inside himself or herself?
9. Is your partner able to communicate with you or, if not, is he or she willing to learn better communication skills?
10. Has he or she become a chronic liar?
11. Is he or she willing to give up the lover?
12. Does your spouse have enough control over his or her impulses to be able to pass up immediate gratification in favor of long-term goals?
13. Is your partner willing to work on your relationship?
14. Can your spouse give up being the controller of everything that happens in your relationship?
15. Is he or she willing to allow you to change?
16. Is he or she willing to give up liquor or drugs if these contributed to the infidelity?[4]

If on the basis of these questions you decide to end the marriage, I would definitely urge you to pray and seek counsel from one or more trusted people before taking such an important step. The benefits of staying with your partner and reconciling the differences, if at all possible, are numerous and are worth repeating. Such a choice avoids the anguish of divorce; it avoids the disruption of setting up separate households; it makes unnecessary the pain of living alone; the children are spared the turmoil of a family breakup; and the faithful partner is not faced with the often-frightening prospect of reentering the dating scene.[5]

The following steps apply to those who decide they want to try to continue their marriage:

Remember that you have every right to oppose your mate's intentions to abandon you. Everyone ends up losing in a divorce. On the average, divorced women and children experience an immediate 73 percent drop in their standard of living.[6] Fathers usually lose regular contact with their children and their homes. Children lose the security that an intact father-mother relationship provides, a home that includes both a mother and a father, the ability to spend special days such as birthdays and Christmas with both parents, and all the things that severely reduced finances bring.

An experienced divorce lawyer put the issue this way: "You know, I don't think people try hard enough. At the first sign of any real trouble, they assume the marriage is dead, and they come in to ask me to help them bury it."[7] Weber and Simring, two writers who are convinced that the present state of easy divorce is very unhealthy for people, say: "Insist, don't beg, that your mate stay. . . . Remind them of their vows . . . the children . . . the things you've accomplished together. . . . You have every right to put up a fuss, not to go meekly, but to oppose your mate's intention to abandon you."[8] Even an increasing number of secular therapists agree that you have a right to fight for your marriage. You have your shared history, your children, and your shared property on your side. With assertiveness, you can often be successful in pulling the marriage back together.[9]

Be honest and direct with the information you have. Don't try to play games with the information you have, such as trying to manipulate or trap your partner into telling you about the affair. Tell your partner what you know and how you have come to know it.[10] In an honest but nonvindictive way let your partner know that you are hurt. An honest expression of your hurt is likely to produce sympathy, whereas a vindictive expression of anger is likely to create barriers.

Ask your partner for more complete information about the affair(s). When you are able to talk calmly, find out how long the affair has gone on. Find out how often your partner sees this other person. If he or she sees the affair partner a lot, find out if it is basically a convenience affair (using the affair for variety rather than deep emotional involvement). Find out if he or she has had other affairs in the past. Ask if he or she is involved with anyone else besides this one person. Find out the sex of the affair partner—this is not always obvious. Ask what your mate feels he or she is getting out of the affair. Try to genuinely understand his or her point of view. Attempt to understand what role you played in the affair. Try not to be defensive, judgmental, or attacking.[11]

Commit yourself to learn, not to leave.[12] Tell him or her that you are willing to look at ways the marriage can be improved, and that you are willing to work on changes. Find out specifics of what your spouse wants, add some things that you would like, and see if you both can make commitments to make specific changes in the coming weeks. Recommend that you both read Willard Harley's book *His Needs, Her Needs: Building an Affair-Proof Marriage* and discuss it together.

Use your partner's choice of an affair partner to identify unmet needs in your marriage. Pittman says: "The choice of an affair partner seems based on the other person's [the affairee] differences from the spouse rather than superiority to the spouse. The point of difference may diagnose a problem for which the affair is seen as a cure. The problem could be sexual, most likely it is not."[13]

Ask for a commitment. Tell your marriage partner that you would like an apology from him or her, and that you would like a commitment to leave the affair and work on strengthening the marriage.

Remember: The greatest strength you have in holding your spouse is your love. Build on this. Let your spouse know this regularly in words, in writing, through your gaze or touch; not pathetically or weepily but openly and graciously. Make conversation. Talk about your relationship. Write a letter about positive experiences you have shared in your home, with the children, with each other. You can even write about the difficult times, and how you worked together to go through those valleys. You may have a host of significant life experiences that you have shared. Spend some money on personal gifts. Invest some money on a shared experience, just for the two of you. Your partner will not want to give up all of these things.[14]

If your partner says that time is needed to break free from the affair, agree to be involved in counseling if that would be helpful. But indicate that eventually he or she must make a choice. It is frequently true that a person, whether Christian or non-Christian, may be so driven by unconscious psychological needs that his or her emotions feel out of control. In order to regain control he or she may need some time in counseling. Just as none of us can turn off a strong feeling by saying, "I'm not going to feel that," it may take time to work through the emotional entanglement of an affair and extricate oneself. One of the lies Satan often feeds a person in such a predicament, is that everything would be okay if you would just accept the fact that your mate loves two people. It is important that you consistently and firmly (but not harshly) make the point that your partner cannot be involved in a love relationship with you and someone else—eventually he or she will have to make a choice.

Don't be obsessed with the details of the affair. Being obsessed about the other man or other woman will either make you feel inadequate or enraged, or both, and produces nothing positive for you or your relationship (it usually detracts considerably). Instead of thinking about your partner's relationship to the lover, use that time and energy to think about your relationship to your partner, what is happening in it now, and what you can do to strengthen it.[15]

Set a time limit on how long you will allow yourself to be left in limbo. Your partner may need some time to extricate himself or herself from the affair. How long it takes depends on many factors—the length of the affair, the manipulative skills of your partner's lover, the former healthiness and attractiveness of your marriage in comparison to the affair relationship, and your partner's own mental health. Together with your counselor and perhaps your spouse, set a date by which the spouse commits himself or herself to making a decision. You may wish to ask that if your partner is not willing to leave the relationship by the agreed time, he or she is to find separate lodging in order to think more objectively about the two relationships and the choice that must be made.

If you continue to be sexually involved with your partner, take precautions. The question of whether or not to be sexually involved has to be decided on a personal basis, and there is much to be said for not being involved while your mate is undecided. The most important thing to be doing at this point is rebuilding a deep *friendship* between the two of you, and most couples find that sexual involvement drains away energy that could probably be more importantly used in building the relationship.

If your mate is not sure he or she wants to leave the affair, ask if the other relationship can be suspended for a time during which you both will work on the marriage. Assertively ask that he or she try to make the marriage better for one year. If you cannot get a one-year commitment, ask for six months; and if not six months, three months. J. Allan Petersen tells a story which illustrates what can happen with only two months' effort at trying to improve the marriage.

> Newspaper columnist and minister Dr. George Crane tells this enlightening experience. A wife came into his office full of hatred toward her husband and committed to getting a divorce. "I do not only want to get rid of him, I want to get even with him. Before I divorce him I want to hurt him as much as I can because of what he has done to me." Dr. Crane suggested an ingenious plan. "Go home and think and act as if you really loved your husband. Tell him how much he means to you. Admire all his good qualities; praise him for every decent trait. Go out of your way to be as kind, considerate, and generous as possible. Spare no efforts to give of yourself to him in every way, to please him, to enjoy him. Do everything you can possibly think of to make him believe you love him. After you've convinced him of your undying love and that you cannot live without him, then drop the bomb. Tell him how much you hate him and that you're getting a divorce. That will really hurt him."

With revenge in her eyes, she smiled and exclaimed, "Beautiful, beautiful. Will he ever be surprised!"

And she did it, with enthusiasm. Acting "as if." For two months she initiated love actions, kindness, listening, giving, reinforcing, sharing, "doing the very best for the object of one's love."

When she didn't return, Dr. Crane called. "Are you ready now to go through with the divorce?"

"Divorce?" she exclaimed. "Never! I discovered I really do love him." Her actions had changed her feelings. Motion resulted in emotion. The experiment became an experience.[16]

Whether we conceptualize what happened here in terms of paradoxical therapy, behavior therapy, cognitive dissonance theory, or George Kelly's fixed-role therapy, one thing has been consistently shown—changes in overt behavior over a period of several weeks often produce corresponding changes in one's thoughts, beliefs, attitudes, and feelings.[17] Thus, a commitment to act "as if" one deeply cares for one's partner for even a period of three months may often provide significant changes in feelings. More will be said about Kelly's fixed-role therapy in the next chapter.

Insist that your mate, who wants to leave the family, tell the children. Often this difficult task is left to the faithful spouse, although the responsibility surely belongs to the deserting spouse. If your partner does tell the children, the children's response may have the effect of causing him or her to reconsider. At this point in an affair your partner may be more moved by a strong plea from the children than by the same plea from you.

Remember that an "open marriage" is neither biblical nor has it been shown to be a viable solution. Some unfaithful spouses—and this is probably much more common among non-Christians than among Christians—have tried to convince their partners to attempt an open marriage. For both Christians and non-Christians, a strong consensus exists among those who have studied the issue carefully: Open marriage does not work. For example, George and Nena O'Neill are best known for their advocacy of open marriage in a book by that title which they published in 1972. Five years later Nena O'Neill, a social anthropologist who had spent years researching modern marriage, retracted much of what she had said in that earlier book. In *The Marriage Premise*, she endorses sexual exclusivity and the need for loyalty, fidelity, and trust in marriage. One of her conclusions, based on interviews with several hundred men and women, both single and married was: "The more accustomed we become to the new freedoms and opportunities, the more open we become in our attitudes toward sex, the more couples are affirming their need for sexual exclusivity."[18]

Dr. Shirley Zussman, a former vice-president of the American Association of Sex Educators, Counselors and Therapists, says that she has never come across a single open marriage that worked. She considers it an intellectual football people enjoy tossing around. As a lifestyle, she asserts, open marriage is not viable.[19]

Dolesh and Lehman have come to the same conclusion. They say: "Some couples, upon the discovery of an affair, will turn to 'swinging' or 'swapping.' This belief, as far as we were able to determine, does not stand the test of time. Usually jealousy and anger enter in and the primary relationship is seriously jeopardized, if not destroyed."[20]

Make sure to have honest discussions with your spouse, even if it means confrontations. Sally Conway suggests tuning in to your partner by asking nonthreatening questions, genuinely listening to what he or she has to say, empathizing, showing tenderness, encouraging and respecting the person, and by being sensitive to timing.[21] Weber and Simring offer the following suggestions for encouraging dialogue: Don't let there be physical obstacles between you. Maintain eye contact when talking and listening. Be willing to share your point of view and consider your partner's. Reminisce about positive memories. Join with (agree with) your partner when you can. Be specific and positive. Agree that there will be no physical violence. Listen without criticizing. Focus your mind on what your partner is saying.[22] Spend time talking about how you can improve the quality of your relationship, rather than always focusing on the affair.[23]

Remember that angry betrayers try to blame their spouses for deterioration in the relationship. Betrayers who feel guilty about their unfaithfulness sometimes deal with that guilt by finding fault with the partner; in a sense, they are trying to find some justification for the affair.[24] Richard Brzeczek explains this from his own personal experience:

> Liz and I began fighting—about everything. I began to criticize her and everything she did. But the harder she tried, the angrier I got. I wasn't angry with her, I was angry with myself for what I was doing to her, and to us. I guess finding fault with Liz allowed me to justify my own actions.[25]

Begin to look at your own possible contribution to the affair. Because of our finite capacities, our imperfect family models (i.e., parents or stepparents), and the effect of our own needs, we are all imperfect spouses. Perhaps this is true, not in large ways, but in small ways that are nevertheless important. It may be that you didn't give your spouse your full attention, believing that you could listen to him or her while doing something else. Perhaps you gave advice when empathy was what was needed. Perhaps you reassured your mate of his or her abilities when he or she was trying to ask your permission to make a change (such as leaving a job he or she felt ill-suited for). Perhaps you began taking your partner for granted, and quit giving the encouragement that was needed on a daily basis.

Perhaps you responded to conflict by withdrawing and, over the years, have withdrawn so much that there was no intimacy left. Perhaps you haven't put any energy into finding hobbies or activities of mutual interest, so that now the two of you do very little together. Perhaps you have looked on sex as something to be endured, and have let your partner know it. Perhaps you have used your partner as a dumping ground for the day's frustrations, and didn't have a healthy balance of sharing joys, humorous incidents, hopes, as well as problems.

Paradoxically, you, the faithful partner, are likely to find that a pivotal moment in your own recovery occurs when you begin to see realistically how you may have contributed to the failure of the marriage. Without self-accusation, you are able to reflect and, possibly for the first time, develop insights into why your mate was drawn to someone else.[26]

Dr. Ruth Neubauer, a New York marriage and family therapist, has said: "Reconstruction of a marriage depends in large measure on how quickly a couple can move beyond the stages of simply assigning blame. Partners who never move beyond the blaming stage may stay married, but the problems which led to the affair in the first place go unexamined and may result in a cycle of repeated infidelities."[27]

Separate facts from negative self-talk. In an earlier chapter we discussed the relationship between our conscious and subconscious beliefs and our feelings (the A-B-C-D-E theory of emotions). This process of disputing can be used by the faithful as well as the unfaithful partner in a marriage. Some typical examples:

- Belief 1: My partner loves someone else more than me; our marriage has no future.
- Dispute 1: My partner is infatuated with someone else; hopefully over the next month or two he or she will recognize the differences between infatuation and mature love and begin to realize that we have much more to rebuild our marriage relationship on than infatuation.

- Belief 2: My partner is considering leaving me for someone else; I really don't have much to offer anyone anymore.
- Dispute 2: People are tempted into affairs for all sorts of reasons, many of which come from sources other than their marriage partner. Although I'm imperfect, I have the ability and willingness to be a good marriage partner to him or her if given the opportunity.

- Belief 3: My partner has been untrustworthy; I'll never be able to trust him or her again.

- Dispute 3: My partner's unfaithfulness hurts a lot, and it may take some time before I can trust him or her the way I used to. However, if I see genuine repentance and a recommitment to our marriage, with God's help we can rebuild trust within our relationship.

- Belief 4: Our marriage will never be as good as it was before the affair.
- Dispute 4: We had let our marriage drift for the last several years; we needed to realize that a good marriage doesn't just happen, but is something we need to work on regularly to keep it healthy.

Recognize that a period of separation may be needed for any one of a number of reasons. Before a decision can be made to terminate the affair, the unfaithful partner may need the extra motivation of experiencing how much he or she would lose by leaving the family. Your partner may need a separation to make it clear that you will not allow him or her to have both a marriage partner and a lover. Family counselor Norman Wright says: "No matter what advice he receives, the [unfaithful spouse] will probably not end the affair until he/she becomes uncomfortable with it or so dissatisfied and stressful that he or she begins to reconsider."[28]

Hopefully, in the event of separation, financial arrangements can be worked out without a formal legal arrangement. In those cases where a partner is not willing to provide financial support voluntarily, the partner who keeps the children may file a petition for separate maintenance. In most states this petition can remain in force indefinitely, until the spouse either decides to return to the marriage or files for divorce.

Be prepared for a previously honest spouse to become a habitual liar. Almost every person who has an affair starts becoming deceptive in order to hide it. His or her statements may not be outright lies; the person tells half-truths that cause the hearer to assume that one thing is meant when something else is actually the case. If he or she continues an affair, there is every reason to believe that the deceptive practices will continue as well.

Develop a variety of coping strategies. If you have a sense of humor, use it. Dress and look your best. Amaze your mate and yourself by doing something independently that you have never done before. Develop one or two close friends of the same sex who can be confidants. Join or form a support group. Allow yourself to be alone, and realize you don't die. Use creative writing to chart your emotional progress, to identify things you are learning about yourself, to express your feelings to your mate or your mate's lover through letters (which usually aren't mailed).

If your partner is no longer living at home and you have children, set up a regular visitation schedule. There are several reasons for this. Never knowing when your mate will drop in keeps you feeling very vulnerable. Your emotions will be more controllable if you know when you will see your spouse. This also helps him or her experience more of the loneliness that will be felt if the marriage is allowed to end, and helps your children have more predictable interactions with the absent parent.

The same principle should hold for you. This is a good time to reinstate some of the processes you used when dating. For example, when dating, probably neither person would "drop in" unannounced, but would call beforehand. Setting up a date for later in the week can give you both something to look forward to. Good dating etiquette can guide you in other things as well—being as warm and accepting as possible, looking good when you see your mate, asking how things are going in his or her life, and sending a love note every once in awhile.[29]

Give the affair time to self-destruct. Dr. Barbara Matthews states that only one in twenty affair relationships is viable eighteen months after a man leaves his wife. She also states that four out of five men ultimately ask their wives for reconciliation.[30] As mentioned earlier, affairs self-destruct for quite a number of reasons. One is that problems which seemed minor when a couple were only together for a few hours a week may become much larger if experienced daily. The unfaithful partner may become lonely for his or her wife and family, or may discover that he or she or the lover is using the affair to work out something in his or her own personal life (e.g., a developmental issue). Once that is worked out, there may be no compelling reason to continue the affair. Since the affair was conceived in infidelity, the partners may begin not to trust each other, and this distrust may eventually destroy the relationship.[31]

If the lover is a female and the man is much older than she, she may want children and find that he does not. Even if she initially agreed not to have children, a year or two later, as she recognizes that her "biological clock" is ticking, she may raise the issue again or may make a "mistake."

Finally, affairs often self-destruct when two people start putting demands on each other. One or both may take a dislike to the way a partner makes such demands, or the way the partner responds to one's expectations.

If your mate ultimately decides to tell his or her lover it's over, ask if someone (whom he or she chooses) may be witness to this final good-bye. If your mate has truly decided to end the affair, the moral support of having someone there as an aid in not being manipulated to continue the relationship should be welcomed. If he or she balks at taking someone, it may be a sign that there is still some ambivalence about ending the relationship permanently.

Use lawyers wisely. In the previous chapter we discussed how lawyers can sometimes make a tense situation worse by introducing adversarial litigation when there is still the possibility of reconciliation. However, a carefully chosen lawyer can safeguard your financial interests and provide important legal information without jeopardizing the chances of possible reconciliation. I would recommend that anyone who thinks his or her partner may be involved in an affair and who has reasonably solid information to substantiate such a suspicion should ask for a consultation with a lawyer who specializes in family law. An initial consultation does not commit you to proceeding with a divorce or even using that lawyer for any further legal action. Some lawyers provide this consultation free of charge. Before setting up such a meeting, I would recommend that you read chapter 9 ("Using Support Systems: Legal Aid") in the book *Love Me, Love Me Not: How to Survive Infidelity,* by Dolesh and Lehman, which has been mentioned frequently in these pages. That chapter provides excellent information which will make you a much better consumer of legal services—should you engage a lawyer—and which could save you a considerable sum of money.

PHASES OF ADJUSTMENT TO KNOWLEDGE OF THE AFFAIR

SUSAN JACOBY'S MODEL

There is no one accepted model of the phases one goes through when the discovery is made that the partner is in an affair. Several authors have developed their own particular models or conceptualizations. In Susan Jacoby's three-stage model, the first stage is that of *discovery*. She comments:

> The initial confrontation between a woman and her husband does not determine whether the union will survive, but it usually indicates whether there is any possibility that it will. Anger and blame—on the part of both spouses—are common, but other elements are present, too, in the kind of confrontation that occurs between partners who are serious about continuing their marriage.
>
> The first of these elements is some expression of remorse on the part of the husband [Jacoby is discussing the situation where the husband is the unfaithful partner]. The second is an indication from the wife that forgiveness may be possible. The third—and probably most important—is an expression of continuing commitment to the marriage. "I did the classic thing," says Karen, whose husband admitted he was having an affair after she questioned him about his late nights at the office. "I threw a plate at him. I told him he could just walk straight out the door, that I didn't want any man who didn't want me." "I don't want

to walk out," he said. "I love you, I love the kids." That made me even madder—in fact, I threw a glass at him—but the words did register. He had said he didn't want to leave. And although I was throwing things, I didn't threaten to leave him, either."[32]

Jacoby's second stage is *blame*, each partner usually attempting to put the entire blame on the other. Her third stage is *talking—negotiation and reevaluation*. This is that phase when the couple shifts from their emphasis on blaming one another to taking some personal responsibility for their contributions to the affair.

Norman Wright's Model

In Norman Wright's slightly more detailed four-stage model,[33] the first stage is called the *impact stage*. It lasts from a few hours to a few days. During this time the faithful partner is trying to adjust to the impact of this new information. He or she is making a decision about whether to fight or flee from the situation. He or she has lost the sense of having control of one's life, and is trying to regain it.

Wright's second stage is called *withdrawal and confusion*. During this phase, which can last from a few days to a few weeks, the person feels numb and depressed as he or she tries to adjust to this emotionally devastating news. Wright calls the third stage *adjustment*—a time when personal insights and optimism gradually start to replace the shock and depression of the impact stage. The person may verbally affirm the value of the insights he or she has gained, and say those insights have been worth the pain.

The fourth stage, suggests Wright, is *reconstruction and reconciliation*. During this time the person goes on to reconstruct a new life, either with or without the partner. He or she gradually becomes reconciled, either to the partner or to the fact that the partner is not coming back. And in the latter case he or she begins building a support system that does not depend on the former partner. Wright does not give average durations for his third and fourth stages.

THE KÜBLER-ROSS MODEL

There have been some attempts to apply Elisabeth Kübler-Ross's five stages of grief to this situation. However, even as those who have experienced the loss of a mate through both death and adultery have said, the latter seems to be more painful, and probably more complex. The first three stages—denial, anger, and bargaining—seem to fit quite well with the experience of affair victims. However, if the bargaining is unsuccessful, another anger stage (instead of Kübler-Ross's depression stage) often recurs. After that second anger stage, the faithful partner may experience depression as he or she adjusts to the fact that the marriage is over. This is followed by an acceptance stage. The fact of the infidelity, with its attendant anger and shame and humiliation as well as the possibility of marital reconciliation, seems to require some modification of Kübler-Ross's five-stage model.

THE DOLESH AND LEHMAN MODEL

Probably the most thorough discussion of the emotional phases of the affair victim has been developed by Dolesh and Lehman.[34] Although they say there is much variability in the amount of time spent in each stage, they also believe that certain common, repeated patterns are experienced by most people upon learning of a spouse's adultery.

The First Stage. In their model, the initial phase of finding out about the affair lasts from a few minutes to a few days. It includes first shock and possibly a physical reaction, followed by disbelief, then anger, a sense of loss, and then a regrouping of inner forces as the person tries to regain control of his or her world through action.

The Second Stage. This stage recapitulates the first one, but each substage now unfolds more slowly. There will be times of denial, when the person acts normally, almost as if the affair and its acknowledgment never occurred. In a way similar to how an ego defense mechanism keeps a person from being overwhelmed by knowledge of the affair, in this phase the person recognizes that the affair has occurred, but acts as if it had not.

Frequently during this stage there will be psychosomatic reactions—headaches, stomach aches, rashes, and nightmares. These are often worse when the person is unable to talk about the affair, but decrease in intensity when talking can begin. During this period he or she is likely to be more clumsy and accident-prone than usual. Some people totally withdraw into a shell of noncommunication and others displace their anger onto their children.

Another ego defense mechanism, rationalization, frequently becomes operative at this time. The person may not deny that the affair has taken place, but denies that it has any real significance. He or she may excuse the partner on grounds that the partner was overworked, or was seduced, or was depressed or in a midlife crisis and needed some cheering up. In rationalization the person doesn't attempt to understand the partner's affair, but attempts to explain it away. These defenses usually crumble after a short period of time.

The Third Stage. Dolesh and Lehman call Stage 3 the "Please love me" stage. The faithful partner may buy new clothes, get a nose job, become more interested in what the other partner likes, get in shape, and become sexier in bed. Much of this behavior is motivated by an intense fear of abandonment. The faithful partner experiences a great loss of personal power— over one's emotions, one's partner, and one's life situation. This partner may feel as helpless as a child, and may take the blame for the partner's affair.[35] This often results in overcompensation, with the faithful partner trying to make up for the areas of the relationship in which he or she fears there was a deficiency. He or she may talk and listen to the partner for hours or engage in terrific lovemaking.[36] People in this stage (and the unwary counselor) may interpret this to mean that everything is fine now, which is incorrect. The excellent relationship is due to the faithful partner's overcompensation, coupled sometimes with the faithful partner's attempts to atone for his or her own guilt. This is not the time for the couple to end therapy. The final healthiness of the marriage will be determined by how they cope in the following two stages.

The Fourth Stage. Stage 4, the "How could you!" stage, is characterized by depression and anger. During this time the faithful partner is likely to have widely fluctuating emotions. One day he or she may feel elated about life, and the next day be seriously depressed. During this time he or she often asks, "Tell me the details," trying to answer the question for themselves, "what did he (she) have that I don't?"

If the unfaithful partner gives in to the request for details, this almost always leads to anger, because the details allow the faithful partner to imagine the sexual activity between the spouse and the lover in graphic detail, which drastically increases one's sense of being betrayed.

"Letting go" of the previous conceptions of the marriage—realizing it will never be what it was before—and accepting the reality of the affair, is a prerequisite to either separation or rebuilding the marriage. There are likely to be moments of fury during this time, fury at being mistreated, lied to, cheated, and abused. This is a time when the danger of retaliatory behavior, including a revenge affair, is greatest. This alternation between anger and depression usually continues for three to six months, but may last longer depending on what is happening in the relationship and the psychological healthiness of the betrayed partner.

The Fifth Stage. Stage 5 is called "Beyond Betrayal" by Dolesh and Lehman. After a period of alternating between anger, depression, and confusion, the faithful partner comes to a point where he or she realizes it is time to take charge of one's life. This is decision time.

Counselees cannot be rushed into this time before they are ready. Sometimes it comes when a betrayer commits one incident too many, and the faithful partner believes that this last move reveals his or her true character. This decision may not lead to immediate action, but a calmness comes, because the faithful partner has decided to take control of his or her life again rather than let the affair or one's partner control his or her emotions. Sometimes the calmness is a sad calmness, because the faithful partner concludes that he or she must leave a chronically unfaithful partner. Sometimes it is a happier calmness, as the person recognizes one's growth, one's partner's growth, and the growth in their marriage.

POST-CRISIS COUNSELING WITH THE FAITHFUL PARTNER

Let us recapitulate the counseling process we have suggested thus far. Initially a couple may come to a counselor or pastor after the discovery or confession of an affair. After an initial joint session, the counselor may suggest individual sessions for each partner.

In sessions with the unfaithful partner the counselor helps him or her understand what the affair means (i.e., the contributions both partners made) and the differences between infatuation and mature love. The counselor helps the person look at the advantages and disadvantages of remaining in the marriage versus continuing the affair. If the unfaithful partner is willing to leave the affair, the counselor helps him or her with the process of grieving the loss of this relationship and emotionally "letting go" of the other person. The counselor helps the unfaithful partner move toward sincere contrition and to realize the amount of healing time the other partner will need. He or she does this by helping the person recognize the multiplicity of wrongs that have been done.

In sessions with the offended spouse the counselor can offer a safe, confidential place where this partner can repeatedly grieve and rage over the loss of the faithful relationship he or she believed existed. If the unfaithful partner is going through a period of prolonged ambivalence, or even if he or she has definitely decided to leave the affair, the counselor can provide support and practical guidance so that the faithful partner does not react in ways that significantly decrease the chances for eventual reconciliation.

After dealing with the initial response to discovery of an affair, a number of issues can be profitably explored in individual counseling with the faithful partner before commencing marital counseling.

Is There a Personality Disorder or an Addiction?

In this post-crisis stage, the counselor can help the faithful partner understand what kind of marital problem, personality disorder, or sexual addiction the other partner may have. This can usually be done without breaking the confidential relationship with the unfaithful partner. Of course, if that partner is unwilling to see the counselor, the issue of confidentiality does not exist. But if the unfaithful partner is in counseling, it is still possible to help the faithful one understand what kind of problem his or her mate may have. This is done by asking questions which help *the faithful partner* bring out in the open important features of the partner's behavior.

Using the empathic-Socratic method described in chapter 6, the counselor can help the person discover things in the guilty partner's behavior which the faithful partner may have been denying, repressing, or rationalizing away prior to counseling. By employing empathy statements, the counselor may assist this partner in pulling together the meaning of what is being uncovered. Any information about the unfaithful partner discussed in these individual sessions comes from *the counselee*, and any conclusions about the likelihood of change come from him or her; thus there is no sharing of what might be considered confidential information.[37]

If the spouse is a chronic adulterer, or if the adultery started within the first two years of marriage, such adultery usually has little to do with the faithful spouse or the quality of the marriage. And the prognosis for change in such a marriage, unless the adulterer is willing to let God work in his or her life, is not high.[38] The sixteen questions listed on pages 190–191 (Decide Whether You Are Willing to Work on the Marriage) provide another gentle way to help the faithful partner recognize the potential for change in the mate.

Are Conditions Present for Working on the Marriage?

There will be very different directions for counseling from this point on depending upon whether the two partners desire the marriage to continue. If both partners want to preserve the relationship, the counselor can help the faithful partner state conditions under which he or she is willing to continue the marriage.

If there is evidence of a sexual addiction, the conditions may include the unfaithful partner's participation in a sexual addiction group, either on an inpatient or an outpatient basis. If there is no evidence of such an addiction, the conditions developed will be unique for each couple. In addition to helping the faithful partner identify conditions, it may be necessary to help him or her work through any fears regarding the setting of limits on the partner's behavior. This should include a consideration of such matters as when and where to discuss such limits, what medium to use (speaking to the mate in person, or perhaps writing a letter, for example), who is to be present if this is done face to face, and what responses from the partner might be anticipated.

IDENTIFYING REPRESSED FEELINGS

An ongoing goal of counseling with the faithful partner will be to help the person identify and deal with repressed feelings. Because of a Christian upbringing, many Christians will be loath to own the depth of rage they feel, the total lack of loving feelings they may have at particular moments, and the desire for revenge they may experience at times. An important part of helping them not become "stuck" in the grieving process will be to help them "own" those very human reactions, and then to talk those issues through. It may be helpful to use the phrase, "If I were not a Christian, I think I would be feeling . . ." to help them identify repressed feelings.[39]

REASSURANCE REGARDING SEXUAL PROBLEMS

It will also be helpful for the counselor to reassure the faithful partner regarding sexual problems which may surface after the discovery of the mate's infidelity. If a wife has had an affair, the husband may become impotent for a time. If it is the husband who has been unfaithful, his wife may become nonorgasmic, or may develop inhibited sexual desire or dyspareunia (painful intercourse). Some betrayed women feel like crying or vomiting after intercourse. It is probably not wise for the counselor to volunteer information about "what may develop," for to do so may increase the likelihood of any one or more of these problems occurring. If the counselee says that one of these conditions exists, he or she may be reassured by the knowledge that such is normal and, usually, temporary.

DEALING WITH SOCIAL ISOLATION AND THE QUESTION "WHY?"

When someone has an affair, it is not uncommon for both marriage partners to feel that their friends pull away from them. Several reasons can be suggested for this. First, no social guidelines have been commonly adopted for handling an affair. If someone dies, friends bring casseroles and covered dishes, but what does one do for someone whose husband or wife is having an affair? People who are uncertain about the correct thing to do often end up doing nothing.

Second, many friends do not know how widely the illicit relationship is known. They fear that it would embarrass the couple whose marriage is threatened by an affair if the couple discovered how many people know about it.

Other reasons exist. Many friends of the couple may not want to seem to be taking sides by contacting either marriage partner. Also, people's time is usually overcommitted; they simply may not think of the couple or consider a partner's loneliness except when they see the couple. Some of the couple's friends may feel threatened by what has happened, and a part of their withdrawal is due to the fears caused for their own marriages. None of these things mean that friends do not care, but they do add up to the fact that the one whose mate is involved in infidelity may have to assertively ask for support from close friends during the crisis, rather than wait for friends to call.

When tragedy strikes, the victims cry out to God—and sometimes to their friends—"why?" Their initial cry is not usually a plea for theological or intellectual understanding. It usually is a plea for empathy, for someone to be with them in their pain. We as counselors and pastors need to realize that the cry of "why?" immediately after infidelity is usually a cry of anguish; such individuals are crying out for someone to understand them rather than to provide them with psychological reasons for the betrayal. Later on, after the initial pain has decreased somewhat, a cry of "why" from these people may be reflecting a desire to understand the reasons for the infidelity. Knowing the reasons will not reduce their pain, but it does help them make sense out of what happened and aids them in restoring order to a chaotic situation.[40] Understanding helps them take the first step in assuming responsibility for how they may have contributed to the affair.

WATCHING FOR BIOLOGICAL DEPRESSION

When a person learns of his or her partner's affair, a prolonged period of psychological depression usually results. Sometimes this psychological depression is severe enough to trigger a biological depression as well (this is not an either/or but a both/and situation). Appendix D, entitled "Understanding Depression," can help the counselor, pastor, and client be sensitized to the possibility of symptoms which indicate that the depression is becoming biological in nature. The appendix also explains the role of antidepressants in treating such depression, and deals with common reasons why Christians oppose the use of antidepressants.

If in the counseling process it becomes evident that one's partner is not going to return to the marriage, the normal procedures and resources used in divorce counseling can come into play. Many excellent books are available, written from either a secular or a Christian perspective.[41]

RESTORING TRUST

The issue of trust must be explored and dealt with as one of the primary foundation blocks when rebuilding a marriage. Trust is usually thoroughly shattered by the revelation of an affair. What are the factors that need to be dealt with in restoring trust? Jennifer Schneider, in *Back from Betrayal: Recovering from His Affairs,* comments on the components that comprise trust and why trust is so thoroughly destroyed by the revelation of an affair.

> One of the biggest costs of affairs is the loss of trust we have as couples. Trust in one another involves predictability, dependability, and faith. A person who is predictable will behave the same way in the future as he has in the past. A dependable person is someone who can be relied on when it matters. Both predictability and dependability reflect past behavior. But since future behavior cannot always mirror the past, faith is the belief—based on past experience that our partner cares—that he will continue to be responsive and caring. According to Erich Fromm, author of *The Art of Loving,* "Faith is an indispensable quality of any significant friendship or love. 'Having faith' in another person means to be certain of the reliability and unchangeability of his fundamental attitudes, of the core of his personality, of his love." The person may change his opinions, but his basic motivations [with regard to us] remain the same.
>
> When an affair comes to light, predictability, dependability, and faith vanish. We learn that our partner's past behavior has been very different from what he had led us to believe, and we therefore have no basis from which to predict his future behavior. We no longer feel we can depend on his concern for us. Moreover, not only can we no longer be certain of the unchangeability of his fundamental attitudes, but we suddenly realize we don't even know what his fundamental attitudes are. All the elements of trust are gone.[42]

One area that a counselor can examine with the faithful partner is what he or she will need from the spouse, in the weeks and months ahead, to begin rebuilding a sense of trust. Each counselee needs to define those things for himself or herself as a first step in being able to ask for them from the partner. Several of the following behaviors may be included:

- Absolute honesty, even when he or she knows that by giving me an honest answer I will be upset
- A willingness to answer my questions fully, without excessive prodding
- An awareness of situations that will cause me to be anxious about his or her trustworthiness, and an attempt either to avoid those situations or to take some action that will alleviate my anxiety
- Consistency in his or her behavior over a period of months
- Commitment to be involved in counseling, and a willingness to share his or her mistakes with others, to help me make the first steps to recovery
- A consistent caring attitude, to help me develop faith in him or her again

FORGIVENESS

Another issue will need working on at this stage of counseling: forgiveness. As a process it will probably be needed again and again over the next several months, but the groundwork for it can begin now. Two closely related problems may manifest themselves regarding forgiveness: one is the unwillingness to forgive, and the other is inability to forgive.

The issue of *willingness* to forgive will eventually come up with the offended partner (and sometimes with the guilty partner too). Initially a person may not *be able* to forgive because his or her pain is too great. But after the initial pain has subsided, this may change into an *unwillingness* to forgive. At this latter stage it is important to understand that pride is usually behind an unwillingness to forgive. Unwillingness to forgive usually means that we have failed to understand that, compared with how much God has forgiven us, the amount that we are asked to forgive others is vanishingly small (Matt. 18:21–35). If we are unwilling to forgive others, we perhaps have never fully appreciated the depth of sin in our own lives for which God has forgiven us.

When a person indicates that he or she is willing, but feels unable to forgive, two methods can be quite helpful, although they work in very different ways and may work best with different clients. One is an experiential method and the other a cognitive-behavioral one.

For those who are open to experiential exercises, inner healing or healing of the memories can be very helpful. The specifics of inner healing are the subject of other books and cannot be treated in depth here.[43] Healing of the memories has produced very profound and lasting healing in many Christians' lives.

The cognitive-behavioral method probably works best with those clients or counselees who, in general, prefer cognitive-behavioral therapy. Many marriage partners who say they cannot forgive believe that forgiveness is a feeling, and cannot produce that feeling within themselves. In such a situation it may be helpful to define more accurately what forgiveness is.

God said through Paul, "As the Lord has forgiven you, so you also *must* forgive" (Col. 3:13 RSV, emphasis added). The forgiveness Paul is speaking of is not a feeling, because feelings cannot be commanded. Hession says: "When we forgive, we have to consent to suffer the loss ourselves. Forgiveness means a willingness to give up our rights in that situation and allowing ourselves to be wronged without retaining the right to repay evil for evil."[44]

Forgiveness involves a decision of the will which includes at least these four elements: (1) a commitment not to bring up the affair verbally anymore. If the faithful spouse says to the partner, "I forgive you," he or she is making a commitment not to remind the partner repeatedly of the wrong. (2) It is a commitment not to punish the person for the offense in indirect ways such as withholding conversation or affirmation or sex. Forgiveness means that he or she promises not to continue to withhold oneself from one's partner as an indirect way of continuing to punish him or her. (3) Forgiveness includes a commitment not to relive the offense in one's own mind. Remembering the affair serves to keep one's feelings of anger stirred up. There is a certain period in the healing process when anger is normal. But if a person continues to mull over the offense beyond that, he or she is responsible for perpetuating his or her anger. (4) All of these need to be practiced with the recognition of one's own need for forgiveness. If a person truly grasps how much he or she needs God's forgiveness, then it is easier for that person to forgive a spouse who sins.

These commitments may need to be remade each day, or at least whenever one is tempted to take back one's forgiveness. We can make a commitment to forgive today, but tomorrow or the next day when we hear or think of a new transgression or remember an old one we may be tempted to withdraw that forgiveness. Therefore our commitment to forgive, in a way analogous to our commitment to fidelity, needs to be remade each time we are tempted to withdraw that commitment. The faithful partner needs to recognize that, while the affair was wrong, it is just as much a sin to feed an unforgiving spirit as it is for one's mate to continue to nurture romantic feelings for another person. If I expect the other person to stop thinking about the affair partner, I must likewise be willing to stop remembering the affair.

Lewis Smedes, in his book on forgiveness, suggests a four-step process of forgiveness that is compatible with what I have suggested.[45] When we are mistreated, our first response is that *we hurt*. In counseling after an affair this is expressed in the deep grief and the loss of ability to trust, even the feeling that life will never hold happiness again. Smedes's second step is that *we hate*. This is represented by the blaming process. "How could he have done such a thing! After all I've done for him, how could he treat me like that!"

His third step is that *we heal*. Healing begins when we start to understand the other person's needs. As the faithful spouse begins understanding the context of the mate's behavior, he or she can begin to see how that spouse became unfaithful, even though he or she may not agree with that action. In marriage counseling after an affair, this step occurs when both partners are able to see the roles they played in making their marriage vulnerable to an affair.

Smedes's fourth and final step of healing occurs when *we reach out the hand of friendship to the person who offended us.* Interestingly, Smedes says that healing (for the offended person) is complete when that person is willing to reach out a hand of friendship, whether or not the other person responds likewise. If the other person does not respond positively the *relationship* has not been healed, but the *person* who took the risk to be vulnerable is healed. His statement can be a reassurance to those whose partners do not return: they can still experience healing regardless of what the former partner decides.

A beautiful story of forgiveness, written by a woman who kept it locked in her heart for half a century, was shared in "Dear Abby" some years ago, in the hope of helping others to forgive.

> I was twenty and he was twenty-six. We had been married two years and I hadn't dreamed he could be unfaithful. The awful truth was brought home to me when a young widow from a neighboring farm came to tell me she was carrying my husband's child. My world collapsed. I wanted to die. I fought an urge to kill her. And him.
>
> I knew that wasn't the answer. I prayed for strength and guidance. And it came. I knew I had to forgive this man, and I did. I forgave her, too. I calmly told my husband what I had learned and the three of us worked out a solution together. . . . The baby was born in my home. Everyone thought I had given birth and that my neighbor was "helping me." Actually it was the other way around. But the widow was spared humiliation (she had three other children), and the little boy was raised as my own. He never knew the truth.
>
> Was this divine compensation for my own inability to bear a child? I do not know. I have never mentioned this incident to my husband. It has been a closed chapter in our lives for fifty years. But I've read the love and gratitude in his eyes a thousand times.[46]

KEY IDEAS FROM CHAPTER 9

Most people who discover their marriage partner is having an affair say that that discovery was the worst experience of their lives.

The most common way an affair is discovered is when a person sees changes in the other partner's habits or established patterns. Common clues include working late at night at the office, taking longer lunches, starting business travel on weekends, renewed interest in appearance, purchasing more attractive clothing or sexier underclothing, sexual changes, emotional changes, encouraging spouse to take trips or vacations alone, difficulty balancing one's checkbook, and unexplained credit card charges.

The spouse of someone involved in an affair almost inevitably senses that something fundamental is changing for the worse in the marital relationship.

A common situation that a counselor needs to work through with a client is the fear of confronting the other spouse. There is strong agreement among marriage counselors that early confrontation of an affair, even though it carries some risks, is healthier for the marriage and carries less risk than taking no action at all.

Spouses invite disrespect by being passive, permissive, or weak when the partner is unfaithful.

Setting limits on what a person will tolerate is not the same as giving ultimatums or trying to control a mate's behavior.

A counselor can help the spouse of an unfaithful partner work through his or her fears of a confrontation, develop an assertive statement, decide how and when to deliver it, and who should be present when it is delivered.

Immediate counseling with a person who has discovered that the other partner is having an affair can be likened to crisis intervention. The initial interventions should focus on supportive counseling and practical guidance to minimize reactions that would reduce the likelihood of eventual reconciliation.

Post-crisis counseling involves:

- allowing the faithful partner to grieve about the affair,
- helping the faithful partner understand what kind of marital problem, personality disorder or sexual addiction their partner has,
- helping the faithful partner identify and deal with repressed feelings,
- letting them know that experiencing sexual problems at this time is normal and usually temporary,
- helping them become assertive in asking two or three friends for support during the crisis,
- referring them for antidepressants if indicated,
- helping them identify what will be necessary from their partner in order to begin rebuilding trust, and
- helping the spouse begin working on the issue of forgiveness.

NOTES

1. Rita Rogers, M.D., quoted by Natalie Gittleson, in "Infidelity—Can You Forgive and Forget?" *Redbook*, November 1978, 191.

2. Richard Fisch, M.D., Assistant Clinical Professor of Psychiatry at Stanford University Medical School. Cited in Sally Conway, *You and Your Husband's Midlife Crisis* (Elgin, Ill.: David C. Cook, 1980), 70–71.

3. For example, John Murray, *Divorce* (Philadelphia: Presbyterian and Reformed Publishing Co., 1975); Guy Duty, *Divorce and Remarriage* (Minneapolis: Bethany Fellowship, 1967), and Stanley Ellisen, *Divorce and Remarriage in the Church* (Grand Rapids: Zondervan, 1977).

4. Carol Botwin, *Men Who Can't Be Faithful: How to Pick Up the Pieces When He's Breaking Your Heart* (New York, Warner Books, 1988), 205–13.

5. Jennifer Schneider, *Back from Betrayal: Recovering from His Affairs* (New York: Harper and Row/Hazelden, 1988), 171–72.

6. Lenore Weitzman, *The Divorce Revolution*. Cited in Gordon, 135.

7. Quoted in Eric Weber and Steven Simring, *How to Win Back the One You Love* (New York: Macmillan, 1983), 174.

8. Weber and Simring, 120–23.

9. Shirley Eskapo, *Women Versus Women: The Extramarital Affair* (New York: Franklin Watts, 1984); George Levinger, "Social Psychological Perspective on Marital Dissolution," in George Levinger and Oliver Moles, eds., *Divorce and Separation: Context, Causes and Consequences* (New York: Basic, 1979), 37–60.

10. Dr. Richard Fisch, quoted in Natalie Gittleson, 192.

11. Botwin, 188–92.

12. J. Allan Petersen, *The Myth of the Greener Grass* (Wheaton, Ill.: Tyndale House, 1983), 127–29.

13. Frank Pittman, *Private Lies: Infidelity and the Betrayal of Intimacy* (New York: Norton, 1989), 42.

14. Weber and Simring, 80, 85, 99.

15. Botwin, 244.

16. Petersen, 200.

17. David Rimm and John Masters, *Behavior Therapy: Techniques and Empirical Findings* (New York: Academic Press, 1974), 139.

18. Nena O'Neill, *The Marriage Premise* (New York: M. Evans and Co., 1977), flyleaf.

19. Cited in Elaine Denholtz, *Having It Both Ways: A Report on Married Women with Lovers* (New York: Stein and Day, 1981), 132.

20. Daniel Dolesh and Sherelynn Lehman, *Love Me, Love Me Not: How to Survive Infidelity* (New York: McGraw-Hill, 1985), 44.

21. Conway, 72.

22. Weber and Simring, 19–42.

23. Dolesh and Lehman, 27–28.

24. Dolesh and Lehman, 9.

25. Richard and Elizabeth Brzeczek, *Addicted to Adultery: How We Saved Our Marriage/How You Can Save Yours* (New York: Bantam, 1989), 40–41.

26. Barbara Gordon, *Jennifer Fever: Older Men, Younger Women* (New York: Harper and Row, 1988), 126.

27. Ruth Neubauer, quoted by Susan Jacoby in "After His Affair," *McCall's*, February 1982, 120.

28. H. Norman Wright, *Seasons of a Marriage* (Ventura, Calif.: Regal, 1982), 123.

29. Weber and Simring, 167–73.

30. Original source not found.

31. Laurel Richardson, *The New Other Woman: Contemporary Single Women in Affairs with Married Men* (New York: The Free Press, 1985), 124–44.

32. Susan Jacoby, "After His Affair," 122.

33. Wright, 125–26.

34. Dolesh and Lehman, 3, 48–100.

35. Notice that according to Dolesh and Lehman these characteristics are considered part of the developmental stages one goes through in adjusting to a partner's affair, rather than codependency features that may have been there for years.

36. Not every faithful partner going through this stage will become sexually active. Some people's response to a partner's affair will be to feel contaminated by sexual contact with the partner, and so even the thought of sex produces revulsion. These people, if there is a successful reconciliation, will usually have a return of sexual feelings, but it will occur later.

37. I do not think it is that helpful, and it probably would constitute breaking of confidentiality, to share the clinical diagnosis of the unfaithful partner with the faithful spouse. It will generally be more helpful to let the faithful spouse develop a "common-sense" psychological analysis of the partner and the partner's likelihood for change. The exception to this would be when the "common-sense" analysis he or she makes contains significant errors. Even then, the counselor should help the client become aware of facts he or she is overlooking, and let him or her make a new common-sense diagnosis.

38. Petersen, 130; Pittman, 123–25.

39. Charles Mylander, *Running the Red Lights: Putting the Brakes on Sexual Temptation* (Ventura, Calif.: Regal, 1986), 100.

40. Dolesh and Lehman, 29.

41. Some of these include *Growing Through Divorce* by Jim Smoke, *Finding Your Place After Divorce* by Carole Streeter, *How to Survive the Loss of a Love* by Melba Colgrove and others, and *The Boys and Girls Book About Divorce* by Richard Gardner.

42. Schneider, 193–94.

43. Good books on inner healing include *Healing for Damaged Emotions* and *Healing of Memories* by David Seamands, *Healing Life's Hurts* by Dennis and Matthew Linn, and *The Broken Image* by Leanne Payne.

44. Roy Hession, *Forgotten Factors: An Aid to Deeper Repentance of the Forgotten Factors of Sexual Misbehavior* (Fort Washington, Pa.: Christian Literature Crusade, 1976), 87.

45. Lewis Smedes, *Forgive and Forget: Healing the Hurts We Don't Deserve* (San Francisco, Harper and Row, 1984).

46. Abigail Van Buren, "When Your Husband Is Unfaithful," *McCall's*, January 1963, 74.

Chapter Ten

Marriage and Family Counseling Following an Affair

Randy was deeply in love with a female co-worker; his marriage to Cindy seemed to have little chance of surviving. Over a period of two and a half agonizing months Randy and Cindy each saw a counselor—Randy to help him decide whether to leave or stay in the marriage, and Cindy to find support while Randy made his decision.

Over the ten weeks Randy came to an understanding of some unmet needs and desires which had left him vulnerable to an affair. And he also came to see why he felt such a different intensity in his love for his affair partner in contrast to his feelings for Cindy. He painfully debated within himself the pros and cons of leaving the affair partner versus leaving Cindy and his family. He experienced intense confusion, depression, and guilt as he gradually came to realize that either choice would result in terrible pain for someone about whom he cared deeply. Eventually Randy decided to recommit himself to the marriage and asked Cindy to take him back.

During this time Cindy had been receiving supportive counseling to help her through this very painful and anxious period. She and her counselor had also spent much time talking about and considering wise responses to Randy's various actions as he struggled to decide. In counseling Cindy vented her anger. She began forming hypotheses concerning the changes that might be necessary in order to strengthen the marriage if Randy was willing to return. Her counselor and she also discussed her response in the event Randy desired to return.

When Randy decided he would like to recommit himself to the marriage and Cindy decided to accept him back, an important milestone in the counseling was reached. However, for them and for any couple whose marriage has been endangered by an affair, several important therapy tasks remain. These include:

Beginning the process of rebuilding trust

Examining *together* and assimilating an understanding of what led to the affair

Identifying other problems in the marriage that need to be worked on in addition to those which are a result of the affair

Teaching the couple skills—especially for communication, conflict resolution, and individual coping—which will enable them to work through present and future problems

Continuing the process of working toward forgiveness

Receiving sexual therapy to restore mutually satisfying sexual functioning

Deciding what and how to tell the children, and working on rebuilding their trust, which usually has been undermined because of the affair

BEGIN REBUILDING TRUST

During post-crisis individual counseling the faithful partner will have defined what he or she would like from the other partner in terms of behavior so that trust can be restored. In this phase of counseling those ideas can be communicated to the spouse.

Trust in the marriage relationship is that emotional feeling which grows when a person knows his or her partner is committed to fidelity. At this point, the counselor may ask the couple to develop a definition of fidelity which satisfies them both. Such a definition will usually include the following components:

- A commitment to invest time and energy in their relationship, and a willingness to be vulnerable so that they become each other's closest friend
- A commitment, when something is done that produces frustration in either mate, to draw closer to each other and work through the frustration, rather than withdrawing from one another
- A commitment never to allow someone else to meet personal needs that should only be met by each other

Overcoming the effects of dishonesty and beginning to build a relationship of trust will, of course, require time. Frank Pittman comments in his book *Private Lies*: "If you've been lying to your partner long enough, your partner is bound to seem rather crazy. People who are lied to become dependent, anxious, delicate and overreactive. They can even become paranoid, and believe they are being lied to even when they aren't. Your partner may seem a great deal saner after being better oriented to reality."[1]

It is good to ask the couple what specific behavioral commitments are necessary to begin rebuilding a sense of trust. These will be different for every couple, and the priority of the different behaviors that are desired will vary. Both the faithful and the unfaithful partner may have done something to damage trust. The counselor will find that regularly included among the now-desired behavioral commitments are these: willingness to answer a partner's questions, to be absolutely honest, and to be accountable to one's mate. Also included are an openness about how each is spending time and money, a willingness to give up personal mailboxes and separate telephone lines, a willingness to decrease the amount of contact one has with persons of the opposite sex who make the other spouse uncomfortable, and a voluntary, *self-initiated* accounting for self when a situation might arouse suspicion (this relieves the partner from having to be a parole officer). Further, each partner—especially the faithful one—will want a consistent, caring attitude from the other partner, willingness to talk about problems, and a recommitment to spiritual values.

The faithful partner also should commit himself or herself to making "I statements" when situations arouse suspicions (rather than brooding or trying to get information through manipulative questions). He or she also needs to understand the process of catastrophizing,* and what can be done instead of catastrophizing. Below is one couple's eight-step plan for rebuilding trust—trust which had been shattered by the husband's three affairs within ten years.

Don and Alice were both near fifty years of age; he had been a traveling salesman who was usually away from home Monday through Friday. Both were Episcopalians, Don with a fairly nominal involvement, and Alice with a deeper one. Their plan included:

1. A commitment to the marriage, as demonstrated by continued marriage counseling until both felt their marriage was strong.

2. Honesty, which meant not telling untruths and not withholding important information (a behavior Don had frequently engaged in).

---

*Catastrophizing involves stating unhealthy beliefs to oneself which are unlikely to be true, but which would be extremely anxiety producing or painful if they were. For example, when someone's partner is five minutes late coming home from work, the spouse begins self-talk to the effect that the partner has probably become reinvolved in the affair. A person can add to the emotional intensity of the catastrophizing by visualizing the feared situation with graphic images.

3. Accountability, especially through volunteering information about whereabouts and schedule.
4. A commitment to fidelity, especially by avoiding places of temptation (such as bars when Don was away from home), and by taking appropriate action whenever Don recognized he was in a high-temptation situation.
5. Don's accepting of responsibility for the pain caused to Alice and their two daughters.
6. Don's seeking a job in their home town (all of the affairs had occurred when Don was "on the road").
7. Making an effort to put their financial affairs in order.
8. Seeking to become involved in shared spiritual activities.

SPUR-OF-THE-MOMENT RETURNS NOT ALLOWED

If the unfaithful partner has moved out of the family home because of a continuing relationship with the lover and then decides that he or she wants to leave the lover and return home, it is probably wise to ask him or her to stay in separate housing for a while to make sure the commitment to return is firm. There are several reasons for this.

First, unfaithful partners who make a spur-of-the-moment decision to return home and who are allowed to do so *immediately* have a high rate of relapse back into unfaithfulness. The immediate move back home seems not to allow them enough time to work through the ambivalences that are inevitably experienced. Thus, the unfaithful spouse may leave the family home again. Second, an immediate return gives the *faithful* partner no time to adjust to the spouse's return. Third, a premature return home followed by a subsequent departure can be very traumatic for that partner and any children in the home—it destroys whatever trust might still exist. If the unfaithful partner waits in a neutral residence for a few weeks after his or her recommitment to return home, and that time is used to develop a reentry plan for both spouses, much of his or her ambivalence can usually be dealt with before the move back home.

Sometimes such a transitional period is impossible because of the circumstances, and an alternative plan is needed. For example, John and Sally were in their thirties and had a history of much sexual experimentation before becoming Christians. Since their conversions John had taken what he believed was a Christian leadership role in the marriage. In reality, however, he was often dogmatic, simplistic, and emotionally insensitive. Sally eventually responded by having an ill-conceived, blatant affair with a professing Christian in the rural community where they lived. The lover had been involved in a long series of affairs with simple, trusting women. Sally had left her children and husband and moved into her own apartment, which represented independence to her.

When she wanted to return to her family immediately, it was because she feared that she would not have the strength to fend off the lover's advances if she remained in the apartment. However, she also feared returning home, for her husband still had a great deal of unresolved anger within him, and he sometimes had been physically abusive in the past.

A compromise was developed that was satisfactory to both. Sally would leave her apartment and stay with an older Christian couple who knew of the affair and were desirous of helping them. John and Sally would gradually spend more time with each other as they both felt ready to do so, and they would gradually volunteer more information to each other to begin rebuilding trust. If Sally felt tempted to return to the affair she would talk with the older woman and use her in a way analogous to an AA sponsor. Sally would make an appropriate confession to her children (who were well aware of the affair) and would ask their forgiveness. She would move back permanently when she and John and their therapist agreed that it was time to do so.

AN UNEXPECTED COMPONENT IN RESTORING TRUST

The faithful partner's development of trust can be hastened as he or she begins to see that the other partner is also experiencing a time of emotional devastation. Marriage and family therapist Don-David Lusterman has observed:

> Restoring trust also involves the victim's recognition that the infidel [the unfaithful partner] needs her support as well. After breaking off an affair, he may feel depression, grief, shame, and the fear that, no matter what he does—stay or leave—he is going to hurt someone. When the victim can accept these emotions and really listen to the infidel, progress is more rapid. And it is very touching to see two people in so much pain reach out to comfort one another.[2]

EXAMINE THE AFFAIR TOGETHER

A second step in marital counseling involves helping the couple *as a couple* examine and assimilate an understanding of what led to the affair. This has been done individually, but now the couple has an opportunity to interact with each other and see how the entire picture fits together. In most cases they find that there were multiple factors, and in many cases there was a sequence of factors leading to the affair.

For example, Joe, a Christian who had been married for fourteen years, came for counseling because he had almost had an affair with a woman at work. The experience had shaken him to the core. He had always been strongly committed to fidelity, but this relationship had grown so gradually over a year and a half that he was surprised to realize the intensity of his feelings for this other woman.

Joe believed he had a healthy, strong marriage. He and Donna, his wife, had a good friendship as the core of their marriage, they shared a common commitment to their faith, and they enjoyed talking about things and doing things together. The only dissatisfaction he had was that Donna was quite inhibited during sexual intercourse. She seemed to participate in sex only because it was her duty, rather than out of any enjoyment or initiative of her own, and she did not care to introduce variety into their love-making. However, since there were so many other positives in their marriage, Joe had chosen not to focus on or emphasize his unhappiness in that area.

In counseling Joe realized that he had been repressing his feelings about how important sex was to him, and that the intensity of his unmet needs (or desires) was contributing to his attraction to the co-worker/friend who had tried to seduce him into an affair. He also became aware that the intense feelings he had about the co-worker relationship were not simply due to anxiety over succumbing to temptation. They were an indication of strong sexual arousal itself. He realized that he had almost welcomed the advances of the woman at the office because of a desire for sexual connection. But he had repressed his conscious awareness of those feelings because such feelings were incompatible with his own moral code.

Joe chose to confess the "almost affair" to Donna, as well as what he had learned about himself through counseling, and ask her forgiveness, which he did in a joint session. Joe's disclosure brought tears to Donna's eyes, and she responded with some disclosures of her own. When they had been dating some sixteen years earlier at college, they had become sexually involved, even though both were Christians at the time. Joe had taken the initiative in this, and Donna had not felt secure enough in herself to say no, even though she did not want sexual involvement. For fifteen years she had kept these feelings of resentment bottled up inside, and they had affected how she experienced sex, making her a less-than-enthusiastic sex partner ever since. Joe asked her forgiveness for the years of pain his behavior had caused her, and Donna asked Joe to forgive her for keeping her resentment bottled up inside and for being so passive-aggressive for fifteen years. In the coming months they went on to develop a much freer and mutually enjoyed sexual relationship.

Because marriage is so interactive, it is unusual for both people not to have contributed to marital vulnerability, either through their actions or their reactions. The marriage and the individuals involved are a long way on the road to healing when they can "own" their contributions and genuinely ask a partner's forgiveness.

In a group setting couples often learn vicariously as others tell about the factors that led to an affair. They can learn from both healthy and unhealthy models (other couples who are struggling to put their marriages back together after the intrusion of an affair). The WESOM (We Saved Our Marriage) groups described by Richard and Elizabeth Brzeczek in *Addicted to Adultery* appear to be an excellent adjunct to individual and marital therapy. These groups provide several benefits. They provide emotional support for members going through the emotional difficulties of rebuilding a marriage, and involvement by the guilty partner demonstrates to the spouse his or her commitment to admit mistakes and make changes. Further, they provide couples with the opportunity to have a ministry to other couples once they have solidified their own marriages.

IDENTIFY OTHER PROBLEMS IN THE MARRIAGE

In addition to the unmet needs which led to the affair and the negative results of the affair itself, a number of other frustrations have usually bothered one or both partners. The chance of avoiding a relapse into infidelity or a divorce are increased if those problems are addressed in counseling.

Knowing that frustrations other than those which are related to the affair will be dealt with in counseling can increase a couple's motivation to work, for each partner sees the potential for developing a more fulfilling marriage. After the crisis is past is often an ideal time to work on frustrations, for many couples tend to repress awareness of dissatisfactions in the marriage. During the aftermath of an affair their defenses are often down, and they may be more honest about bothersome issues than previously. Whatever methods the counselor has found to be effective in normal marriage counseling (i.e., when no affair is involved) can be used here.

Some couples have become so discouraged about their marriages that little motivation remains for staying in counseling or attempting to change their behavior. In such a situation it is sometimes helpful to use Richard Stuart's *Caring Days* to increase motivation.[3] For those not familiar with this technique, the counselor usually introduces it with a brief statement that people generally feel positive toward those who do pleasing things for them. During courtship these "pleasing" behaviors are normally quite frequent, but they gradually decrease during marriage. And if significant marriage problems develop, they may decrease precipitously. With positive behaviors occurring infrequently, few positive feelings are generated. In *Caring Days* a method is given to help the caring cycle begin again.

Each marriage partner is given a pad and pencil and asked to list the other partner's behaviors which elicit positive feelings toward that spouse. The counselor avoids the word *loving* because in a seriously deteriorated relationship neither mate may experience feelings which he or she would call love. Each item on the list should meet these four criteria:

1. It should be a specific behavior (e.g., "greet me when you come home from work with a kiss and a hug," not "be more loving").

2. It should be positive (e.g., "try to listen to me until I'm finished" rather than "don't interrupt me all the time!").

3. It should be something that can be done on a daily or somewhat regular basis (e.g., not something so expensive that it can occur only once in several years).

4. It should not be a behavior which is the object of serious contention between the couple (i.e., one that either partner feels uncomfortable with or unwilling to do).

Each mate is encouraged to list twelve to fifteen items that meet these criteria. It is often helpful to let both persons write down five or six items, then ask them to read them aloud. The counselor and clients can work with the items until they meet the four criteria. After both clients have a clearer understanding of how to compose items, they can complete their lists.

It will usually take most of a fifty-minute session to complete this exercise. When the lists are as complete as possible using the time available, the counselor can make two copies of each list, one for the spouse and one for himself or herself.

The assignment is to try to do at least three things from the partner's list each day, and to express appreciation when one's partner does something from his or her list. Other caring behaviors can be added as either spouse thinks of them, thus giving the partner more items from which to choose. Often a week or two of Caring Days, and the positive feelings generated by this exercise, can increase a couple's motivation to work on other aspects of their marriage.

DEVELOP COMMUNICATION AND CONFLICT-RESOLUTION SKILLS

Most couples in marriage counseling complain that they do not communicate effectively, or that they do not know how to resolve conflict when they want different things. A method that I have found helpful is to take the role of a coach who teaches the couples explicit communication skills and coaches them in their use until the couple can use them effectively without my intervention.

This approach can be used with any book that teaches specific communication skills. My favorites are *Talking Together* and *Connecting*.[4] In my use of these books I have couples read a chapter each week. We spend a few minutes at the beginning of each session discussing questions they have about that week's content or any personal applications they see. Then we discuss an issue (something that bothers one or both persons), using the skills from that week's reading and from those of previous weeks. As a coach, I help them learn to use the skills to resolve their own problems. Before each person speaks he or she must summarize what the partner said to that partner's satisfaction—which quickly helps people learn to listen more carefully to each other. If one partner starts to deviate from healthy skills, I may stop that person, even in midsentence, ask for an identification of what he or she is starting to do wrong, and then help the person rephrase the statement in a healthier way. Often we will resolve one issue per session. Sometimes the issue is resolved when each person understands the other's perspective; at other times the issue is resolved by having one or both partners agree to some change in their behavior. The following week serves as an opportunity to see if the agreed-upon change resulted in the goal they had in mind.

If an issue is too complex to be resolved in one session, the couple can be asked to continue the discussion at home until it is resolved or they get stuck. If the issue cannot be resolved in one session but the couple is not ready to continue discussing it on their own, they can be asked to spend the week thinking about their own goals and what the other partner has said. We then resume the discussion in session the following week unless some urgent issue needs to take priority.

As a coach, the therapist or counselor can help the couple learn the skills, interrupt an unhealthy style before someone becomes angry or hurt, assist the sender in finding a healthy way to send the message, and ask questions which help the couple look at parts of the issue that may have been suppressed, denied, or repressed. The coach can gradually reduce his or her level of involvement as the couple becomes adept at completing discussions of complex or emotionally loaded issues on their own.

By using a book to teach couples communication skills and practicing them on real issues in the sessions, two important goals are accomplished simultaneously. Couples resolve real issues in their marriages, and they also learn skills which, hopefully, they will use for the rest of their lives to resolve issues before they become problems.

Couples can be asked to consciously attempt to use the skills twice a week at home to work on issues they feel ready to tackle on their own. By giving a structure of twice a week, it helps couples not to feel that they must be trying to practice continuously the new way of talking, and it introduces a structured time when they purposely are trying to use healthier skills to resolve their problems.[5]

Another finding that can be used with couples is George Kelly's *fixed-role therapy*.[6] In fixed-role therapy, the therapist and counselee compose a role sketch that includes desired behavior patterns as well as desired attitudes, feelings, and goals. In order to minimize resistance to change, the counselee is asked to *act like* the person identified in the role sketch, not try to *be* that person. He or she is to try this as an *experiment* to see what happens (not asking the person to make a permanent commitment to remain a certain way), as another approach that reduces resistance. It has been found that people who act according to the roles prescribed by the fixed role sketch make gradual but significant shifts in their perceptions, attitudes, feelings, and behavior.[7] While I do not use fixed-role therapy explicitly when counseling couples, the research on this method does suggest that if people are willing to experiment with new (i.e., more gentle, loving) behavior toward their spouses, they will begin to experience emotional changes which are consistent with their new behavior.

A number of individual coping methods have been suggested for this period of time as well. It seems to help if each partner stays moderately busy. If a person cannot get a job, he or she can do volunteer work. Some people elect to continue their education. The most unhealthy situation is for a man or woman to have nothing mentally stimulating to do, and to think about the partner's affair much of the day. One former client who did this would be so enraged by the end of the day that she would launch a physical or verbal attack against her husband almost every evening as he came in the door. Their lives and their relationship dramatically improved when she took a job at a neighborhood store.

It is important to realize that a couple cannot simply return to their old way of functioning once the affair is over. For one thing, the affair has drastically changed their relationship. For another, while the affair was going on, the unfaithful partner probably developed some methods of nondisclosure to keep information from the other mate. The relationship will not become healthy unless the couple consciously makes an effort to become more honest, more caring, and more open with each other than previously.

CONTINUE THE PROCESS OF FORGIVENESS

Forgiveness has already been discussed in chapter 9. I believe forgiveness is a process, because as the faithful partner sees further evidences of his or her spouse's repentance and commitment, he or she is able gradually to let go of more of the hurt and anger.

Within Scripture sin is often considered a debt. In one sense, when the unfaithful partner sins, he or she incurs a debt to the faithful partner. The sin of marital betrayal causes a large debt because of the tremendous pain it causes. Forgiveness means a willingness to let go of the debt that is owed—to cancel it so that it no longer exists. Forgiveness cannot be complete as long as one is minimizing the pain one feels because of the adultery. It is only when a person is fully aware of the pain, fully aware of the debt the partner owes, that he or she can truly cancel the debt.

Sometimes a Christian may repress the full extent of his or her anger at the spouse because of socialization messages that have come through the family of origin or through Christian upbringing. In such cases the person may need permission and help to fully experience the anger that is there. This can be done through Gestalt-type exercises. Some have found it helpful to vent their hostility through talking or screaming in an empty room, through writing, or through hitting an inanimate object. The offended person needs to find an effective way to express the deep pain, and know that the other partner has heard the depth of that pain, as part of the process of forgiveness. When this is not done the pain may be repressed, rather than worked through.

ATTEND TO THE SEXUAL RELATIONSHIP

For some couples the sexual relationship revives without any specific attention from the therapist. In other cases there may be a need for explicit intervention. If the unfaithful partner has a sexual addiction and his wife has become a coaddict, a sixty- to ninety-day period of celibacy may have advantages for them. For such couples an extended period of mutually agreed-upon celibacy can have the following benefits:[8]

1. It prevents the person or couple from using sex inappropriately to meet other needs.

2. It shows one or both persons that they can survive without sex.

3. It helps one or both partners to begin to view his or her spouse as a human being rather than a means of sexual gratification.

4. It helps the couple do loving things together.

5. It forces people to develop new coping strategies and face problems more directly.

Not every couple wants or needs a period of celibacy. This should be a mutual decision, and not a way of punishing the other.

It is important for every couple, whether or not there has been a sexual addiction, to talk about the meaning of sex for themselves, either within or outside a counseling session. The majority of couples engage in marital sex for forty or fifty years without ever talking about it. This can be an excellent time to talk about what pleases them, what is arousing to them, and changes they would like the partner to make in their love-making. Prescribing Masters and Johnson's Sensate Focus I and II exercises can be an unpressured way of helping the partners begin to become sexual again, helping them become aware of the many enjoyable ways of pleasuring the other partner before actually having intercourse, and helping them begin talking with each other about their sexual relationship.

A therapist or counselor can determine whether areas exist regarding sexual functioning that need further discussion. In some cases standard sex therapy may be required for common after-effects of affairs (e.g., secondary impotence). The following four books are written from a Christian perspective and contain much useful information. They are given in the order from the most basic to the most detailed:

The Act of Marriage by Tim and Beverly LaHaye

Love Life for Every Married Couple by Ed and Gaye Wheat
The Gift of Sex by Clifford and Joyce Penner
Counseling for Sexual Disorders by Joyce and Clifford Penner

TALK WITH THE CHILDREN

Children living at home inevitably become involved when one parent has a protracted affair. They sense the tension or lack of closeness in their parents' relationship, or they hear heated arguments, or they may overhear telephone conversations which tell them something is wrong.

In general children can deal more healthily with a situation when it is explained at their level of comprehension than when they are given no explanation or an untrue explanation. Most parents decide to talk openly with their teens, but less explicitly with their younger children. If their younger children hear of the affair through gossip or some other way, it is probably best to tell them the truth objectively. If there is a dual addiction (e.g., substance abuse and sexual), most parents choose to tell about the substance abuse problem only. If children, especially teen-agers, know a great deal about the parent's behavior stemming from the sexual addiction, it may be best to acknowledge both.

In the parent's explanation time, it is considered wisest to talk with one child at a time, so the explanation can be geared to his or her level of understanding. This also allows the child maximum opportunity to ask questions or express feelings. As with divorce, where an affair is involved it is best not to ask the children to take sides. Running down the other parent, even though he or she may be biblically wrong, does nothing helpful in the situation. It is best also for the parent not to fall apart in front of the kids or ask them to be that parent's support system. They are devastated enough by their own loss. A parent should look to his or her peers rather than the children for emotional support.

Parents should be aware that the sound of an angry discussion travels through the house especially well at night. It is best that any major confrontation of one parent by the other not be in front of or within earshot of the children. Nor should either parent displace anger onto the children. If there is going to be a separation, a parent should seek to prepare the children in advance. The spouse who is leaving should tell the children, although both spouses should be present. Parents should plan in advance what they are going to say, preferably conferring with a counselor about how they will communicate this information.

If there is a sexual or substance addiction, it is probably wise for a parent to *eventually* talk with one's teen-aged children about addiction, coaddiction, and codependency. Such discussions, along with children's involvement in appropriate support groups, may help young people prevent similar problems in their own lives or learn to deal with the problems early. While many honest confessions of parents to their teens have produced greater closeness and have perhaps prevented pain by educating them concerning dangers to which they are predisposed, there is always the risk that a teen will respond negatively to the parents' confession. There is also the danger that, out of their hurt or anger, they will tell relatives whom a parent would rather not be informed. Most parents, especially when their children know of the affairs already, decide that the benefits of an appropriate confession to one's children outweigh these risks.

It is not uncommon for children to have nightmares, tantrums, and school problems when problems develop between the mother and father. They may be unresponsive or rebellious to parental authority. Children may love and hate the offending parent simultaneously. If the faithful spouse has accepted the offending spouse back, the children may be angry at the faithful spouse for doing so before they were emotionally ready to do likewise. Both parents should be aware that, even if the offending spouse has made a biblical choice to stay in the marriage, it will take time to rebuild the children's trust in the offending parent. Affairs are as painful for children as they are for their parents.[9]

DO AFFAIRS HAVE ANY REDEEMING QUALITIES?

Though terribly painful, an affair can have a beneficial end result. Marriage and family counselor Marcia Laswell states: "The person involved in an affair has made an undeniably dramatic statement that cannot be ignored, and has opened up the possibility for the couple to do constructive work on the relationship."[10]

Psychologist Ruth Westheimer agrees: "I would never recommend an affair . . . because the other consequences are too painful. Nevertheless, it is a fact that some spouses are jolted out of their complacency by a partner's affair."[11] A woman who discovered her husband was having an affair said: "In a sense, I'm almost grateful for discovering the affair. [Otherwise] we might never have come to know each other."[12] Dr. Sandra Finzi says this about her counseling methodology and goals when she counsels couples following an affair:

> When I coach couples through the aftermath of an affair, I focus away from the vivid drama of the pain, betrayal, gory details, and strong passions, and ask them to look at the silent world of companionship, understanding, affection, and solidarity in their relationship. At times, of course, we find that these emotional resources are lacking and these marriage[s] end because they are empty, not because of the affair.
>
> In most of these cases I have found that when the protagonists learn to distinguish between long-term, unshakable solidarity and passing infatuations, when they stop expecting passion from the person who has seen them before breakfast for 20 years, the marriage becomes more solid, based less on charged feelings—that change from moment to moment—and more on the solid ground of shared experience and compatibility tested by the years. . . .[13]

She goes on to say that there is a change in the attitudes with which each partner regards the drama of the affair. The adulterer no longer thinks his or her infatuated feelings mean that one's "true love" has been found. The faithful spouse no longer believes that something terrible is wrong with him or her, or that the marriage has always been a charade.

Finzi's end goal of therapy with the faithful partner is a good description of noncodependent living—that she not feel guilty about having devoted time to things other than her spouse, and that she be able to enjoy spending time on her own pursuits. The healthy graduate of her counseling is not consumed with worry about whether her spouse will be unfaithful again, for she has faith in their years of shared companionship, in God, and in her ability to make it alone. She shares the responsibility for making the marriage work.

Affairs are never right and never a good way to build a better marriage. But as good can come out of evil, so benefits can come from affairs, even though there are less painful and less sinful ways to accomplish these same purposes.

KEY IDEAS FROM CHAPTER 10

In marriage counseling following an affair, the following therapeutic tasks should be addressed: assisting in the rebuilding of trust, examining the affair together, identifying and working on other frustrations in the marriage, teaching communication and conflict-resolution skills, continuing the process of forgiveness, providing needed sex therapy, and helping the couple decide what and how to tell the children.

NOTES

1. Frank Pittman, *Private Lies: Infidelity and the Betrayal of Intimacy* (New York: Norton, 1989), 66.

2. Don-David Lusterman, "Marriage at the Turning Point," in *Family Therapy Networker*, May/June, 1989, 48.

3. Richard Stuart, "An Operant Interpersonal Program for Couples," in *Treating Relationships* D. H. L. Olson, ed. (Lake Mills, Iowa: Graphic, 1976)

4. Sherod Miller, Elam Nunnally, and Daniel Wackman, *Talking Together* (Littleton, Colo.: Interpersonal Communication Programs, 1979), and Sherod Miller et al. *Connecting with Self and Others* (Littleton, Colo.: Interpersonal Communication Programs, 1988). Further information about these books can

be gained by calling (303) 794–1764 or by writing to ICP, 7201 South Broadway, Littleton, CO 80122.

5. Les Carter, *The Prodigal Spouse: How to Survive Infidelity* (Nashville: Thomas Nelson, 1990), 212.

6. George A. Kelly, *The Psychology of Personal Constructs* (New York: Norton, 1955).

7. Leon Festinger, "Behavioral Support for Opinion Change," *Public Opinion Quarterly* 28 (1964), 404–17. Albert Bandura, E.B. Blanchard, and R. Ritter, "The Relative Efficacy of Desensitization and Modeling Approaches for Inducing Behavioral, Affective, and Attitudinal Changes," *Journal of Personality and Social Psychology* 13 (1969): 173–99.

8. Taken from Jennifer P. Schneider, *Back from Betrayal: Recovering from His Affairs* (San Francisco: Harper and Row/Hazelden, 1988), 174–79.

9. The above suggestions were taken from Schneider, 197–201 and Daniel Dolesh and Sherelynn Lehman, *Love Me, Love Me Not: How to Survive Infidelity* (New York: McGraw-Hill, 1985), 139–46.

10. Marcia Laswell, quoted by Susan Squires in "Extramarital Affair," *Glamour,* September 1980), 278.

11. Ruth Westheimer, quoted by Susan Jacoby in "After His Affair," *McCall's,* February 1982, 121–22.

12. Don-David Lusterman, "Marriage at the Turning Point," in the *Family Therapy Networker,* (May/June, 1989), 51.

13. Sandra Finzi, "Cosi Fan Tutte" in *The Family Therapy Networker,* (May/June, 1989), 32–33.

PART THREE

Affair Prevention for Couples and Church Groups

Chapter Eleven

Premarital Preparation

IDEALLY, AFFAIR PREVENTION BEGINS with the lives of one's parents and grandparents. For reasons we do not fully understand, the likelihood of infidelity in a marriage is increased by the presence of infidelity in the family of origin. And the likelihood of infidelity there is affected by the faithfulness or unfaithfulness of the grandparents. However, since couples have no control over either their parents' or grandparents' behavior, the earliest point at which they can intervene to decrease the likelihood of infidelity in their marriage is during their dating relationship. This can be done in a number of ways.

DEVELOPING A STRONG FRIENDSHIP

A large percentage of couples marry on the basis of romantic feelings or sexual attraction. Many do not recognize that the core of any good marriage is not romantic feelings nor sexual attraction, but a deep friendship.

Such friendships take time to develop. In the process of developing friendships people find that they have more in common with some people than with others. They also find that their expectations and preferences are more compatible with some people than with others. With certain people more effort is required to keep a positive relationship going or to keep problems from disrupting the relationship. Conversation is more difficult with them and they have fewer interests in common. In the process of developing a relationship, some people discover they have important differences of opinion, or that they tend to misinterpret each other's characteristic behavior. The only way one can know that a comfortable friendship will be possible with another person is through spending time, allowing that relationship to develop, and becoming aware of similarities and differences in expectations, preferences, opinions, and characteristic behaviors.

There are many reasons why it is best to postpone sexual involvement until marriage. The most important is that God commands it, but there are several others. Many sexual problems have their origin in premarital involvements. Sexual activity before marriage can cause guilt for both partners, guilt that affects their sexual relationship in marriage. If one person was less willing to become involved sexually than the other but did so out of fear of losing that person, or out of a lack of assertiveness, he or she may transfer conscious or repressed resentment into the marriage which may affect the marital sexual relationship for many years (see the case of Joe and Donna, pp. 228–29).

Premarital sex can result in venereal diseases, some of which are incurable or fatal. A premarital pregnancy can cause a hastily planned marriage, with ensuing problems that often emerge in coming years, or can lead to an abortion with its attendant guilt.

Postponing sexual involvement until after marriage is particularly relevant in this discussion for three reasons. First, if a couple becomes sexually involved, this drains off much of the energy that could otherwise be spent developing a quality friendship. Second, sexual excitement may sweep a couple into marriage and so cloud the decision making process that neither person knows if a deep enough friendship exists—a friendship that can sustain a lifelong marriage. The couple may discover after marriage that there is little depth to their relationship besides the sexual. Third, learning the discipline of feeling very close to a person without allowing the relationship to become sexualized provides important training for later temptations to infidelity and also gives both persons the opportunity to learn whether the potential partner is willing to say no to an improper sexual relationship.

Some individuals cannot form friendships because they have difficulty talking with others on a deep, personal level. This may be due to a lack of knowledge of conversational skills, or the person's own self-talk may cause such anxiety that he or she cannot relate easily. Or it may be because the person has never known people who have deep friendships with members of the opposite sex. For some people, all of these factors are relevant. Two helpful resources for couples with these problems are the books *Conversationally Speaking* and *The Friendship Factor*.

Conversationally Speaking, by Alan Garner, is an easy-to-read book which teaches people basic conversational skills and also discusses self-talk and its role in creating anxiety. Although it is not a Christian book and contains a few elements of a secular mind-set which one might wish were not included, this is a helpful book to recommend to any adolescent or adult who has difficulty conversing.

The Friendship Factor, by Alan Loy McGinnis, is a well-written Christian book that shows the importance of setting aside time to allow friendships to develop. In an age when many young men may have questions about whether having deep friendships is a "manly" thing, this wise book easily dispels that misconception. This is an excellent, nonthreatening book for any young couple to read before marriage, for it will encourage them to let their friendship become the core of their marriage.[1]

BECOMING AWARE OF MARITAL EXPECTATIONS

In conversations as friends a man and woman will become aware of many of the dreams, hopes, and expectations each has for their marriage and their life. However, because each of them wants the acceptance of the other, they may consciously or unconsciously avoid discussing areas where they think incompatibilities exist. One way gently to lead such a couple to look at all areas of their relationship is for the counselor to take a comprehensive marital inventory. This tool can help them see themselves and each other's perceptions of themselves. One such inventory is the PREPARE premarital inventory.[2]

The PREPARE inventory is a carefully developed psychological test that can be used effectively by pastors as well as mental health professionals. The test results are presented in ways that do not require graduate-level training in statistics and psychometrics in order to understand or interpret them. There are two parallel versions of the test, one to be used when neither person is bringing a child into the marriage, and another when one or more children are brought to the present marriage. (This is a very important difference, for if couples do not work out their separate expectations about how to relate to children from a former marriage, the new marriage has a strong likelihood of failing.)

In addition to the counselor's emphasis upon the use of conversation and a structured premarital inventory to help couples recognize the expectations they are bringing to marriage, the counselor will also want to do something further. Each potential marriage partner needs to look at the potential spouse's family for clues concerning expectations the future spouse may have. Then the couple needs to discuss anything which, based on their observations, has made either of them uncomfortable.

For example, Roy and Sandy had been dating for some time before Sandy had an opportunity to see Roy's parents interact in their home. When she did, she became highly indignant. Roy's parents were both professionals, and both worked full-time in the same field. However, when they arrived home in the evening Roy's father habitually retired to his favorite recliner while he read the paper or watched television, and his wife took care of all of the housework and the meals. If he wanted something to drink or eat, he would call out what he wanted, and his wife would bring it to him. This had been customary behavior with them for many years, and Roy's mother gave no outward indication that she was unhappy with this "division" of labor.

Sandy, a mild feminist at heart, was incensed at Roy's father's behavior. However, she thought that Roy might not be open to criticism of his parents, and she did not want to lose Roy (no one else had dated her seriously). Therefore she said nothing, hoping that Roy would not imitate his father in this regard. Unfortunately, within a few weeks of their wedding Roy started to expect of her the same things his father had expected of his mother. Sandy soon found out that Roy had a long list of services which he believed a male was entitled to from his wife. He had not expected these services from her as his girlfriend or even as his fiancee, but once she became his wife he let her know what they were. He looked upon her indignant protests as totally unreasonable, for the expectations he had of her were no different than his father's expectations of his mother. And his mother had never indicated that she was unhappy with their arrangement. Roy looked upon Sandy's anger as an indication of her spiritual immaturity and unwillingness to be biblically submissive. Sandy was quite sure that his sense of entitlement and his expectations were the things that were biblically out of line.

When last I heard of Roy and Sandy they had gone through several Christian counselors, with little change in their attitudes and little improvement in their relationship. It would have been much better for them both if Sandy, upon viewing the behavior of Roy's parents, had discussed that with Roy before their marriage. Then they could have experienced each other's intransigence on this issue, and made a decision about the viability of marriage in light of it.

DEVELOPING A PERSONAL DEFINITION OF FIDELITY

It is wise for every couple to realize that at several times throughout their marriage one partner will not perfectly meet the needs of the other. Frustrations will develop between them, and one or both of them may be tempted to become involved with someone else. Such couples will be better prepared to meet those situations if they have thought about it beforehand and made commitments to each other concerning their actions in such circumstances.

It may be well for each individual to identify the kind of situation in which he or she believes the most vulnerability could be experienced, and to plan a response that could be used. If either partner comes to the marriage with additional risk factors (e.g., one's parents had affairs, he or she was active sexually before marriage, or one [or both] of them was emotionally or sexually unfaithful to the other while dating), it is even more important for the couple to define what "fidelity" means and make explicit commitments to each other in this regard. Some couples might even write out personal commitments, and read those promises to each other as part of an anniversary tradition.

LIVING ON YOUR OWN BEFORE MARRIAGE

I believe it is wise for every young woman to live on her own (either with or without roommates, but away from her family of origin) and become trained in a skilled vocation before she marries. I have three reasons for making this recommendation.

First, if a woman goes directly from her parents' home to her own home as a bride, at some time during her life she will probably resent the fact that she never had a time when she was able to make her own decisions. She may become angry, realizing that she has never known a time when she has not had to submit either to her father or her husband. With Satan's tempting influence, she may start to believe that she needs to experience this kind of freedom if she is ever to be truly happy.

Many Christian wives have left their families either temporarily or permanently in pursuit of the happiness they believed they would find once they were no longer under the authority of a man. Having a period of autonomy before marriage gives women a more realistic picture of the advantages and disadvantages of that condition, and allows them to develop their own identities.

Second, the experience of learning a skilled trade or profession increases the woman's self-esteem and sense of confidence in a way that is probably as valuable as the actual skills themselves. It is hard for a person with no skills or profession not to feel codependent to some degree.

Third, most young married couples will need two incomes in order to provide many of the necessities of a young family today. Not having any marketable skill puts a woman in a very dependent position if her husband becomes unfaithful. Both of them know that it would be extremely difficult for her to divorce him and live on child-support payments (if they have children) and what she could make as an unskilled worker. Such knowledge by itself puts a woman in a codependent position. For all of these reasons, a husband and wife will have a better chance of a healthier marriage based on mutual respect and healthy self-confidence if the wife has spent some time on her own and developed her vocational skills before marriage.

I believe it is also wise for a young man to spend some time on his own between living in his family of origin and marriage, although for different reasons. First, when living at home he may be accustomed to having much of his income available as spending money, never having to restrict his spending because most living expenses are paid by the parents. He may continue those patterns into marriage unless he has an interim time of being responsible for his own expenses and learning conservative spending habits.

Second, many young men grow up accustomed to having their mothers take care of many family necessities (e.g., buying food and clothes, preparing meals and cleaning up afterward, washing and ironing clothes, and keeping the house clean and picked up). If they never learn to do these things themselves, they may not be able to help with these chores when necessary nor will they have an adequate sense of empathy and appreciation for their wives.

Third, with the economic realities that face us now, it is probably going to be necessary increasingly that both marital partners work part- or full-time. In that situation it is clearly unfair for men not to share housework. For these reasons I believe it is beneficial for young men to experience living on their own, as well as women, before marriage.

DEVELOPING REALISTIC EXPECTATIONS ABOUT BEING "IN LOVE"

We have talked about this point at various places throughout this book. To be healthily prepared for marriage, a couple needs to realize that the psychological experience of being "in love" is a very specific experience which is not permanent. It is important that they replace the unrealistic expectation that being in love lasts permanently with a more realistic understanding of mature, committed, married love. Otherwise they may assume, as the in-love experience fades, that something vital is waning in their marriage, and they may go searching for it in other relationships.

In an analogous fashion a couple may be encouraged to decide which of the in-love behavior patterns they wish to retain as permanent behaviors in their marriage, and which ones are unnecessary. If there is not an explicit discussion of this, it is not uncommon for many of the caring behaviors of the dating relationship to cease during the first year of marriage, especially if problems develop in the relationship.

A longer rather than a relatively brief dating period helps couples learn more about each other's expectations and behavior patterns. Also, it allows both people to make a more fully informed decision about whether they will be easily compatible.

A longer relationship also gives each of them a more accurate picture of what the other partner is like. People can usually hide behind an agreeable façade for a few months. Longer relationships will help both potential marriage partners know the other person more fully. A longer dating relationship will help each person discern whether one's partner has a personality disorder or a sexual addiction that will make infidelity likely. For those who believe that they have found the perfect person for them, and must get married immediately, Botwin's statement is always relevant: "Relationships that take off like rockets are generally fueled by neurosis."[3]

CHANGING CODEPENDENT BEHAVIOR BEFORE MARRIAGE

Many a woman adapts to everything she believes her partner wants while dating (sometimes men do this also, but more commonly it is women). If he loves football, she attends football games with him, never giving him the slightest hint that she really believes that watching football is boring and a terrible waste of time. If he is on three softball teams, she adapts to this, without having an honest discussion about whether this pattern will allow them to have a healthy marriage relationship. If he makes impulsive financial decisions without discussion or long-range planning, she says nothing and secretly hopes that he will become more mature in his financial dealings when he is married. If he has a habit of making decisions that he knows would be unpopular with her without consulting her, she says nothing and hopes that he will become more sensitive once they are married.

All of these codependent behaviors allow the marriage to get off to an unhealthy start because they reinforce the typical male's expectation that his wife should do most of the adapting, especially in areas about which he feels strongly. If she passively adapts to him throughout their dating period, and then becomes assertive after marriage, he may respond negatively because he had grown accustomed to her making most of the adjustments. Now he believes she has changed the rules of the game.

What more frequently happens is that a woman is codependent during the dating period, and during the marriage

tries to suppress her anger about his insensitivity and failure
to consider her in decision making. Her anger may erupt in an
occasional aggressive outburst, but when she is aggressive she
feels guilty and often retracts her legitimate frustration in the
process of apologizing for how she expressed that frustration.
As a result the husband's behavior does not change. And often
these frustrations, because they are not dealt with, allow walls
to develop that put one or both partners at risk for an affair.

In contrast, being willing to share opinions and preferences
openly during the dating period helps both people approach
the relationship as one in which there will be mutual give and
take, where each one's opinions and preferences are treated
with equal respect. This helps the couple recognize whether
there is genuine compatibility based on many shared interests
and beliefs, as opposed to the pseudo-compatibility which occurs when one or both persons in the dating relationship are
codependent. Equally as important, this helps the woman see
how the man will respond to her differentness. If he responds
with respect and a willingness to meet her halfway, this is
healthy. If he responds with frustration to her differentness
and attempts to manipulate or intimidate her into doing things
his way, and is not willing to reexamine his responses, it is best
for her to look for another marriage partner.

Even when the future mate displays behavior that makes
them feel uncomfortable, some women maintain their
codependent behavior during dating because of two self-
statements they make, either consciously or unconsciously.
These are: (1) Hopefully, he will change after marriage, and
(2) having him is better than having no man. Both of these
self-statements need to be disputed. In regard to the first, if
she is codependent throughout their dating period and suddenly becomes assertive after they are married, she should
not expect him to welcome her "new personality" with enthusiasm. He married her thinking she was one way. It now
seems unfair to him if she says that the way she was during
dating was not her true personality, and she now wants him
to respond positively to who she really is. He is more likely

to believe she tricked him than embrace his newly discovered wife with joy. Secondly, the dating period is the time when she has the most psychological leverage with him. If he is unwilling to change for her then, he is even less likely to do so after marriage.

The second self-statement (having him is better than having no man) is both codependent and wrong. The reason it is *codependent* is that she is looking for a man to make her happiness complete. It is neither healthy nor fair to expect someone else to make us happy—our happiness and our sense of identity should be based on our recognition of who we are in Christ, and on knowing that we are living a life of obedience before him. This statement is *wrong* based on both clinical interviews and objective measures of happiness—as a group, women in unhealthy marriages are less happy than women who are single.

The practical implication of this research for women is this: You will be happier if you express yourself assertively while dating, allowing your partner to clearly experience your true personality and preferences. This is true even if it means losing one or more boyfriends. The woman who "captures" a man by behaving codependently while dating, and then finds out in marriage that he is not interested in valuing her ideas and goals when they differ from his, may find herself overwhelmingly vulnerable to an affair.

There is one other codependent behavior that is important to identify here—the tendency some women have to drop all their women and men friends once they meet "Mr. Wonderful." This is unhealthy for a number of reasons. First, by dropping her other friends she becomes overly dependent on her boyfriend, expecting him to meet all of her emotional needs. This is an unrealistic expectation, even in the best of marriages.

Second, this does not allow the couple to work out mutually acceptable guidelines about friendships outside the marriage. A woman may find, once she is married, that her husband resents any time she spends with other friends, no matter how innocent the reasons for gathering are, and she may find that he is totally unwilling to reconsider his position. If she had continued to be involved with these friends while dating, she would have experienced his jealousy or insecurity before making a final decision about marriage, and may have been able to make a wiser one as a result.

Third, if a woman drops all of her other friends to focus exclusively on her boyfriend, she is implicitly saying that he is so important that she will drop everything else in her life to attend exclusively to his needs. We men have enough narcissism that we do not need women encouraging us to believe that that is a reasonable expectation. In the dating relationship we need to experience the real person our partner is in his or her own right, with real needs, expectations, and friendships. The way men and women respond to that reality can be an important clue as to the wisdom of marriage to a given person.

SOME IMPORTANT PREMARITAL COMMITMENTS

A large church in the Atlanta area has a rather unusual requirement before their pastoral staff will agree to marry a couple: The couple must agree to take a course in marriage communication skills (offered as one of the adult Sunday School electives) during their first year of marriage.[4] A church that incorporates such a program into the Sunday School electives can offer it to all newlyweds and also to any other couples in the church who wish to take it. In this way it can serve a preventive function for all the families in the church, not just the newly married.

Another premarital recommendation is to have every couple voluntarily commit themselves to read Willard Harley's book *His Needs, Her Needs: Building An Affair-Proof Marriage* sometime between the third and twelfth months of their marriage. As discussed in an earlier chapter, Dr. Harley identifies the five most important psychological needs of men and women. He spends a chapter discussing each one. His insights are crucial for strengthening marriages, for the top five needs of men and women are different. Therefore, if we love our mates as we would like to be loved, we may miss their most important needs unless we are helped to see them.

There is a reason for recommending both of these activities during the first year of marriage rather than before marriage. During the premarital period, the in-love phenomenon causes many couples to be oblivious to the practical issues they will face as a married couple. They are convinced that love will cause every problem to disappear as if by magic, and there is little that anyone can do to convince them otherwise. By about the third month of marriage most delusions of this sort have been adequately dispelled, and a couple may be more motivated to learn skills and gain other knowledge which can help their marriage work better. Of course, there are premarital couples who come to a pastor or counselor because their relationships are already foundering. In those instances a couple is ready to benefit from programs such as *Talking Together*, and they will also find much that is useful in Harley's book.

KEY IDEAS FROM CHAPTER 11

Couples who are dating or engaged can reduce the chances of infidelity occurring within marriage in the following ways:
- Developing a strong friendship during the dating period, postponing sexual involvement until marriage
- Ascertaining whether their expectations, preferences, opinions on important matters, and characteristic behaviors are compatible
- Observing the marriage of one's dating partner's parents, and discussing any marital patterns with which they feel uncomfortable
- Identifying the situations in which one believes he or she would be most vulnerable to infidelity and developing a plan should the situation arise
- Living on one's own and developing career skills before marriage
- Developing realistic expectations about being "in love"

- Changing codependent behavior *before* marriage
- Committing themselves to take a course in communication and conflict resolution either before or during the first year of marriage
- Reading and discussing a book such as *His Needs, Her Needs* during the first year of marriage to sensitize oneself to the emotional needs each person has.

NOTES

1. Alan McGinnis, *The Friendship Factor* (Minneapolis: Augsburg, 1979).

2. Further information concerning the PREPARE inventory can be gained by writing to PREPARE, P.O. Box 190, Minneapolis, Minnesota 55458–0190, or by calling 1–800–331–1661.

3. Carol Botwin, *Men Who Can't Be Faithful* (New York: Warner Books, 1988)

4. They use the twelve-hour Talking Together course developed by Interpersonal Communication Programs, 7201 South Broadway, Littleton, CO 80122. The telephone number is (303) 794–1764. This course comes with a very thorough syllabus so that it can be led by anyone willing to study it. There are many different skills-based programs available: Essential ingredients are that the program teaches discrete communication skills, gives couples a chance to practice those skills, and allows couples to receive feedback on their use of the skills as they practice them.

Chapter Twelve

Maintaining a Strong Marriage

THROUGHOUT THIS BOOK we have discussed many factors which can lead to infidelity, even in marriages of committed Christians. This chapter will attempt to summarize some ways we can use those awarenesses in a preventive manner to reduce the likelihood that we, or our marriage partners, will become vulnerable to affairs.

CONVERSATION, COMMUNICATIONS, AND FRIENDSHIP

Several lines of research evidence indicate the importance of communication and friendship to a healthy marriage. And conversely, the lack of a solid core of friendship in a marriage puts that marriage at risk for infidelity. Dolores Curran received input from more than five hundred professionals in the areas of education, church, health, and family counseling in her attempt to identify the marks of positive family life. From a list of fifty-six choices, the respondents selected the fifteen traits they believed were most prominent in healthy families. They are listed here in the order in which they were chosen by these respondents.

According to this interdisciplinary group of professionals, the healthy family

1. communicates and listens
2. affirms and supports one another
3. teaches respect for others
4. develops a sense of trust
5. has a sense of play and humor
6. exhibits a sense of shared responsibility
7. teaches a sense of right and wrong
8. has a strong sense of family in which rituals and traditions abound
9. has a balance of interaction among members
10. has a shared religious core
11. respects the privacy of one another
12. values service to others
13. fosters family table time and conversation
14. shares leisure time
15. admits to and seeks help with problems.[1]

Although there are role distinctions between parents and children, the hallmark of a healthy family is that family members treat one another as good friends treat each other.

Conversely, as we have seen in a number of studies reviewed in previous chapters, in research with both men and women who have had affairs the primary problem cited, which led to their affairs, was lack of communication. Both men and women wanted someone with whom they could be open, and who would listen to them nonjudgmentally.

Alan McGinnis put it succinctly when he said, "If 'love' has fled, it probably means that some of the things that can go wrong with any friendship have gone wrong, and usually those can be corrected."[2] What are the components of a healthy friendship? First, a good friend is a good listener. Dr. Robert Sternberg has said, "If you want to make a major improvement in your relationship in a minimum of time, try listening carefully to what your partner says, and—equally important—show your empathy by putting yourself in his or her place."[3]

If you want a long-term marriage, let your partner know you appreciate him or her. Make sure you spend enough time together. Participate in activities you both enjoy. Spend time talking about topics of mutual interest as well as sharing deeply with each other. Develop the various kinds of intimacy within your marriage.

Friends establish priorities that allow their friendship to grow. A partner should always come before one's job and children. One's career provides a way to meet the material needs of his or her spouse and family. It is a means to an end, not the end itself. Unfortunately, a career can begin to absorb all of one's time and energy: it can become a mistress of sorts, and can destroy a marriage just as surely as any other mistress.

The marriage partner should always be closer to the other spouse than to their children. When marital problems develop, however, we may be tempted (and this is more common for women than for men) to withdraw our emotional energy from the marriage and invest it in the children. A husband resents this, for his wife is putting their children first in her emotional priorities, rather than him. Children feel most safe in a family when the core of the family is the husband and wife's relationship to each other.

Each spouse should take the initiative in meeting a partner's needs. In many distressed marriages, spouses say through their behavior "I will meet your needs once you start meeting mine." As one partner waits, so does the other, and neither's needs are met. If both spouses take the initiative in meeting the other's needs, usually both sets of needs will eventually be met.

A good friendship allows the relationship to change, for people are constantly growing and changing. A relationship with unchangeable rules eventually dies as the unchanging rules start to feel like emotional strait jackets to the imprisoned partners. Healthy relationships allow the people in them to change, and make that change easier for the people involved by discussing the reasons for change.

No controversy exists on this point: An unfulfilling sexual relationship places men at high risk of infidelity. From objective psychological assessments such as those of Harley to more informal interview research such as that of Penney, Botwin, or Gordon, a primary reason for male infidelity within marriage was found to be nonexistent or infrequent sex, or very inhibited and uncreative sex play. A partner who is *significantly* overweight is also listed as a risk factor, but not as frequently as nonexistent or infrequent sex.

Alexandra Penney found that, according to most men, women do not know how to satisfy them sexually.[4] In her book, *How to Keep Your Man Monogamous*, she identifies five mistakes that she believes women commonly make that cause them not to fulfil their partners' sexual needs or desires. Those five are:

1. Women don't make time for sex, and they don't take adequate time for sex.

2. Women aren't active enough during sex play.

3. Women aren't willing to surrender themselves totally to the joys of love-making, either because of anxiety or because their minds are wandering.

4. Women confuse sex and love. They always associate the two, whereas men sometimes want to express pure sex, sometimes sex and love.

5. Women believe that the importance of sex goes down over time. There are differences among researchers and writers on this point. Most believe that sexual desire in men gradually decreases with age. However, research by Cimbalo, Faling, and Monsaw found that "over time the importance of sex increased."[5]

Penney articulates what she calls The Golden Rule of Love-Making, which is, "Don't do unto him as you would have him do unto you."[6] Women usually want pleasuring over their entire bodies, and with regard to genital stimulation, a very light, slow touch. Men generally want stimulation primarily directed to the genital area, and want a firmer, stronger pressure. Thus if women stimulate men the way they themselves would like to be stimulated, their men may not be aroused. Penney suggests that a woman can satisfy her man more fully by finding out what he wants, and she can do this by asking two simple sets of questions: "Do you like this better than this?" and "How does this feel?" "Is this as good?"

Women appear less likely to have an affair primarily because of sexual dissatisfaction, although this does not necessarily mean that husbands do a better job of fulfilling their sexual needs. One interesting piece of information is that religious women, as a group, reported a higher level of satisfaction with their sex lives than less religious women.[7] In a *Redbook* survey 100,000 women, most of whom were married, answered questions about their marriage and sexual lives. The more religious a woman described herself, the more likely she was to describe her marriage and sex life positively. Religious women were more likely to discuss sex freely with their husbands, feel satisfied with the frequency of intercourse, and consistently reach orgasm during intercourse. This research would seem to discredit the notion that religious people live more sexually repressed and less sexually fulfilling lives than their less religious counterparts, at least with regard to women.

Penney's Golden Rule of Love-Making applies both ways: We men need to constantly remind ourselves that the same kinds of touch that might be stimulating to us may be unpleasant or even painful for our wives, and use the same sensitivity in asking what pleases them as we would like them to use with us. Men and women differ in another significant way. A woman needs much more pleasuring than does a man in order to experience a climax. And this means more time must be given her in foreplay. Whereas a young man can be ready for orgasm with less than a minute of stimulation, most women will need between ten and twenty minutes of pleasuring before they reach orgasm.

Another important difference between men and women, alluded to earlier, is that men sometimes enjoy sex for a variety of nonromantic reasons, such as tension relief, distraction from unpleasant situations or feelings, or in response to something or someone other than their wives. Women, who usually want sex to be paired with romance and affection, sometimes feel hurt or frustrated when their husbands do not feel likewise. We men need to be sensitive and responsive to that fact.

Developing mutual sexual fulfillment in marriage is related to three main factors—the general healthiness of the marriage relationship, the comfort both partners feel in talking about what pleases them sexually and in asking the same from their partners, and acquiring information on male and female sexual response. In chapter 11 I have given the names of four books which are widely used within Christian circles and which contain much good information on male and female sexuality.

With the resources available today, no Christian couple needs to have a boring or unfulfilling sexual life. If discussions with one's partner and reading do not provide the information needed to improve this area of one's marriage, consultation with a counselor who has specialized training in sex therapy may provide the needed answers.

NONSEXUAL AFFECTION

According to Harley's research, the most important emotional need of married women as a group is the desire for nonsexual affection. Just as strongly as the average man wants a fulfilling sexual relationship, his wife desires affection that does not have sex as its end goal. This causes conflict for many couples because men, in the expression of affection, easily become sexually aroused. A woman, wanting simple affection, may be turned off by her husband's preoccupation (or so it seems to her) with sex, and may begin refusing to display affection (which she really wants) because that always seems to lead to intercourse.

How can husbands and wives learn to show nonsexual affection to each other again? One way is to adopt the Caring Days exercises found on page 230–32. Another way is to begin doing things which the majority of men and women have indicated please them. A number of years ago psychologist Michael Campion asked several hundred women what actions of their husbands made them feel loved and happy. Their most common responses were:

A wife felt loved when her husband:

- prayed with her
- complimented her in front of the children
- cleaned the bathroom
- asked her for her opinion on a decision he had to make
- went to church with the family
- kissed her without sex as an object
- complimented her
- babysat so that she could have a night out
- opened the door for her
- accepted her for what she was and let her be herself
- took her for a walk
- fixed a meal
- sent her a flower
- told her she was beautiful
- had a good, open conversation with her[8]

Dr. Campion also asked several hundred husbands what things, when their wives did them, made them feel loved and cared for. Listed below are some of their most common answers:

A typical man felt loved when his wife:

- prayed for him while he was at work
- had a good, open conversation with him
- kept his favorite food in the refrigerator
- told him she was happy with his salary

- did not criticize him in front of others
- supported him in the disciplining of their children
- gave him a chance to express his frustrations when he arrived home from work
- listened carefully to what he had to say without prejudging
- respected him and let him know it
- told him she was proud of his success[9]

Dr. Carl Brecheen, who has led many seminars on marital intimacy, suggests that an important way to build marital intimacy is to show nonsexual affection for one minute at each of the following four critical junctures of the day: the first moment you are awake together in the morning, the last moment before the first one leaves for work, the first moment when you see each other after returning home from work, and the last moment of your waking day. By suspending other activities and thoughts and showing nonsexual affection at each of these times we can help our partners be without us for significant periods of the day and still know they are loved.[10]

Another way of keeping romance alive in a marriage is by dating. Rick Bundschuh and Dave Gilbert, who have written *Dating Your Mate*,[11] recommend going out for a date, even as infrequently as once every other month. They suggest that dating can enrich a relationship that is stagnating because of an overly full schedule. By planning the date a week or so ahead of time, the couple can enjoy the anticipation of the date for several days and thus increase their enjoyment of it. Group activities that can enhance affection in a marriage include involvement in planned activities, such as Marriage Encounter or Marriage Enrichment.

RECREATIONAL COMPANIONSHIP

According to Harley's research, the second strongest need that men have is the desire to do enjoyable, recreational things with the marriage partner. A common reason given by men for an affair is that they wanted a relationship in which they could get away from constant responsibilities. They wanted a break, and usually they wanted someone pleasant to enjoy that break with them. If the wife always has more work to do, or if she can never leave responsibilities behind and just focus on recreation for its own sake, the man might decide to go alone; and eventually he may find someone there who enjoys the same activity.

Developing intimacy in recreational activities probably requires changes for both husbands and wives. Both need to recognize the importance of taking time away from the constant demands of work and other things to spend a while together in a recreational setting. For some this will mean laying aside perfectionistic tendencies about housework or workaholic tendencies toward one's career (there will always be something more that could or should be done). For others it may mean looking at the combination of activities which are using up all of one's time, and cutting out one or more "good" activities so that one has time for recreation as a couple. Many of us may have difficulty here, for if the choice is between a "good" working activity and recreation, we feel we must choose the working activity. But God designated one day in seven for rest. Constant working leads to psychological burnout and distressed marriages. It is appropriate to take time for recreation.

Doing this will generally mean putting a moratorium on discussing problems during recreational times. For both it will mean experimenting with different kinds of recreational activities until they find one or more that both enjoy. Probably no activity should be scratched from the list of possibilities until both people have seriously tried it at least twice. Husbands should not expect their wives to join them in activities that are unfulfilling for them, nor should wives expect their husbands to join them in activities which their husbands don't enjoy.

This is not intended to imply that husbands and wives should spend all of their recreational time together. In a healthy marriage there should be time for activities together and those enjoyed separately. However, building the marriage may mean shifting the relative amounts of time spent in various activities so that a larger portion of one's recreational time can be spent on activities the couple enjoys together. If the couple resist this, they may need to explore other issues in the relationship, issues that relate to why one or both of them want to spend their recreational time separately.

For couples who are very cautious, Weber and Simring suggest that it is healthy to allow a little excitement into their lives. They suggest that a person is less likely to look for excitement elsewhere if he or she can do exciting things with the other partner.[12] Norman Lobenz has said, "There is no better safeguard against infidelity than a vital, interesting marriage."[13]

CONFLICT RESOLUTION

It is important to address problems as they arise. Lawyer Harriet Pilpel, who specializes in family law, comments: "I have seen a number of women whose husbands, according to them, 'walked out on them without any warning.' When I talked further with them it turns out there were serious problems in the marriage. But the wife did not confront them herself, no less ask her husband to confront them with her."[14]

Weber and Simring agree. They advise marital partners to take a proactive stance when either one senses something is wrong in the marriage. If a person sees signs that his or her partner is unhappy, or if he or she is unhappy, the authors urge that partner to talk with the other about it. The spouse should push for honest discussion, even if it means angry words at first. He or she should not remain passive, allowing the marriage to drift toward an affair or a divorce court, but should fight for a healthy marriage.[15] The Apostle Paul was probably referring to the idea of not letting problems go unresolved when he commanded, "Never go to bed angry—don't give the devil that sort of foothold" (Eph. 4:27, PHILLIPS. See also Matt. 5:23–24).

Most people unconsciously approach a conflict with the idea that either my opponent wins and I lose, or I win and my opponent loses. This kind of mentality often causes conflicts to be more aggressive than they need to be. In the last several years counselors have identified several kinds of workable compromises, approaches in which both parties can end up gaining part or all of what they desire through negotiation.

Negotiation takes into account both person's goals. It keeps us from entering a discussion as if the other person were an opponent. The other person, instead, becomes a collaborator and partner who is also trying to develop a mutually satisfying solution. A workable compromise might take any of the following forms:[16]

1. *Find a mutually satisfying alternative.* This approach involves having both people identify their goals and the plans they have for reaching those goals. Then they try to find an action plan which allows both of them to reach those goals (or at least an equal portion of each person's goal).

2. *Develop a quid pro quo contract.* This Latin term means "this for that." Person A agrees to help Person B reach one of her goals if Person B will agree to help Person A reach one of his goals.

3. *Take turns* (this is self-explanatory).

4. *Seek separate solutions.* Two people agree to separate temporarily and pursue their respective interests, and come back together again after accomplishing their goals.

5. *Allow an involved third party to decide.* If Person A and Person B both want different things, and Person C will be going with them, ask Person C to voice his or her preference (without telling C of the previous conflict). A and B agree to accept whatever C decides.

6. *Practice positive yielding.* If none of the above solutions creates an acceptable compromise, practice positive yielding. This means that one partner, out of love and respect for the other, defers. It is good if both people are willing to positively yield part of the time. The biblical base for trying to find workable compromises and positive yielding is Philippians 2:4, "Each of you should look not only to your own interests, but

also to the interests of other," and Ephesians 5:21, "Submit to one another out of reverence for Christ."

AVOIDING HIGH-RISK SITUATIONS

In chapter 2 we discussed several high-risk situations where affairs can develop. Using Kreitler's typology, some of the more common ones are the "Be a Good Neighbor Affair," or the "Cup of Coffee Affair," or the "Office Affair." A statement by Carlfred Broderick, which Kreitler cites, applies to all high-risk situations: "If you find yourself in a situation involving delicious privacy with an attractive member of the opposite sex, you should begin to look for ways to restructure [i.e., avoid or change] the situation."[17]

In addition to avoiding or restructuring situations that would put us in repeated, private contact with an attractive member of the opposite sex, it is wise to heed Mylander's words of caution: "A wise Christian husband will make a personal pact never to share love language or tender talk with someone other than his mate. This includes a note or card in the mail or even a phone call just to talk."[18]

Pittman discusses how people who form a friendship with a member of the opposite sex—a relationship that meets some of their normal and appropriate needs for friendship—may unintentionally be drawn into an affair. "Most often people are not seeking an alternative to their marriage but a supplement to it," he says. "They just want a friend for whatever [emotional needs] aren't getting [met] at home. Some people don't realize they can have friends of either gender without having to sexualize the friendship. . . . So they sexualize the friendship, and turn it inadvertently into something quite different from its original function [i.e., it becomes an affair instead of a friendship]."[19]

Not everyone agrees that it is wise for married persons to have deep friendships with members of the opposite sex. It is probably unwise to attempt close relationships with people of the opposite sex under the following conditions:

- if a person has had difficulty with infidelity in the past
- if one's marriage is poor (here it may be helpful to develop deep friendships with people of the *same* sex)
- if it is clear that the "friend" is not committed to recognizing the sanctity of one's marriage relationship

Alan McGinnis is one Christian psychologist who believes that under certain conditions it is possible and healthy to develop deep friendships with persons of the opposite sex. The following are excerpts from six guidelines he suggests for keeping sexual feelings under control and still enjoying deep friendships.

1. Don't trust yourself too far. Be aware of the ebb and flow of your sexual desire. . . . If you [are experiencing strong sexual feelings] exercise extra caution.

2. Select companions who have strong marriages themselves. If your friend is hungry for love, it may be very difficult to keep the relationship within bounds.

3. Be sensible about when and where you meet. Some settings are more sexual than others. . . .

4. Talk to your mate about your friendships. When meetings become clandestine, it is a danger signal that things are getting out of hand. Either bring yourself to tell your spouse about the progression of the friendship or get out.

5. Draw a line for physical contact. Find the amount of physical affection that is comfortable and safe for you, since no one can stay in control once sexual touching and kissing cross a certain boundary.

6. Bail out if necessary. Once in a while, no matter how much we try, a friendship with the opposite sex gets out of hand and we know where it is going to lead. If your marriage is precious to you, there is no question of what must be done, however great the pain—you back away.[20]

PREPARATION FOR HIGH-TEMPTATION DEVELOPMENTAL CRISES

It is important for each couple to make themselves aware of developmental situations that increase vulnerability to affairs. Chapter 2 discussed these developmental transitions more thoroughly. Some of the particularly dangerous ones include:

- Making the transition from romantic to married love
- Pregnancy and birth of children (the couple should plan for some private time [e.g., a date] at least once a month). The very fulfilling and demanding role of mothering can crowd out the important role of being a wife
- Extraordinary stress at work (the nonworking spouse needs to be particularly supportive during times of increased job stress)
- Experiences of failure or rejection
- Success (this can be dangerous in two ways: increased responsibilities may mean more fatigue with consequent loss of judgment, and pride)
- Male peers who are divorcing and enjoying the single life (may make fidelity sound boring to the husband)
- Female midlife crisis (if it occurs, it usually happens between ages thirty-five and forty)
- Male midlife crisis (if it occurs, it comes between forty and forty-five)
- End-of-decade birthdays (the spouse may wish to expend extra effort in strengthening the marriage relationship at these times)
- When one's partner is chronically ill

In short, whenever a couple is experiencing a developmental transition their lives are more unstable and unpredictable than usual. Particularly during such times it is important that each partner be physically and emotionally available to the other.

With the passing of time people change—their ideas, their expectations, and their needs are different. If partners do not stay emotionally connected to each other and allow each other to grow and change, they often find out that they have "grown apart." This can become an excuse for either an affair or a divorce.

Marriage relationships continually change as the individuals within that relationship change. At any given moment one or more emotional needs of one or both partners may go unfulfilled. This may be because the mate does not recognize the unmet need. Or there may not be time or energy to meet the need. Or this particular need was not important until now. Rather than allowing an unmet need to become an excuse for an affair, marriage partners should commit themselves to tell one another of changes in their needs. They should give and receive the assurance that they will be faithful to each other even when it is impossible to meet each other's needs at every moment. There should be a reciprocal commitment between them that both will make a best effort to meet the other's needs, given the energy and time available.

Of all of the developmental transitions, the male midlife crisis seems to be the one most vulnerable to an affair. A male "falls in love" with a woman twenty to forty years younger than himself. Barbara Gordon, who has studied this phenomenon of older men with younger women extensively, has identified ten factors which she believes help *prevent* these kinds of affairs. These factors are:[21]

1. A parental model of a strong, committed marriage,

2. Quiet confidence in self, not performance oriented [those persons with personality disorders that lead to promiscuity often have a very low self-esteem, which they try to buttress by constant "conquests," sexual or otherwise],

3. Belief that the adoration some young women give older men is false,

4. Having a wife who is a best friend,

5. Recognizing that all men have occasional fantasies, but making a clear distinction between having a fantasy and acting it out,

6. Deep involvement in a social community [religious community] that reflects their values,

7. Interweaving their lives with their spouses and changing along with them,

8. Belief in each other's trustworthiness and capabilities,

9. Recognizing the difference between pleasure and joy, and choosing the latter, and

10. Giving each other permission to become what they want to become.

DEVELOPING ANTI-TEMPTATION STRATEGIES

IDENTIFYING PERSONAL AREAS OF VULNERABILITY

Anyone who is serious about affair prevention should think about the various situations that would place himself or herself at high risk for infidelity. A counselor can also help both individuals identify situations or types of relationships which are particularly dangerous for each of them.

For example, one male when thinking about this found that he was at that time tempted by two women, but he was surprised to realize the particular two toward whom he was attracted. They were physically unattractive and neither one appealed interpersonally to him. But both women showed him very high respect, and he realized that this was what made him feel attracted to them.

The particular area of vulnerability, and the reason for it, will vary from person to person. This may even vary for the same person over time. The important thing is for the man or woman to identify the area or areas of personal vulnerability and think about them in order to be better prepared for temptation when it comes.

Earlier in this book we discussed the situation of the Christian who says "affairs will never present a temptation to me." To such believers I would repeat the words of Ellen Williams, "If you are thinking to yourself, an affair could never happen to me, you are in trouble. To believe that we are immune leaves us wide open and unprotected."[22]

MAKING AN EXPLICIT COMMITMENT TO FIDELITY

No one can be a good enough partner to ensure that his or her mate will never cheat (this is one of the burdens the codependent spouse puts on himself or herself). Occasional unmet needs will always exist within any marriage because of time limitations, human finiteness, one's failure to be aware of one's own needs, the failure to communicate those needs to the partner, as well as other reasons. Even if one could meet the partner's needs perfectly, that person might be tempted due to boredom.

"An old canard says that people never get interested in someone outside their marriages unless something is lacking at home, but that is patently untrue," notes McGinnis. "There is no way that a long marriage, no matter how good, can keep from being ho-hum at times."[23] Both partners need to make an explicit commitment to fidelity that will continue in force even when their needs are left unsatisfied. In the traditional wedding vows people make a commitment to fidelity, but since this is part of a formal ceremony, it may never be personalized to the degree it could be. Some couples make their vows more personally meaningful by rewriting the traditional vows in their own words, adding points of emphasis that are important to them. By the term "making an explicit commitment to fidelity" I am referring to a personalized statement that both persons make to each other. This can be included in the wedding ceremony or privately between them.

Some who have felt the strong pressure of temptation may feel uncomfortable making an explicit commitment to fidelity for they fear that some temptation may come along which would be impossible to resist. However, God has promised that he will not allow us to be tempted to sin beyond what we are able to bear, and he further says that, with the temptation, he will provide a way of escape (1 Cor. 10:13). As we have seen in previous chapters, we can control our *behavior* as long as we are wise about the situations we get involved in. And we can control our *thoughts and feelings* (not every spontaneous thought and feeling but the ones that regularly occupy our minds) through the use of thought-stopping and thought-replacement and the images we nurture in our minds. We can make a commitment to fidelity because, with God's help, we can be in control of our thoughts, feelings, and behavior.

It can be helpful for the couple to reaffirm their commitment to fidelity from time to time, especially when they know they may be tempted, as this story illustrates:

> A Christian salesman friend was attending a dealers' convention in New York City. On a free evening he was waiting for a car with others to see some of the city's sights. But he got into the wrong car. These salesmen were not headed for the tourist attractions but for a famous swinging bar. Before my friend knew his mistake, they were on the way with no turning back. Upon entering the bar, each man was immediately joined by a girl who took him by the arm and led him to a table. His girl was saucy, pert, and dressed seductively. "As the evening continued, the temptation was like a steam roller," he told me later. "This girl was luscious. I had all I could do to keep from grabbing her impulsively and taking her to one of the back rooms. But the thing that held me and protected me—the only thing—was that before I had left home, I had told my wife that I was hers alone, and that regardless of any enticements, we belonged to each other and we would be praying for each other." His [commitment] ahead of time saved him.[24]

DEVELOPING A HEART OF GRATITUDE AND A BIBLICAL CONSCIENCE

One principal reason God chastised David for his sin with Bathsheba and his murder of Uriah was David's lack of gratitude for all that God had given him. In the same way, if we take time to ponder all the good things God has given, and if we think of all the other partner's good qualities and past behavior, we should be able to come up with many reasons for gratitude. It is hard to be unfaithful to someone for whom one is grateful.

God's Word teaches us that one of the best ways to avoid giving in to temptation is by memorization and meditation on Scripture (Ps. 119:11).[25] A number of biblical passages warn us of the dangers and judgment for those who fall into infidelity. A beginning list would include some of these:

Proverbs 2:11, 16–18	Malachi 2:15
Proverbs 5:3–4	1 Corinthians 6:18–20
Proverbs 5:15–23	1 Thessalonians 4:3–8
Proverbs 6:25–32	Hebrews 13:4
Proverbs 9:13–18	

EXPANDING OUR AWARENESS OF THE HIGH COST OF INFIDELITY

Like most other temptations, infidelity promises rich enticements at very little cost. As does all sin, infidelity ends up being extremely costly in many ways. An unfaithful marriage partner sometimes loses the marriage, relationships to and contact with one's children, good relationships to one's extended family and close friends, and one's job. He or she often suffers extreme financial losses as one tries to pay for two residences, divorce attorneys' fees, child support, and counseling fees for family members. Most painful are the emotional and spiritual costs, however. By the time an affair has ended the initiator usually realizes that he or she has damaged or destroyed the emotional happiness of every person he holds most dear.

Satan never tells us beforehand about the terrible costs of an affair, for this is part of his strategy. At the beginning of an affair hardly anyone will believe the tremendous pain that will be experienced in the coming months; by distracting us from an affair's problematic results, Satan keeps such thoughts out of our conscious awareness.

One of the best ways to become aware of the tremendous costs of infidelity is to hear the story of people who have been through it. By reading one of the numerous books on the subject, a person can learn of the costs before ever contemplating an affair. Of the books which tell about people's affairs, I will suggest two. *A Healing Season* by Karen Kuhne is about a woman (a pastor's wife) who had an affair with a Christian man who stayed in the pastor's home for a summer. *Addicted to Adultery*, by Richard and Elizabeth Brzeczek, is about a former Chicago police superintendent, one of Illinois' brightest politicians, who lost his job, his career, and nearly his family to an affair. Reading either of these books will help any of us become aware of the tremendous pain that infidelity causes.[26]

DECIDING IRREVOCABLY IN FAVOR OF FIDELITY

E. Stanley Jones has said, "If you don't make up your mind, your unmade mind will unmake you."[27] Nowhere is this truer than in the area of sexual temptation. J. B. Phillips has stated this memorably in his translation of James 1:2–8:

> When all kinds of trials and temptations crowd into your lives, my brothers, don't resent them as intruders, but welcome them as friends! Realize that they come to test your faith and to produce in you the quality of endurance. But let the process go on until that endurance is fully developed, and you will find you have become men of mature character with the right sort of independence. And if, in the process, any of you does not know how to meet any particular problem he has only to ask God—who gives generously to all men without making them feel foolish or guilty—and he may be quite sure that the necessary wisdom will be given him. But he must ask in sincere faith without secret doubts as to whether he really wants God's help or not. The man who trusts God, but with inward reservations, is like a wave of the sea, carried forward by the wind one moment and driven back the next. That sort of man cannot hope to receive anything from the Lord, and the life of a man of divided loyalty will reveal instability at every turn.

As we discussed in chapter 5, the Christian may have ambivalence about sexual temptation. At a conscious level he or she may be strongly committed to fidelity. At a subconscious level, the pull of temptation toward an affair is there. Because of the subconscious nature of the attraction, a Christian may put himself or herself in a situation that is unwise for one who is thoroughly committed to remaining faithful. This ambivalence between one's conscious beliefs and one's subconscious attraction causes him or her to be like a wave of the sea, carried closer to an affair one moment, then retreating the next.

Failure to recognize and confront our subconscious attraction to an affair puts us at risk.

PLANNING AHEAD FOR POTENTIAL TEMPTATIONS

Psychological studies of compulsive sexuality, whether involving compulsive homosexual or compulsive heterosexual behavior, sometimes discuss "behavioral-completion mechanisms." This term refers to the fact that, in certain situations, a person almost inevitably becomes sexually involved. The relationship between that stimulus situation and the person is so strong that he or she feels impelled to complete a sexual act.

For example, consider the following scenario: A couple works together for several months, or even a few years. They like each other and help each other out in their work, so an emotional attraction develops. They see each other at times when they both look their best, so there may be a physical attraction. If they begin working together in the evenings when their inhibitions are decreased because of fatigue and because they are alone, the principle of behavioral-completion mechanisms will work itself out. They can easily end up in each other's arms, and hugs will eventually lead to sex.

The concept applies to anyone. Most of those reading this book are counselors, or pastors who spend time regularly in counseling, persons who are not normally involved in compulsive sexual behavior. However, any of us, given a seductive set of circumstances, might find it difficult not to say yes to a sexual temptation. Knowing this, it is important to identify such situations and avoid them. Even though the stimulus is not sinful of itself (e.g., working with a co-worker in the office in the evening), we should avoid it if it could lead to sin.

Another concept from behavioral psychology is applicable here—the concept of "chaining." Often one behavior is connected to another and regularly follows it—the two behaviors seem to be "chained" together. For example, an obese person has often developed the habit of eating high-calorie foods while watching television. The behavior of watching television has become chained to the behavior of snacking. Behaviorists frequently identify the specific behaviors in a chain that leads to some unwanted behavior, such as smoking, overeating, or compulsive sexuality. There are likely to be several steps in such a chain before one gets to the item that directly precedes the unhealthy behavior. It is possible to break the chain at the link directly before the unwanted behavior, but because of behavioral-completion mechanisms, trying to break it there may prove unsuccessful. What is more likely to succeed is identifying a step further back in the chain, and identifying an alternative behavior there that would break the chain at that earlier point.

Several years ago a Christian student sought out a professor's counsel on a matter that was troubling him. He found that when he would date a girl and take her to her apartment afterward, he would became sexually involved with her, even though this caused him a great deal of guilt and remorse afterward. It was a recurring pattern with him. The elements of his "chain" were the anticipation of an enjoyable evening with the girl, a nice dinner or movie, perhaps a pleasant walk, a time of sharing and becoming vulnerable to each other, driving his date to her home, walking to her door, being invited in, having more conversation and a snack, engaging in some casual expression of affection, which usually led to sexual intercourse.

The professor asked the student to identify the link in the chain where, if he took an alternate step, he would probably be able to stay free of sexual involvement. The young man recognized that if he was truly serious about avoiding sex he would have to say goodnight at the door and end the date there.

READY STRATEGIES FOR SPECIFIC RELATIONSHIPS

If we find ourselves tempted to become wrongfully involved with a specific person, particularly if the temptation is coming from within ourselves, we should first try to understand why it is happening.

A Christian young man suddenly found himself having sexual fantasies about someone in his church, fantasies which "seemed to come out of nowhere." However, as his counselor asked him to think about interactions he had had with that person recently, he found several things had happened. Not long before this he had been in her home to deliver something. While he was there she had been extremely pleasant and gracious (and her husband had not been home). He had been asked to substitute teach one of the elementary Sunday School classes one Sunday, and she had volunteered to help and had been very supportive. Also, she and her husband had begun sitting quite close to him during church services, and so he had been seeing her and talking with her more frequently. And finally, he realized that she had the type of figure that was most attractive to him. As he put all this together he realized that his feelings had not "come out of nowhere," but that plausible reasons could be given concerning why he was feeling some attraction to her. Simply understanding why he was feeling attracted helped increase his sense of control over his feelings.

Second, we can use the A-B-C-D-E method to dispute tempting thoughts. Recalling Scripture that has been memorized and thinking on the costliness and destructiveness of an affair can aid in disputing the thoughts with which Satan is trying to seduce us.

Third, we should not allow ourselves to daydream about sexual fantasies with that individual. Constantly associating pleasant sexual feelings with the person will cause anyone to feel more tempted to a sexual liaison.

Fourth, if sexual fantasies come unbidden, we distract ourselves by focusing on something else (for example, returning to on-task thinking). Or, we can admonish the tempting thought and its originator to leave ("Out, in the name of Jesus!" or, "Get behind me Satan, in Jesus' name I command you to leave!"). Or we can replace the pleasant fantasy with a negative one (imagining being caught in the illicit relationship by the pastor or someone else, and feeling all the shame and embarrassment such a discovery would cause).

Fifth, we can structure our time so that opportunities to be with the person are minimized. Most temptations will decrease in strength if we do not feed them through fantasy or actual contact.

Sixth, if the problem persists, we can form a small accountability and support group with one or two Christian friends of the same sex with whom we can share the problem. These friends can provide prayer support and suggestions, and they can hold us accountable. If none of these strategies is successful, it may be worthwhile to consult with a Christian counselor for more specific guidance.

PRAYING FOR A SAFETY NET

If we follow the above guidelines, we will probably be in much better control of sexual temptations that come. Yet there is still the possibility that we will be faced with unexpected and highly tempting situations for which we have not planned (as the man at the sales convention in New York City). This shows the need for a safety net.

One Christian man had been praying for just such a safety net. On a particular evening he knew that he would be alone with an attractive female who had indicated several times that she desired a sexual relationship with him. There was no way to avoid the encounter, though he had tried. Even though he was strongly committed to fidelity, he knew that this woman could be very seductive, and he was anxious about his ability to stand strong in the face of her behavior.

God provided a "safety net" for him in an unexpected way. Two hours before he was about to be alone with this woman, a friend came to see him. This friend shared how he had become involved in an affair, and the awful devastation that had come about as a result. After hearing about his friend's pain for two hours, the Christian man had no difficulty refusing the propositions the woman made that evening.

DOMESTIC SUPPORT AND FAMILY COMMITMENT

In healthy families there is a balance between domestic support (males' fourth highest need according to Harley) and family commitment (females' fifth highest need). By *domestic support* Harley means the male desire to have his wife "simplify his life by cooking his meals, washing and ironing his clothes, keeping the house [neat], calling a repairman when necessary, and attending to the basic needs of their children. To the extent that she gives him this kind of domestic support, he enjoys his responsibility to provide his family with the income it needs."[28] *Family commitment* refers to a woman's need that her husband be strongly committed to the care and nurture of their children.[29] This involves not only spending time with the children, but a strong commitment to learn how to be a good father. To a lesser extent it also involves the woman's desire that he be committed to having good relationships with their extended families, both his and hers.

In a culture in which increasing numbers of women work part-time or full-time outside the home, and where professional responsibilities often consume much more than forty hours per week, these reciprocal expectations are often difficult to meet. Most men nurture the fantasy of a wife who runs a well-organized and efficient home, who takes care of problems with common sense and decisiveness, and who does the majority of the disciplining so that the children are well-behaved and rarely require discipline from him. This fantasy is present even when his wife works full-time!

Most wives have slightly more realistic expectations for their husbands. They would like a husband who initiates contact and interest in the children's activities, who supports their discipline and is willing to discipline the children himself when he is there, and who is committed to learning how to be the best father he can be.

These two interrelated areas need to be discussed by nearly every couple, and need to be rediscussed as children grow older, and as work and family responsibilities change over the years. While few women have an affair because the husband fails to be a good father to the children, many husbands have affairs because, in their perception, the wife does not run a well-organized home, and because they are regularly besieged with complaints within the family. Most men want to come home and be able to retreat from pressures; they do not wish to experience a whole new set of them.

The answer is not for women to try to meet men's expectations: We men have to discard some of our unrealistic and unfair expectations about domestic support. In some cases women can become less dependent on involving their husbands in every decision or every disciplinary problem with the children. It may help to develop some "buffer zones," times immediately after either parent returns home from work when the problems of the day are not unloaded on him or her (unless an emergency exists). Each couple needs to develop a means of sharing these interrelated responsibilities in ways that seem fair to both of them.

CHURCH-INITIATED AND CHURCH-RELATED PROGRAMS

I believe there are several reasons why pastors should not try to be the primary counselor for those from their own congregations who become involved in affairs. First, such counseling is very time consuming. To help the involved person decide whether or not to end the affair, to help that person become emotionally detached from the affair partner, to provide support for the faithful partner during this process, to help the couple examine contributing reasons for the affair, to help them forgive and rebuild trust, and to strengthen the marriage afterward will usually require a minimum of thirty hour-long counseling sessions. This is more time than most pastors can reasonably spend with one couple.

Second, because of time constraints upon them, pastors may have a tendency to confront prematurely. A premature confrontation usually raises the unfaithful partner's defenses, and increases the chances that he or she will leave the church and his or her family. If the unfaithful partner leaves the church in anger, the other mate may feel the need to follow him or her to a new church if there is to be any chance of reconciliation. Thus the couple loses the support of their church family at the very time they need it most.

Third, serving as pastor and as counselor simultaneously places the pastor in a dual relationship that sometimes will present role conflicts. As counselor you are bound to keep what is said in the counseling sessions confidential, but as pastor you may feel, especially when blatant public adultery occurs, that you must play a role in leading church discipline. You cannot do both.

Fourth, the dual relationship can produce another problem of a different kind. Many females unconsciously project father-figure needs onto their pastors, needs that make such a woman feel close to her pastor. If at the same time the woman is the one who has been betrayed, she may have a strong desire for you to meet needs that are not being satisfied by the unfaithful husband. The vulnerability for both of you in this situation is increased because of your role as pastor.

Finally, even if you are able to give a couple the extensive time they need and are able to help them successfully be reconciled to each other, they may leave the church because they are embarrassed about how much you know of their personal lives.

For these reasons I believe it is best for a pastor to refer the couple involved in an affair to a Christian counselor whom he or she trusts. However, it is important for the pastor to continue to be involved with them in a supportive role, for they will need to feel his or her support and prayers in the struggle, perhaps more than in any other crisis they could face.

Having said this, it is still important for pastors and pastors-in-training to be aware of the material within this book. It is crucial that they understand the dynamics that can unconsciously lead a person into an affair, both for their own protection and also in order to develop affair-prevention programs for the church. It is important for them to know the process and time needed for a couple to work through an extramarital crisis and to forgive and rebuild trust in a marriage relationship so that they can show the necessary patience with the process.

While it may be unwise for pastors to take on the primary counseling of couples after an affair, pastors probably have an unparalleled opportunity to implement affair-prevention programs within their congregations. Within our society no other place than the church is so ideally suited to teaching couples that affairs can happen, even in Christian marriages, and to conducting marriage-strengthening and affair-prevention programs. Pastors are the persons best able to see that these various topics are addressed in sermons and that the necessary concepts and skills are taught within the adult electives of the Sunday School on a regular basis.

What might this involve at a practical level? Several things, all of which could be adapted to the personality of the pastor and the needs of the congregation, could be added:

- Obviously the material discussed under Premarital Preparation could be added to the regular premarital counseling a pastor gives.
- A commitment to enroll in a course in communication skills (offered as a Sunday School elective) in the first year of marriage could be part of a couple's premarital agreement.
- Possibly a course on "Affair-proofing Your Marriage" or "Strengthening Your Marriage in a World of Temptation" could be offered at least once a year for couples during the second year of marriage.
- Marriage-strengthening courses could be offered as a regular part of the adult elective curriculum. A new good course could be introduced each year and offered in several successive quarters until every couple in the church has the opportunity of taking it.
- At least once a year a message on marital fidelity could be preached, with an encouragement that each couple renew their vows to fidelity.

SUCCESSFUL LONG-TERM MARRIAGES

What is the relationship between affairs, affair-proofing, and successful long-term marriages? An affair is usually (but not always) a sign, a symptom, that something is lacking in the marriage. Affair-proofing is like the preventive maintenance done on a well-designed machine: It is not a substitute for a well-designed machine, but every well-designed machine can benefit from preventive maintenance.

What are the characteristics of a well-designed marriage? From the pages of Scripture and the findings of modern psychology we might describe it in the following way. A successful Christian marriage involves two people who:

- believe that the most fulfilling way to live is to focus their lives around loving and serving God
- model their own relationship to each other around the love God has demonstrated to us and the submission seen within the Godhead
- believe that their true wealth lies, not in what they can accumulate on earth, but in the spiritual investments they can make by loving and helping other human beings
- are willing continually to be in the process of discovering areas where personal growth is needed within themselves, committing themselves to grow and encouraging the growth of the mate, their children, and others around them
- have a growing awareness of their own internal dynamics, of being able to recognize their own unconscious thoughts, feelings, and goals, and nurture the same process in the partner
- are willing to share their inner selves, to encourage the same in the partner, and to allow themselves to be changed by that sharing
- each have a host of friends of varying levels of intimacy
- have a strong commitment to sexual exclusivity and fidelity, with a consequent high level of trust
- are willing to accept things that one cannot change
- have a balance of power between partners
- have a balance of depending on each other and ability to be independent when needed
- share an assumption of permanence in the relationship
- have an enjoyment of each other

- share a history that is cherished
- recognize one's own and one's partner's humanity[30]

May God help us all develop that kind of relationship.

KEY IDEAS FROM CHAPTER 12

Couples can reduce the chance of an affair after marriage by consciously keeping conversation, communication, and friendship strong in their marriage.

Maintaining a healthy, mutually enjoyed sexual relationship is an important part of affair prevention.

Men need to remember that their wives want nonsexual affection just as strongly as they (husbands) want sexual fulfillment.

It is important for couples to have some regular kind of recreational companionship where they leave work and problems behind and enjoy having fun together.

If couples do not resolve conflicts as they occur, the resulting frustrations can put them both at risk for an affair.

It is possible for people to have deep friendships with others of the opposite sex without those relationships becoming sexualized if one observes careful guidelines such as those developed by McGinnis.

Couples need to inform themselves of developmental situations that put one or both of them at risk for affairs, and build extra support into their relationship at such times.

The following anti-temptation strategies are recommended:
- Identify your personal areas of vulnerability
- Make an explicit commitment to fidelity
- Develop a heart of gratitude
- Develop a biblical conscience by memorizing and meditating on Scripture
- Expand your awareness of the high cost of infidelity
- Decide irrevocably in favor of fidelity
- Plan ahead for situations in which you might be tempted

Strategies one can use if tempted by a specific relationship include understanding why we are being tempted by this particular person, using the A-B-C-D-E method to dispute tempting thoughts, not focusing on sexually arousing fantasies, minimizing time spent with that person, and if necessary, forming a small accountability and prayer support group.

Wives need to be aware of their husbands' desire for domestic support, and husbands need to be aware of their wives' desire for family commitment.

While pastors probably should not become involved in the primary counseling of couples when there is an affair, they can play a very important supportive role in such couple's lives.

Pastors and churches are probably uniquely positioned to do affair prevention through sermons, premarital counseling, and adult Sunday School electives which regularly encourage couples to keep their marriages strong and healthy.

NOTES

1. Dolores Curran, *Traits of a Healthy Family* (San Francisco: Harper and Row, 1983), 23–24. Cited by Jake Heerema in *The Chaplain's Newsletter*, Pine Rest Christian Hospital, 1990, 7.

2. Alan Loy McGinnis, *The Friendship Factor* (Minneapolis: Augsburg, 1979), 167.

3. Robert Sternberg, quoted in Penney, *How to Keep Your Man Monogamous* (New York: Bantam, 1989), 118.

4. Penney, 143.

5. Penney, 164. The full documentation for point 5 is: R. Cimbalo, V. Faling, and P. Monsaw, "The Course of Love: A Cross-sectional Design," in *Psychological Reports*, Vol. 38, 1976.

6. Penney, 147.

7. Susan Sadd and Carol Tavris, *The Redbook Report on Female Sexuality* (New York: Delacorte, 1977), 97–106.

8. Michael Campion, *Especially for Husbands* (Minneapolis: Bethany Fellowship, 1978).

9. Michael Campion, *Especially for Wives* (Minneapolis: Bethany Fellowship, 1979).

10. Carl Brecheen, "Marital Intimacy." Part of the Counseling Today audio cassette series published by The American Association of Christian Counselors, P.O. Box 55712, Jackson, MS 39296–5712.

11. Rick Bundschuh and Dave Gilbert, *Dating Your Mate: Creative Dating Ideas for Those Who Are Married or Those Who Would Like to Be* (Eugene, Ore.: Harvest House Publishers, 1987).

12. Eric Weber and Steven Simring, *How to Win Back the One You Love* (New York: Macmillan, 1983), 71.

13. Norman Lobenz, "Make Your Marriage Affair-Proof," *Woman's Day* (March 13, 1979), 150.

14. Cited in Barbara Gordon, *Jennifer Fever: Older Men, Younger Women* (New York: Harper and Row, 1988), 90–91.

15. Weber and Simring (this idea occurs throughout the book).

16. Several of the workable compromises listed in this chapter are adapted from ideas in Virginia Satir, *Conjoint Family Therapy* (Palo Alto, Calif.: Science and Behavior Books, 1967).

17. Cited in Peter Kreitler, *Affair Prevention* (New York: Macmillan, 1981), 15.

18. Charles Mylander, *Running the Red Lights: Putting the Brakes on Sexual Temptation* (Ventura, Calif.: Regal, 1986), 42.

19. Frank Pittman, *Private Lies: Infidelity and the Betrayal of Intimacy* (New York: Norton, 1989), 43.

20. Alan McGinnis, 170–71.

21. Gordon, 239–52.

22. Ellen Williams, "The Day the Fairy Tale Died," *Today's Christian Woman* (Winter 1981–82), 49–51.

23. McGinnis, 167.

24. J. Allan Petersen, *The Myth of the Greener Grass* (Wheaton, Ill.: Tyndale House, 1983), 96–97.

25. Petersen, 92.

26. See Appendix A for full bibliographic details.

27. E. Stanley Jones, *The Way to Power and Poise* (Nashville: Abingdon, 1949), 258.

28. Willard Harley, *His Needs, Her Needs: Building An Affair-Proof Marriage* (Old Tappan, N.J.: Revell, 1986), 130.

29. Harley, 138.

30. Some of the items in this list are adapted from Francine Klagsbrun, *Married People Staying Together in the Age of Divorce* (New York: Bantam, 1985). Those items are 4, 8, 9, 10, 11, 12, 13, 14.

Appendix A

Annotated Bibliography

Botwin, Carol. *Men Who Can't Be Faithful: How to Pick Up the Pieces When He's Breaking Your Heart*. New York: Warner Books, 1988.

> Written by a popular columnist on sexuality and relationships. While the author takes a nonjudgmental stance on sex outside marriage, she has many excellent insights into why men are unfaithful, how to predict the likelihood of unfaithfulness in the future, and how to respond when there has been infidelity.

Brzeczek, Richard and Elizabeth. *Addicted to Adultery: How We Saved Our Marriage/How You Can Save Yours*. New York: Bantam, 1989.

> This is the very open story of how adultery shattered this couple's life, their family, and Richard's very promising career. From this experience they started WESOM (We Saved Our Marriage), a support group modeled after AA and Al-Anon. This group uses the Twelve Steps to help couples put themselves and their marriages back together after an affair.

Carnes, Patrick. *Out of the Shadows: Understanding Sexual Addiction*. Minneapolis: CompCare Publishers, 1983.

The first of two books by the man who pioneered the concept of sexual addiction and who suggested that the Twelve Steps of AA may be the best treatment approach available for sexual addictions also. Someone who seems to be compulsively and indiscriminately involved in one sexual experience after another may be suffering from a sexual addiction.

Carter, Les. *The Prodigal Spouse: How to Survive Infidelity.* Nashville: Thomas Nelson, 1990.

A fine book, written for the Christian spouse of an unfaithful marriage partner, it integrates scriptural teaching with counseling practices. Well balanced in its advice, it addresses a number of practical issues in more depth than many books in this bibliography.

Chapman, Audrey. *Man Sharing: Dilemma or Choice? A Radical New Way of Relating to the Men in Your Life.* New York: Morrow and Company, 1986.

Audrey Chapman builds upon the facts that many more women are available than men and society has condoned nonmonogamous relationships for men for some time. She writes from a feminist perspective that women are responsible for finding their own happiness within themselves and thus should not be dependent on any one male for emotional fulfillment. She suggests, in light of these things, that a realistic option for women is that they should have a number of male relationships to meet their sexual, social, and emotional needs. She recognizes this option will not be acceptable to some women, and urges all women to be tolerant of others who do not view reality the same way. She talks briefly about the grief a woman experiences when she finds out the man she has been seeing has also been seeing other women. She never addresses the incompatibility of encouraging women to have several men in their lives with the grief that she and most women go through when they discover that one of their "men" has been sharing himself with several women.

Clinebell, Howard and Charlotte. *The Intimate Marriage.* New York: Harper and Row, 1970.

A good discussion of the many facets of marital intimacy, barriers to intimacy, and means for encouraging growth in intimacy.

Conway, Sally. *You and Your Husband's Midlife Crisis.* Elgin, Ill.: David C. Cook, 1980.

A very helpful book for women on this developmental passage (crisis for some). Practical advice for women about how to respond to all of men's midlife behaviors, including the possibility of an affair. There are differences of opinion about whether all men have an identifiable midlife crisis, or whether some make a series of gradual midlife changes and thereby avert a crisis. For the wives of those who have a crisis, this book is excellent.

Denholtz, Elaine. *Having It Both Ways: A Report on Married Women with Lovers.* New York: Stein and Day, 1981.

The author interviewed more than one hundred married women who had had or were having affairs while they were married. She maintains a morally neutral stance about the practice, discussing the reasons women become involved in such affairs, why they stay involved, and how these relationships usually end.

Dobson, James. *Love Must Be Tough: New Hope for Families in Crisis.* Waco, Tex.: Word, 1983.

This is an excellent book about how to respond assertively when a marriage partner begins an affair. Explains why submission and giving up one's rights usually does not work. An informative book for anyone whose spouse is having an affair and everyone who counsels Christians.

Dolesh, Daniel and Sherelynn Lehman. *Love Me, Love Me Not: How to Survive Infidelity.* New York: McGraw-Hill, 1985.

An excellent book covering the early signs of betrayal, what to do if an affair is suspected, why affairs happen, and the stages most people go through when they realize a spouse has been unfaithful. Includes advice on how to use the legal system, community resources, and personal faith to get through the crisis.

Gordon, Barbara. *Jennifer Fever: Older Men, Younger Women.* New York: Harper and Row, 1988.

An interesting look at what the author has called "Jennifer Fever"— the phenomenon where a middle-aged man leaves his wife of many years to live with or marry a young woman often half his age. Includes interviews with the men, the young "Jennifers," the abandoned wives, as well as psychiatrists, psychologists, and marriage counselors.

Harley, Willard. *His Needs, Her Needs: Building An Affair-Proof Marriage.* Old Tappan, N. J.: Revell, 1986.

This book takes the approach that while men and women have the same emotional needs, the top five needs for most men differ from the top five needs of women. Marriages become vulnerable because husbands and wives fail to realize that they have different needs and, therefore, fail to meet those needs. Highly recommended for those who counsel couples.

Hession, Roy. *Forgotten Factors: An Aid to Deeper Repentance of the Forgotten Factors of Sexual Misbehavior.* Fort Washington, Pa.: Christian Literature Crusade, 1976.

This is a discussion of many of the less obvious factors which often accompany sexual sin and an appeal to the person so involved to repent.

Joy, Donald. *Rebonding: Preventing and Restoring Damaged Relationships.* Waco, Tex.: Word, 1986.

Includes some interesting concepts related to the issues of affairs, healing, and prevention. Be aware that the author defines almost all of his basic terms differently than the majority of evangelical theologians and writers. The validity of his conclusions may be affected by this.

Kuhne, Karen. *A Healing Season: A True Story of Adultery and Reconciliation.* Grand Rapids: Zondervan, 1984.

This story illustrates how unhealthy families of origin can lay the groundwork for an affair, and how overcommitment to Christian ministry can further exacerbate this vulnerability. Reveals the painful torment that is experienced by the faithful spouse, the unfaithful spouse, and the affairee in any affair. This couple's path back to healing and wholeness may have been less painful and required less time if the couple had been in regular counseling with a therapist experienced in treating affairs. The couple's pain might also have been lessened if antidepressants had been prescribed, for they both seemed to have experienced depression as a result of the affair.

Lutzer, Erwin. *Living with Your Passions: A Christian's Guide to Sexual Purity.* Wheaton, Ill.: Victor Books, 1983.

This book and Mylander's (see below) cover the same topic, but in slightly different ways. This volume is more basic and draws its insights almost totally from Scripture; Mylander's book provides a little deeper reading, and integrates more psychological insights with biblical truth.

McGinnis, Alan. *The Friendship Factor.* Minneapolis: Augsburg, 1979.

An exceptional book on friendship. The author takes the position that it is possible to have deep heterosexual friendships between Christians. He recognizes the temptations that can come with such friendships and identifies several excellent guidelines to keep friendships from becoming affairs.

Mylander, Charles. *Running the Red Lights: Putting the Brakes on Sexual Temptation.* Ventura, Calif.: Regal, 1986.

An excellent book on dealing with sexual temptation in its various forms, it contains two chapters on church discipline that are among the finest written anywhere.

Penney, Alexandra. *How To Keep Your Man Monogamous.* New York: Bantam, 1989.

Over a period of two and one-half years Ms. Penney interviewed psychiatrists, psychologists, and two hundred men to find out what made them stay or stray. Not a Christian book, but very well written, containing many excellent points.

Petersen, J. Allan. *The Myth of the Greener Grass*. Wheaton, Ill.: Tyndale House, 1983.

A good book, from an evangelical perspective, on how people become involved in affairs, how to respond if it happens, and practical preventive strategies.

Pittman, Frank. *Private Lies: Infidelity and the Betrayal of Intimacy*. New York: Norton, 1989.

Written by an experienced marriage and family therapist, this book is full of wisdom and wit. Though Pittman is not a Christian writer—statements occasionally are strongly nonbiblical—there is much helpful material here for Christians to ponder.

Richardson, Laurel. *The New Other Woman: Contemporary Single Women in Affairs with Married Men*. New York: The Free Press, 1985.

Dr. Richardson, a sociologist, has defined what she calls "the new other woman"—a single female, often well-educated and highly career-oriented, who either does not want to let her career take second priority to a marriage, or who has no marriageable prospects, or both. Yet this woman may desire *some* male companionship in her life, so she begins an affair with a married man. The book discusses why these women become involved with married men, how their liaisons progress, and what happens when they end. The author analyzes why so many of these women, even though they entered the liaisons in order to maintain their emotional independence, become emotionally dependent on "their" men.

Schneider, Jennifer P. *Back from Betrayal: Recovering from His Affairs*. San Francisco: Harper and Row/Hazelden, 1988.

An excellent book, written by a physician, for women who are married to sexual addicts. Contains a thorough introduction to the concepts of sexual addiction, coaddiction, and codependency, with theoretical as well as practical material. The material on codependency would be relevant for anyone, male or female, whose mate is being unfaithful, whether or not they meet the criteria for sexual addiction.

Smedes, Lewis. *Forgive and Forget: Healing the Hurts We Don't Deserve*. San Francisco: Harper and Row, 1984.

A very thoughtful, personal, biblically compatible treatise on the process of forgiveness. The author suggests there are four stages to the healing process: hurting, hating, healing, and reconciliation. Very worthwhile reading.

Weber, Eric and Steven Simring. *How to Win Back the One You Love*. New York: Macmillan, 1983.

These men are not writing from a Christian perspective, but they take a strong stand for keeping marriages together, including those threatened by divorce or an affair. They encourage the spouse who does not want the divorce to fight for their marriage, and include a number of good ideas about how to do so. They also have some helpful cautions about divorce lawyers, and how these attorneys can hasten the demise of a marriage or cause damage that significantly lessens any chance of reconciliation.

Wright, H. Norman. *Seasons of a Marriage*. Ventura, Calif.: Regal, 1982. This book examines the normal developmental tasks of men and women during each decade of life, and the consequent stages their marriages go through. It includes chapters on midlife transitions, affairs and unfaithfulness, and the healing process after an affair.

Appendix B

Organizations and Resources

For Alcohol Abusers

1. Most cities have several Alcoholics Anonymous (AA) meetings per week. Times and locations can be found by calling the AA office listed in the telephone directory. Each group has its own personality, so a person may feel more compatible with one group than another.
2. Information about starting a group can be obtained from
Alcoholics Anonymous World Services, Inc.
General Services Office
468 Park Avenue
New York, NY 10016
1–800–252–6465

For Family Members of an Alcoholic

1. Most cities will also have Al-Anon meetings for spouses and friends of alcoholics. The alcohol abuser does not have to attend AA for the spouse to attend Al-Anon. In some cities support groups exist for teen-age children of alcoholics (Alateen). All meetings are free.
2. Information about starting a group can be obtained from
Al-Anon Family Group Headquarters, Inc.
P.O. Box 862 Midtown Station
New York, NY 100188–0862
1–800–252–6465

For Adult Children of Alcoholics (ACOAs or ACAs)

1. Many cities have ACOA groups as part of the Al-Anon network. Also, these groups may be helpful to anyone who grew up in a dysfunctional family and who recognizes that he or she has codependent thinking and behavior patterns, even if no alcohol abuse was present.

2. Information about starting a group can be obtained from either
National Association for Children of Alcoholics
31706 Pacific Coast Highway
South Laguna Beach, CA 92677
714–499–3889
or
Children of Alcoholics Foundation, Inc.
200 Park Avenue
New York, NY 10116

For Drug Abusers and Their Families

1. An adaptation of AA for those who abuse other drugs is Narcotics Anonymous (NA); for those who abuse cocaine or crack, Cocaine Anonymous. Frequently younger substance abusers use both alcohol and drugs, and may be addicted to more than one substance. Usually these people feel more kinship with the people in NA groups than with those in AA groups.
2. A support group for family members is called Nar-Anon, and is available in most larger cities.
3. There are also support groups called "Tough Love" which are available to the parents of substance abusing children. These groups use the philosophy found in the book *Tough Love: How Parents Can Deal with Drug Abuse*, by Pauline Neff.

For Sexual Addicts and Their Families

1. In larger cities there are now groups for sexual addicts patterned after the twelve-step process of AA. Information about where such groups meet may be obtained by calling the AA telephone number.
2. Further information about sexual addiction can be obtained by reading Patrick Carnes's two books, *Out of the Shadows* and *Contrary to Love*, or by writing to the following organizations:
Sex Addicts Anonymous
P.O. Box 3038
Minneapolis, MN 55403
or
Sexaholics Anonymous
General Services Office
Box 300
Simi Valley, CA 93062
3. Information for family members of those who are sexually addicted can be obtained from:
S-Anon
P.O. Box 5117
Sherman Oaks, CA 91413

Appendix C

Marital Intimacy

Instructions: Howard and Charlotte Clinebell* suggest that intimacy, like a diamond, has many facets, and then go on to define ten of those facets. *Intellectual intimacy* refers to the closeness that comes from the sharing and valuing of each other's ideas in a context of mutual respect. *Emotional intimacy* refers to the sharing of one's deepest feelings with one's partner. *Esthetic intimacy* refers to the sharing of experiences of beauty together, such as a beautiful waterfall, a beautiful sunset, a beautiful piece of music. *Creative intimacy* refers to acts of creating something together. *Recreational intimacy* refers to the sharing of experiences of play and fun together. *Sexual intimacy* is the experience of sharing sexual pleasure together in the context of mutual love and commitment. *Work intimacy* refers to the closeness that comes when two people work closely and cooperatively together to accomplish a task. *Crisis intimacy* refers to the closeness that comes when a couple cope with problems and pain and find they are drawn closer to each other as a result. *Commitment intimacy* is the feeling that comes as a result of two people investing themselves in a cause greater than themselves or their marriage (e.g., sponsoring the Special Olympics). *Spiritual intimacy* is the closeness that comes when two people share their spiritual faith, commitments, and goals together.

Couples can discuss each of the above areas and decide whether they are satisfied with the level of intimacy they enjoy in each area. After discussing all of them, they can go back and develop practical action plans in those areas where one or both are not satisfied. It is probably best for couples to work their action plan in one or two areas at a time, rather than trying to make several changes at once.

Nine of the ten kinds of intimacy (everything except sexual intimacy) can be encouraged in friendships outside of marriage or in premarital relationships to help spouses realize the variety of ways they can relate to each other.

---

*The definitions of the various facets of marital intimacy are adapted from Howard and Charlotte Clinebell, *The Intimate Marriage,* Harper and Row, New York, 1970, 23–39.

Appendix D

Understanding Depression

© 1991 Henry A. Virkler

The many stresses which converge when an affair occurs can produce severe depression for all parties involved. Often significant spiritual and psychological components of depression exist in a profound degree, triggering biological changes in the body. For this reason counselors and pastors who work with such couples should be alert to the possibility of biological depression that may require medication. This brief essay is intended to help clients understand how biological depression may be present during or after an affair, and the proper role that medication may play in its treatment.

Depression in Christians can come from a variety of sources—spiritual, psychological, and biological. In order to reduce the depression an individual is experiencing, it is important to understand the specific causes of *that person's* depression. Far too frequently Christians teach a simplistic model of depression and say that every Christian's depression is caused by a single source (e.g., sin, or lack of faith, etc.). Such teaching is often inaccurate and produces further condemnation rather than helping the hurting person.

Spiritual Sources of Depression

Some depression comes from spiritual sources. David was depressed when he realized that Bathsheba was pregnant, and when he later learned that the child conceived with her would die. Whenever we knowingly commit sin, we are likely to experience guilt feelings and depression. The only truly effective remedy for this kind of depression is confession, repentance, and, when necessary, restitution. Christians who are experiencing this kind of depression and who have not made a complete repentance (i.e., they have not decided that they irrevocably want to turn from their sin) will not experience a complete release from their guilt and depression until they do so.

Another kind of spiritual depression has been called *anomie*. Anomie refers to the aimlessness and despair that comes from having no sense of purpose or significance in one's life. Clearly the Christian message that we have a loving Father who imbues our lives with eternal significance and purpose can be a powerful antidote to this kind of spiritual depression.

A third type of spiritual depression occurs when individuals unconsciously transfer their memories of how their earthly parents responded to them onto God. For example, if their parents used criticism much more than encouragement, or if their parents expressed anger and rejection when the children did something wrong, they are likely to unconsciously project these same reactions onto God, believing that he withdraws from and is angry with them when they fail. Since we all fail to live a perfect Christian life, this can lead to a state of spiritual depression.

Psychological Sources of Depression

There are many psychological sources of depression; here we will discuss only some of the more common ones.

We all become depressed when we lose someone or something very important to us. The intensity of grief that we feel is proportional to the importance that person or thing had in our lives. Loss of things can include loss of job, financial security, and health (Job lost all of these and his children simultaneously). It can also include grieving over the loss of a role (e.g., a mother whose last child goes off to college experiences an emptiness because she no longer has someone to mother). We can also grieve over the loss of something we hoped would happen when it becomes clear that it will not occur after all, as when someone else gets picked for a promotion which we felt certain we would be given.

Christians surely grieve, just as do nonbelievers. Our faith gives us *added resources* to cope with loss and disappointment, so that we need not grieve as those "who have no hope." We need not grieve as someone would who believes that his or her loved one has ceased to exist, and that he or she will soon do likewise. We may still grieve, however, because we deeply miss the presence of someone we love, even though our parting is temporary. It is psychologically and spiritually unhealthy to suppress our normal human grief processes based on the mistaken belief that Christians with enough faith should never experience sadness over the temporary (but nonetheless pain-ful) loss of someone or something important to us.

A second kind of depression comes from a state called "learned helpless-ness." Animal researchers first identified this condition in animal experiments. Dogs would be placed in cages which had no means of escape and whose floors contained an electrical charge. At first the dogs would try to flee, but eventually they simply cowered in a corner when the electrical current was on. They continued this behavior even after they were moved to cages from which they could escape. They had learned to perceive their situation as one in which they were helpless to avoid pain. Dogs with "learned helplessness" manifested an emotional state similar to that in hu-mans which is called "agitated depression"; that is, they showed constant signs of being both anxious and depressed.

Learned helplessness, and the depression which comes from this state, is seen with moderate frequency in people who come for counseling. It is particularly common in women and children who receive verbal or physi-cal abuse or who believe they are about to lose a mate (or father) and can do nothing about it. Women and children often are financially and physically dependent on those who are producing the painful situations in their lives. So, like the dogs in the experiment, they are in a position of constant dread that the pain could start again at any moment and that they can do noth-ing to avoid it or stop it.

A third common cause of psychological depression is lack of assertiveness. People often overlook or neglect the needs of timid, shy per-sons, and as a result shy people often believe that no one cares about them. Shy people often miss out on many of the positive experiences that make people happy to be alive, and this can also contribute to their depression. Usually timid people learn to be that way early in life. Now they continue to be timid even though no one in their present world would respond puni-tively if they were more assertive. Such people can often be helped through proper assertiveness training.

A fourth common psychological cause of depression is perfectionism (technically known as obsessive-compulsive personality disorder). The per-fectionist sets unrealistically high goals, then feels guilty, depressed, or anxious when he or she fails to reach them. Perfectionists also typically overlook the things they do right, and only focus on those situations where they make mistakes, causing them to have overly negative views of them-selves.

The perfectionist also usually adheres to unrealistic, high standards for those close to him or her (family and co-workers), and this often causes those relationships to be unpleasant and depressing. Perfectionists who become Christians are likely to translate these same perfectionist strivings into the spiritual sphere and will usually find Scriptures which seem to support their approach to life. People with obsessive-compulsive personality styles will usually not change unless they become convinced that it is healthier and wiser and equally biblical to accept themselves as imperfect humans *in the process* of becoming more like Christ. They fear that accepting themselves as imperfect will condone a life of mediocrity.

Biological Sources of Depression

Our bodies contain approximately five billion nerve cells, of which three billion are found in the human brain. Between each cell and the next is a small space called a synapse. Nerve impulses travel through the nerve cell as an electrical impulse. At the synapse these impulses are changed into chemicals called neurotransmitters, which carry the impulses to the next cell, where they are turned again into electrical impulses. This process happens at the juncture of each nerve cell.

Some people, because of their genetic constitution, have a tendency at times to not produce enough of one or more of the neurotransmitters, and thus the nerve impulses do not get through with the strength they should. This could be likened to how a car would function if each of its spark plugs were fouled with carbon deposits.

This state is sometimes referred to as *endogenous depression.* Endogenous depression will manifest itself in one of three ways: (1) feelings of depression, which may include crying and feelings of hopelessness, (2) lack of energy to carry out the normal tasks, or (3) lack of enjoyment of activities that normally should bring enjoyment, such as eating or sexual activity.

If a person has a *significant* spiritual or psychological depression which lasts for more than two weeks, it *can* trigger an endogenous depression in the person if his or her genetic makeup is as described earlier. However, in some people an endogenous depression may ensue without any psychological or spiritual precipitating event.

When an endogenous depression begins, the depressed mood will often attach itself to whatever is most important in a person's life. In the case of a Christian with endogenous depression, he or she may believe that God no longer hears prayers. Or the person may feel that he or she has lost spiritual joy. In more severe cases of endogenous depression, the individual may believe that salvation is lost or that the unpardonable sin has been committed. If a Christian seems preoccupied with minor sins that have been committed, and if normal counseling and reasoning from Scripture does not seem to change the person's beliefs about being alienated from God, it is very possible that endogenous depression is the problem.

The physical imbalance in the body, which produces this kind of depression will often correct itself in six to nine months. However, if the endogenous depression is moderate to severe, the person may lose the ability to function effectively or may even attempt suicide if not treated with antidepressants.

Misunderstandings About Antidepressants

In the Christian community there are several common misunderstandings about antidepressants that need correcting. First, antidepressants are not addicting or habit-forming. A person can take them as long as he or she has a chemical imbalance and then discontinue them *gradually* when the imbalance is corrected, with no addiction problems.

Second, antidepressants cannot be used as a "cop-out" if the person has a psychological or spiritual problem. Antidepressants will only work when the person has an endogenous depression.

Antidepressants usually take from three to five weeks to produce their maximum benefit. Therefore, people should continue taking them at least that long if they hope to benefit. The side effects from most antidepressants last only a few days and then disappear as the body adjusts to their presence.

The stresses produced by an affair can precipitate an endogenous depression in both the faithful and unfaithful partner. Counselors and pastors who work with these people should be alert to this possibility and make referrals to physicians when they suspect the presence of a biological depression.

Antidepressants will not cause an unfaithful partner to feel less guilty about his or her unfaithfulness. By reducing the biological component of the depression, they can help him or her think more clearly about the situation and the changes one needs to make.

Index